Adventures of a
LANDLOCKED
DIVER

ROGER ROTH

HOLON
PUBLISHING

www.Holon.co

ISBN: 978-1-929765-35-5 (Hardback)
ISBN: 978-1-955342-59-9 (Paperback)
ISBN: 978-1-955342-60-5 (eBook)

Published by:

Holon Publishing & Collective Press
A Storytelling Company
www.Holon.co

Cover photo and "Roger and Nurse Shark" by Cricket Manuel
Bio photo and "Roger in Indonesia" by A. Scott Johnson

This book is dedicated to the three most import-
ant mentors I've had in the diving industry.

Joyce Hayward is known as "The Lady of the Lakes" for her documen-
tation and research of Great Lakes shipwrecks and was later inducted
into the Women Divers Hall of Fame. Her presentations were always
inspiring to me because she told such a fantastic story using the facts.

Stan Waterman is known as "The Man Who Loves Sharks" and
has entertained the world with movies that earned him five Emmy
awards. His delightful way of making anyone feel as important as he
became is an inspiration in itself, and his friendship is cherished.

Jim Church taught thousands of underwater photographers and vid-
eographers easier and better ways to get the shot. He was always there
with his experience and teacher attitude for anyone seeking advice.
As our friendship grew, I realized he was surely a teacher of teachers.

Special thanks to Cricket Manuel, Rudy Whitworth, Scott Johnson
and Andy Sallmon for donating their pictures for this book.

Introduction

When I first started diving, I had trouble finding the words to describe to my friends and family the beauty and wonders I was seeing in the ocean world. That's what led me to begin filming underwater. Many of the things I filmed moved me so much at times, I began writing poems about those encounters underwater, as well as some of the other people I've been privileged to meet in my travels.

Just like many other divers, I consistently get questions like, "How did you get into diving, especially since you are from landlocked Cincinnati, Ohio," or "How did you get into filming underwater," or "Where is your favorite place to dive?" Since 1988 I have been telling the same stories about my diving experiences, adventures and people I've met along the way. I've obviously added to my repertoire of tales with each dive trip.

I have noticed that most people are quite interested in these stories each time I tell them. Then the questions become, "What is your favorite marine animal," or "What is the deepest you've gone," or "Have you found any sunken treasure," or "What is the scariest thing that has happened to you while scuba diving?"

Also, like many other divers, I could probably talk about these things forever. Once I get started, one might be hard-pressed to stop me. Scuba diving and filming underwater has become a serious passion for me and I've been blessed to be able to perpetuate my diving by using my filmmaking skills and producing promotional videos for dive operations all over the world. Scuba diving has taken me on unprecedented adventures and introduced me to a good number of the most famous people in the diving industry, some of whom have taken me under their wings as mentors. When asked why, they told me they knew I'd pay it forward, which I always have and always will.

While growing up, I knew I would never make it to outer space as an astronaut, but scuba diving has now allowed me to visit the frontier of inner space as an aquanaut. Every time I slip beneath the surface, I wonder what new feeling I will experience or what new marine creature I'll find that I've never seen before. Inner space is a whole new world just waiting to be discovered.

It's a world that holds many secrets to be unlocked. There are chemicals and toxins in the oceans that are not found on land that could lead to cures for many diseases. There are fears that people have about marine creatures like sharks, barracuda, eels, and stingrays that can be allayed once people know the actual behavior of these critters. Most importantly, understanding inner space in our rivers, lakes and oceans can help mankind better control the sustainability of these ecosystems.

Having taught junior high science for six years in the 1970's, I find the science of the oceans and mostly their inhabitants to be exciting. I adore watching and interpreting behaviors and relationships of the marine creatures. These behaviors may include predator-prey relationships, other symbiotic relationships whether they are mutual or commensal, courting and mating behaviors, various ways marine creatures lay and incubate their eggs, acts of camouflage for protection, and even learning how marine creatures physically change as they grow from juveniles to adults. In some species, if you saw a juvenile and an adult of the same species next to each other you would swear they were two very different species of fish.

Did you know that there are some species of fish that basically have one breeding male in a school and the rest of the fish in that school will be females? He basically has his own harem. But if anything happens to him, one of the females will change sexes and become a male of that harem for breeding purposes.

But beyond the science of inner space, while traveling around the world I get the opportunities to meet new people and learn about new countries. I learn about their histories and cultures, their languages and dialects, and sometimes even their taboos. I live and eat with them, and occasionally I'm even invited into their homes as part of their families, albeit only for the short time I'm visiting their countries.

If I'm going to a country that speaks a language other than English, I work hard to learn some basic words so that I can communicate with them in their language, even if it's just a few dozen. I've found that most countries see Americans as snobs but if I show them the slightest courtesy of learning their language, they are not only impressed, but I've gained a lot of respect from them as well.

There are times when I push the limits of my diving profiles and there are times when others push my limits. There are misunderstandings because of cultural differences, as well as language barriers. Of course, there are also problems with TSA agents, customs agents, airlines and their staffs, hotels and their staffs, taxi drivers, and even personality conflicts with tour guides, as well as other divers.

But until my body or mind (or wallet) no longer allows me the luxury of dive travel, the above-mentioned negatives will always be overshadowed by the countless positives I experience with every trip I take. Some people get certified, then the newness wears off or it becomes too expensive to travel and they don't dive anymore. I keep hoping that the newness never wears off for me and that I can keep finding a way to afford the dive travel so that I can continue meeting new people and experiencing new adventures like the ones I'm sharing in this book.

Table of Contents

Clean the Pool

It was the summer of 1968 after my junior year of high school. I was tired of babysitting and mowing lawns in the neighborhood for my spending money. I didn't want to work in the pro shop of the local golf course again, nor did I want to smell the cutting oil that permeated the machine tool shop owned by my best friend's father; at least not that summer.

I knew I didn't mind working hard and I also knew I wanted to learn something new. I did want to enjoy my job and I also wanted to get paid well. Being only 16 years old, I just wasn't sure how to go about finding that job.

I decided to get into my car and drive around my community looking for someplace that might be hiring. I filled out applications in a nearby factory, a fast-food restaurant, a local car dealership and even a plumbing company. I didn't have experience for any of these jobs, but I knew I would be a fast learner given the opportunity.

Interestingly enough, it was "PR" from the plumbing company that called me back. He wanted me to come in the next morning to start my new job. I was excited about this because I had grown up in a new subdivision where houses were being built all the time and now, I was going to get the chance to be a part of the construction industry one way or another.

The following morning, I reported for work and "PR" told me I'd be a plumber's helper. Mike was the plumber that I would be working with and he would begin to teach me how to be an effective helper for him. That summer I learned about plumbing fittings and how to solder them, all about specific tools that plumbers use, how to rough in plumbing for a new house, and even how to thread and install black pipe for natural gas lines in the house.

On days when Mike didn't need me as his helper, "PR" would give me other jobs to do telling me that new experiences would be good for me. Sometimes, he assigned me to work with his brother

Austin who was more of a jack of all trades. When working with him, there were days that I learned how to drive a dump truck and other days that I learned how to operate bulldozers and backhoes. Driving the dump truck wasn't too hard but it wasn't as easy learning how to operate the bulldozers and backhoes since I didn't do it that often.

For the first month, I was jumping around from job to job with Mike or Austin, depending on who needed me most, with no specific responsibilities in mind other than just helping. When I was with Mike, I was always only doing plumbing. But when I was with Austin, I could be doing almost anything in construction from moving dirt to framing houses, installing shingles on a roof or even painting.

Since Austin and "PR" noticed that I was good with ladders and a paintbrush on some smaller projects with Austin, my second month was spent with "PR" and Austin's nephew Kim, painting a large two-story wooden house out in the country. Kim was a couple years younger than I and we got along very well from the beginning. Neither of us was afraid of heights, nor were we afraid of hard work.

We had the same routine every day, starting at 7 AM with plugging in the radio then eating our donuts and milk. After that we set up our equipment and painted until 10 o'clock when we took our first break. Austin always took a coffee break at 10 so we decided we should get a break at 10, also.

By 10:15 we were back to painting until lunchtime at noon. That's when we would drive down the road to a local bar where we could get some good hamburgers. We were too young to drink beer, but this bar is where many construction workers went for lunch, so we wanted to be like them.

Within about 45 minutes we were back on the job painting again. At 2:15 we took our afternoon break like Austin taught us. That's usually when Austin or "PR" would stop by to check on us and make sure we were making headway and doing a good job.

By the end of the month, we finished painting the house. "PR's" plumbing and building contracts were getting finished quicker than he could contract more. So, in order to keep us busy he would give Kim and me odd jobs to do around the shop, and even at his home.

It didn't take us long to get the shop well-organized, so then he sent us to his home. He had us cutting his grass, trimming bushes, washing windows, cleaning gutters and even washing cars and boats. "PR" and Mike both had expensive cigarette boats that they would take to the Ohio River on weekends.

By the last week of the summer before I was to go back to school, "PR" had just about run out of work for us to do. We were cleaning the work trucks, sweeping the parking lot, and even washing the windows at the shop. With all that completed, he remembered how the algae was collecting in and overtaking his swimming pool since he was spending so much time down on the river.

So, on our last day of work for the summer we met at his house with our bathing suits to clean "PF's" pool. He gave us bristle brushes to use to clean the algae from the sides and bottom of his concrete pool. He also brought out two scuba tanks that would strap directly to our backs with regulators, masks and fins for us to use while cleaning the algae in the deeper parts. There were no buoyancy compensator vests to help with our buoyancy back then.

I told him I had never really seen scuba equipment close-up and I had no idea how to use the equipment. That's when Kim quickly remarked that he had used some before with "PR." Then "PR" quickly went through how to set up the equipment and showed us how to turn it on and use it before he went back to the shop. He did warn us to not come up from the deep end too quickly while holding our breath as it could cause our lungs to overinflate and burst.

Kim and I donned the scuba gear and he slid into the pool to begin brushing the algae from the concrete surface of the pool bottom. I slowly swam over him and watched and felt his bubbles careen into my body as they rushed to the surface. Interestingly enough, I noticed those bubbles getting larger as they approached me at the surface. I'd even noticed my own reflection in the larger bubbles!

I don't remember much about cleaning the algae that day, although it was probably a pre-cursor for my days volunteering at the Northern Kentucky Aquarium just across the Ohio River from Cincinnati after I got certified. However, there were some things I'll never forget.

Mostly what I remember is lying on my back on the bottom in the deep end watching my bubbles rise towards the passing puffy, cumulus clouds in the sky above, while glistening with the individual rays of sunlight passing through the water. The silence and calm under the water was different than my younger days of springboard diving from junior high through college. Once I was able to stay under water instead of going to the surface for a breath of air, the serenity I felt filled my body and spirit.

This was my first introduction to scuba. It was very relaxing and great fun for me. You would think that I would have looked into scuba diving right at that time. But it would be almost two decades before I would again think about scuba diving.

After high school, I got a summer job doing roofing. Through the next four years, I used what I'd learned, and I contracted a few roof replacements on my own that turned out well. In 1973, I graduated from Miami University in Oxford, OH and began teaching 7th & 8th grade science. I also truly enjoyed coaching wrestling since I wrestled varsity all four years in high school. I also continued contracting roof replacements during holiday vacations and summer breaks. I would always seek good advice from my suppliers when I had questions as to the proper way to do something.

In 1978, my twins (a girl and a boy) were born, and my wife began heavily using drugs. We divorced, and I left teaching by the end of 1979 in order to get custody of the twins. My only option was to go full-time with my roofing experience so that I could be there for the babies in the mornings and evenings before and after day care. I did know that I'd been making more money roofing part-time than I did teaching full time, so I felt confident I could make it work.

Watching the Action

Fast-forwarding to 1986, one of my roofing suppliers decided to give away trips according to material purchases. These trips would be taken in January during roofing's slower season. Being a small roofing contractor, I never really purchased enough in materials to actually earn the whole trip like the larger roofing contractors, but I did trade him my labor remodeling his house and his summer home in order to earn the rest of my way on these trips. We both saw the benefits of this arrangement and were happy with how it worked out.

The first year he offered this vacation in 1987, I found myself fortunate enough to be on a Royal Caribbean cruise ship for a week! Altogether that year my supplier hosted about 40 roofers and their spouses. Some of them I knew and all the others became friends before the end of the week.

After unpacking our luggage in our staterooms, most of us spent the first afternoon sitting poolside, sunning, and drinking beer while the ship plied its way through the waves. The ladies remarked how much they enjoyed having these pool boys constantly bring them their drinks. The men would shrug, smile, and give their drink orders, then just sign the bar tabs that were assigned to our staterooms.

None of us got bored sitting there. The men found plenty of pretty womanly figures and bikinis to stare at while the women were agog at all the good-looking "pool boy" waiters. We were all impressed by the waiters spinning their empty trays atop their finger and even tossing these trays in the air then catching them on their fingertip as if they were tossing a baton at a football game.

Cruises can be spectacular in many ways. I remember well our very first dinner with 10 of us assigned to each table. Dinners were usually formal affairs requiring coats and ties. I never was much of a coat and tie person but I very graciously dressed accordingly given this wonderful (and now free) opportunity.

We were already relaxed and in awe during our first day on the ship, but when we approached our table, we noticed the napkins at each place setting being folded to look like an animal. Since we had never seen this before, this was just another impressive "wow!" we had experienced on our first day.

When each of us sat down at the table, a waiter was there to gracefully place our napkins in each of our laps. Then he would ask us individually how we were doing. As we answered him, his reply to us was, "Excellent!"

While he passed out our dinner menus, he happily suggested various island drinks while taking our drink orders. The island drinks were ones like rum punches, mai-tais, and blue Hawaii's. Most of the ladies chose the island drinks while the men chose beer or mixed drinks. While writing each of our orders on his pad he would remark, "Excellent!"

When the waiter went to get our drinks, we discussed the list of menu items and were impressed by the extensive array of entrées available. These included various kinds of fish, shellfish including lobster tails, different types of steaks, chicken prepared in more ways than you could imagine, as well as vegetarian dishes. The list of side dishes was even more extensive.

When the waiter came back with our drinks, he easily remembered what everyone ordered and placed our drinks in front of each of us correctly. Then he stated he was ready to take our meal orders. After taking each order he would say, "Excellent choice!"

When it was my turn to order I again looked at the menu, but I still couldn't decide between ordering a steak or lobster tails, so I asked him if one was better than the other. It was then that the waiter told me, "No problem, sir, I'll just bring you both!" I asked him if that was really true and possible, his answer to me was, "Yes, absolutely! Excellent choices!"

When the food came out, he had my steak and lobster tails together on one large plate, larger than everyone else's. The food was so delicious it wasn't hard for me to finish everything. The hard part after that was choosing from the dozen or more exquisite-looking desserts he displayed for us on a large tray. There's no doubt that this was an "excellent" evening.

At the end of our week on the cruise ship, we had envelopes in our staterooms for tips and a form to fill out rating the staff from servers, to maids, to bar staff and so on. The best rating possible was "Excellent," thus explaining why the staff always mentioned "excellent" throughout the week.

Cruise ships will sail from island to island giving guests the opportunity to visit and experience a few different islands if they were so inclined. While docked at the islands, the cruise line will offer numerous activities and excursions for the guests to do from playing volleyball in the sand or surfing in the waves to shopping in the numerous stores for our souvenirs. That is of course if guests wanted to leave the ship and its amenities at all.

The first island we stopped at was Puerto Rico and we docked in the harbor of San Juan. Many of our group went ashore, and I was sure to take my video camera with me to film the narrow cobblestone lanes and tightly-packed, colorful buildings. Sometimes I would casually film others in our group while they shopped, picked out merchandise, or even argued about spending the money. This footage would later playfully show up on a video I'd produce for the group after I got home.

The next day, we moored at Haiti. Many of the ladies decided we would spend the day at the beach and told the men that would be the plan. We begrudgingly packed up some beer and ice and we all made our way to the buses that would take us to the beach.

Upon our arrival and before we went down the stone stairway to the beach, many of the women decided they wanted to use the restroom to change into their bathing suits. This came as no surprise to the men so we meandered towards a stone wall that overlooked the large beach and the seashore. As we looked down one of the guys became wide-eyed and stated that this beach thing might not be so bad after all. He began pointing out all the topless women lying in the sun and playing in the surf with their children.

Soon after the wives went in the restroom, two older ladies came out. One asked the other if she had any idea how they would find their husbands. Overhearing this, I quietly whispered to the guys, "I bet it's those two older gentlemen over there ogling the beach." Of course, I was right.

When our wives came out, we all made our way to the stairs but none of the guys mentioned the fact that this was a topless beach. At first the ladies were preoccupied with trying to figure out where we would sit and what lounge chairs we might each be able to grab for ourselves, so they didn't even notice any of the topless women. It was minutes later that one of them finally whispered to all the others that she just saw a topless female over there.

When the wives asked us if we knew this was a topless beach, we couldn't contain our laughter any longer. Of course, we knew by now! We were not blind or dead men. We had already decided that we now had a good enough reason to hang out on the beach all day which the women should appreciate.

The guys gathered lounge chairs for everyone. The ladies lined up all of their chairs next to each other facing the water and the sun. We placed ours more parallel to the waterline for obvious reasons. We could see people playing in the water as well as up and down the beach. As time went on, the ladies talked about how happy they were to be tanning themselves on a tropical island beach. Of course, the guys agreed with them wholeheartedly. We had already decided that we didn't think it could get much better than this.

After being on the beach for a couple of hours, a very pretty girl in a small bikini approached us carrying a large basket full of different women's bathing suits. She asked a couple of the ladies if they liked the bathing suit she was wearing. They answered yes but told her it wasn't anything they could wear.

So, she started holding up some other bathing suits from her basket. One of the wives said she really liked the blue one with yellow flowers, so the girl removed both top and bottom of her bikini and donned the blue one with yellow flowers to model it for everyone. The guys unanimously decided the day did in fact just get better.

The next island we visited was St. Thomas. On that day, we chose to do an afternoon wine and cheese sailboat excursion that included snorkeling. As soon as we all boarded the sailboat, we were offered our first glass of wine accompanied by French baguettes and cheese.

The captain of the sailboat cruised around the island giving us time to relax and get to know others on the sailboat and even let some of us take the helm. It didn't take long to make new friends along with our old ones. After an hour or so of sailing, the captain dropped anchor so we could begin snorkeling.

The first mate pulled out the safety vests and began to teach everyone how to use them. Then he passed out the masks, fins, and snorkels to each of us on the boat. We finished our wine, donned our safety vests, masks, snorkels, and fins and jumped into the water. Once in the water we looked down to see myriad schools of fish around us.

At the time, I didn't know what kind of fish they were. All I knew was that they were colorful and there seemed to be hundreds of them. In thinking back now, I'm pretty sure we were inundated by schools of Sgt. Major Damselfish and yellowtail snappers, both of which enjoyed being fed the potato chips and bread the first mate used to "chum" the water.

While snorkeling, I meandered away from the group and enjoyed just dangling my arms in the water. It seemed as though the longer I remained still, the more the fish would congregate around my hands and arms almost as if they would let me hold them. This was the first time I remember feeling one with the ocean!

Then I swam a little farther from the sailboat and studied different types of corals along with the myriads of fish. The corals were of many different shapes and colors. Some were round and hard and others were soft and flowing back and forth with the current.

After drifting further from the sailboat, I happened to notice a shipwreck about 45' below me. It was probably about 50' long. There were scuba divers on this wreck and I watched for a long time as these divers swam in, out, and around the wreck.

Sometimes it seemed as though the divers were studying things in the sand where the hull met the seafloor. At other times, they seemed to be studying the nearby corals, but I couldn't see what they were looking at. I was definitely much more interested now in watching the divers and what they were doing than I was just watching fish swim.

After about an hour, the captain called us all back to the sailboat. When I got back on board, the first mate suggested to me that now I know the difference between snorkeling and scuba diving. Curiously, I asked why. He said, "When snorkeling, you watch the action; when scuba diving, you are the action!" That is when I was sure I would be certified for scuba diving before our next sponsored vacation, which would be an all-inclusive week at a resort on a beach in Runaway Bay, Jamaica.

And now you know.

GARDENS OF MEMORIES ~ ON SNORKELING

Beneath the surface a shipwreck is found;
  The start of memories that will ever abound.
A cruise, a sailboat with cheese and wine,
  Snorkeling St. Thomas with friends of mine.
Schools of fish brightly colored and near
  Swim through my hands showing no fear.
Corals and sponges spread over the sand,
  While sun rays stream down to backs all tanned.
Swimming further away to be all alone
  A shipwreck is spied that would set a new tone.
The divers exploring both in and out;
  Being bound to the surface elicits a pout.
Bubbles ascending tickle my chin;
  Pain in my foot from rented fin.
Snorkel is filled with water and salt,
  Wondering if divers are finding a vault.
I only watch as divers have fun,
  Decisions are made, I'll soon be one.
Next time I visit, the action I'll be,
  Gardens of memories in open sea.

January in Jamaica

Upon returning from an "excellent" Caribbean cruise, I quickly did some research on various dive shops in Cincinnati. At the time, there were about 13 shops in the Greater Cincinnati area. I'd later find out that Cincinnati was ranked as the second largest landlocked dive retail market in the United States at that time!

Somehow, I also convinced my father to get certified with me. He was a family physician and had taken me golfing (or I should more accurately state, caddying) every Thursday and Sunday during the summers since I was probably around 10-12 years old. I thought it was finally time for him to join me in something about which I began to develop my own passion.

We went to the evening classroom sessions and pool sessions twice a week for 10 weeks. After each session, we'd shower then our instructor and assistants would suggest we join them at a nearby restaurant or pizza place and we could listen to their tales about their dive trips. Food, beer, and their dive stories (whether true or not) only whetted our appetites more to become certified divers and begin making our own stories.

After completing the NASDS (National Association of Scuba Diving schools) certification course and written exam, our only other responsibility would be to do our open water dives with an instructor. For most, this meant spring or summer camping trips to limestone quarries around northern Ohio or Indiana where water temperatures range from 35-55° and visibility might be 5-20' at the most. The most interesting things to see in these quarries might be a few small mouth basses, some paddlefish, or maybe a bicycle to sit on wearing scuba gear that's next to a school bus that one can swim through or feed fish while on top of it.

I did some serious pondering about whether I wanted to indulge in this cold-water madness to complete my open water dives in a quarry so that I'd be certified for my upcoming trip to Jamaica. That's when I realized that it would make more sense to take a referral letter from my dive shop with me to an instructor in Jamaica stating that I'd completed all necessary classroom and pool work and I only needed the necessary open water dives to complete my certification. So, in January of 1988, I took my referral letter to an instructor at the resort where we were staying in Runaway Bay, Jamaica.

I was again traveling with that same group of roofing contractors and their spouses. Even before we left the airport in Montego Bay, most everyone had already been approached by locals asking if we wanted to buy "weed" or "blow," which was marijuana and cocaine. I think there may have been one or two roofers that bought some marijuana and they said it was pretty good at the time. I personally thought it was quite brazen of the locals to be walking around selling this stuff, but that was on them, not me.

This week would be all-inclusive, meaning we didn't have to buy any of our food or alcoholic drinks and there were even always cigarettes on the bar in a glass for the taking by those who smoked. Since I smoked at the time, I tried them but they were bad enough that I decided I'd stick with my own brand that I'd brought along with me even though the other ones were free.

Meals were served buffet-style. We were told the main dishes on the buffet tables were chicken or beef along with goat, but every one of them tasted like goat to me and many others, so we really didn't know. Goat meat was popular in Jamaica and therefore was included on the buffet tables. The curried goat wasn't too bad, but it wasn't something I'd choose for my main entrée nor was it something I ate often.

I did some research about diving in Jamaica before I left and found out that there weren't going to be many larger fish to see due to overfishing practices of the Jamaican population for decades. I don't remember much about those eight dives I made in Jamaica other than verifying my research about the lack of larger fish. What I do remember is that I was so "wowed" by all the pretty colored fish and how they danced around the colorful reefs that I found it hard to describe to my friends what I was seeing on my dives after each day's diving. That made me wish I had some sort of camera with me for those dives.

At the beginning of each dive, my instructor would make sure

I was OK, then he would put me through the normal drills that I'd practiced in the pool sessions. I'd remove my regulator then put it back in my mouth and clear it of water so I could breathe again. I'd take off my mask, put it back on, then clear the water from it so I could see again. Then we would practice buddy breathing which was my using the instructor's spare regulator called an octopus to breathe from. After these drills, we would swim around the reef for the rest of our dive and he would point things out that he thought were interesting.

These drills are necessary in case your mask gets accidentally kicked off or you run out of air. While on a dive years later, I had just made my entry into the ocean and settled to a sandy bottom at about 30'. I looked to my left quickly and all of a sudden, I tried to breathe, but only got a mouthful of water. This started to confuse me since I still had my mouthpiece in my mouth. Then I realized that my mouthpiece had come disconnected from my regulator which was hanging down to my right. I quickly grabbed my regulator remounted the mouthpiece to it, put it back in my mouth, cleared the water from the regulator and began breathing easily again. Once back on the boat, I tightened the zip tie that was holding the mouthpiece to the regulator and never had that problem again.

On the second day of diving, I'd do the same drills then my instructor had me take off all of my gear underwater then put it back on. This is called doff and don and a drill necessary in case something isn't working properly with your gear and you need to take it all off to check things out. Through my years of diving, I have had reason to do this, usually when my tank strap isn't tight enough thus allowing my tank to slip down and possibly away from my BCD vest (Buoyancy Control Device). That's when I'd have to remove my gear, reweave the strap tighter, then put my gear back on again.

There have been other times when one of my hoses got caught inside my BCD when I put it on but I didn't realize it until after I'd gotten in the water. A simple doff and don would allow me to untangle the hose and put my gear back on properly. Sometimes I still practice this skill just to keep it second nature in my mind.

After a successful doff and don, we began our reef tour again. I remember my instructor once took a rock and pounded it on the top of a coral head. There was some sort of liquid that began oozing out from the coral and lots of little fish began crowding around the coral head and eating at the liquid. I'm guessing this liquid was also filled with the algae that lives in coral and the fish were feeding on it. Since what he did actually damaged that coral, I now understand better why their reefs aren't what others are around the world. (That's besides the fact that Jamaicans dynamited and/or poisoned their reefs for generations to collect the dead fish, but ruined the habitats for the fish populations.)

The next day's dives included swimming through some gullies in the reef. As we swam through, we'd pass more corals and "plant-like things" (gorgonians). Every once in a while, I'd notice small, but colorful trumpetfish hanging vertically in the gorgonians. They almost looked like the branches of the gorgonians and I realized this must have been their type of camouflage. But when I tried to get closer, they would gracefully glide away.

Each evening at dinner, my friends would ask me what I saw on my dives. I would try to explain the camouflage effect of the gorgonian for the trumpetfish, but a lot got lost in my description. Everyone seemed to be quite interested in my adventures, but I don't think any of them were interested enough to consider getting certified. They had done some snorkeling from the beach, but my having tried that once, I knew they weren't seeing anything like what I was seeing on my dives.

By the end of the week, I was still having great trouble accurately explaining to my friends the cool things I was seeing. I knew I had to find a way to document the wonders of the oceans that I was experiencing so I could share these experiences with others without having to try to explain it. Thinking to myself, I knew I already had a video camera that I used on land to document these trips as well as my family's activities. Maybe I could have a waterproof housing made for my camera.

Before leaving Jamaica, I had completed all eight of the open water dives I needed to get my certification card. The instructor filled out the paperwork for me to send in to NASDS so they could issue my C-card, which never expires. I was finally a certified scuba diver!

When I returned home, I looked into having that waterproof

housing made for my camera. Ikelite was a housing manufacturer based in Indianapolis, only 90 minutes away, so I contacted them and made arrangements to have this housing made. I sent my video camera to them and a few weeks later it came back with a custom housing that would keep my camera dry and allow me to work all of the necessary buttons and levers that manipulate the camera.

That would be the beginning of my underwater filmmaking career! The following January, my roofing supplier would be hosting the group on a 10-day vacation in Hawaii.

Rudy Whitworth – Seahorse Productions, LLC

Trumpetfish are 2-3' long and can change colors to match their surroundings for their camouflage.

GARDENS OF MEMORIES~ON THE TRUMPETFISH

Extra stalks in gorgonians; long, not quite round;
    This is where memories are sure to be found.
Within feathered arms new forms seem to appear;
    Soft-slender in shape, subtle motions half-clear.
Hanging head down, they pretend not to be seen;
    Protecting themselves from an eating machine.
They pose with a stealth, like none found ashore;
    With new blends of colors we know and more.
At first you can see them, then think they are gone;
    Then trumpets may blare with a full silent yawn.
A sharp eye or camera can catch what they've caught;
    A small shrimp or fry becomes dinner, as taught.
Curling in currents like curtains on stage,
    Trumpetfish wave their own wallpaper page.
I yearn to move closer and glide in nearby,
    To see what they say with that look in their eye.
But, arching their bodies and dipping so slight,
    With invisible finning, they slip from my sight.
A quest to continue their own hunting spree;
    Gardens of memories in open sea.

Hawaii

Before I left for the 10-day Hawaiian vacation and cruise hosted by my roofing supplier, I'd listed each island that we would be visiting. Then I contacted a dive operator on those islands to arrange for them to pick me up at the cruise ship pier of their island on the dates I'd be on their island. Many of these dive operators were used to this happening and it usually worked flawlessly. I also contacted a couple of friends who lived in Hawaii and made arrangements to meet up with them whenever I'd get to the island on which they lived.

We first landed on Oahu and stayed in a hotel in Honolulu for the first two nights. We were scheduled to attend a Luau that first evening in hopes it would keep everyone awake later in the evening to help begin adjusting to the six-hour time difference. It didn't work very well for me as I was awake before 4 AM, so I decided to take a walk around the city for a while then go to the beach and wait for the sunrise.

A very good friend of mine in Cincinnati had a brother, David, who was based in Oahu while serving in the Navy. We'd planned on meeting up for a couple of dives on my first full day in Honolulu. After breakfast that morning, he picked me up at the hotel and took me to Hanauma Bay, which was a state park with a popular beach for snorkeling and scuba diving. The part he didn't tell me about was the very long walk down the hill from the parking lot carrying our scuba gear and camera systems, then around the perimeter of the beach through the sand, then across some rocks to a point where we could finally gear up and do a backward roll into the waves.

Once in the water, everything was relaxing. David took a number of pictures of me and I got video of him while he used his still camera. He was a pretty good photographer and I was glad to receive a great picture he took of me holding my new video rig, giving an "OK" sign underwater. That was the first picture of me underwater and I still have that picture today hanging in my equipment room.

After our dive, we lugged our gear back across the sandy beach and UP that hill and across the parking lot, only to change tanks and climb down some rocks to the water level. This dive site was called, "Toilet Bowl" and it was easy to figure out how it got its name. The surge washed in and out of a narrow inlet and Dave taught me how to use the surge to my advantage to get to where we were going.

At the end of the inlet, we entered a small cavern. At the back of the cavern, I could see a very large blue parrotfish, maybe up to what seemed at the time to be three to four feet long. As we got closer to it, I guess it got spooked because it flew past us like a blue rocket. There had been no time for me to even get my camera turned on, let alone get video of the parrotfish.

The next day I went diving with a dive shop by the name of South Seas Aquatics who took me to a shipwreck called the Mahi. This was an old Navy minesweeper that had been converted into an oceano-graphic research vessel for the University of Hawaii. Then in 1982, the owner of the dive shop arranged to have the outdated ship sunk as an artificial reef and a great ship for divers to explore.

As I descended, I saw two spotted eagle rays swimming around the wreck, but they disappeared by the time we got to the wreck. Once on the wreck a green moray eel appeared and while I was film-ing it, the divemaster actually petted it. I'm guessing he must have had some food for it, but I missed that part. At least I had video of an eel to share with family and friends!

Our second dive was at a dive site called Makaha Caverns. It was more of a reef dive than cavern exploration, but there were some lava tubes that we swam through. These are conduits where lava flows un-derground away from a volcano. As the lava cuts down through the ground, the upper areas of these conduits then become hollow. In these lava tubes, I saw crabs, a lobster, and scads of squirrelfish. I only know this fish ID because I could now bring my video footage home and identify each and every critter I filmed.

The next day we boarded the cruise ship and headed towards Kau-ai. As planned, Aquatics Kauai picked me up the following morning at the pier and took me on a couple of dives. I was enjoying the fact that the fish and hard corals in Hawaii were larger and much more colorful and beautiful than anything I'd seen in Jamaica. I even saw two turtles playing on the second dive. I wonder now if there might have been more to this than just playing thinking maybe they had been courting each other.

Sadly, my new dive light fell out of my pocket on the second dive. I thought maybe the divemaster had found it since it was a large, four "D" cell light and would have been pretty obvious to someone paying attention the way he should have. But he wasn't admitting to it if he had found it. He said he would contact me if it got turned in, but that never happened. I learned to better secure my dive light from then on.

The next morning, we were moored on the Kona Coast of the Big Island of Hawaii. Dave was the son of the owner of the travel agency that booked the trips for my supplier and he was also a certified diver. Dave was a couple of years younger than I and I knew him from high school. His father was also the president of our local Sycamore Community Schools Board of Education where I'd grown up and eventually taught. I was glad to finally have someone to dive with that would actually experience everything I was experiencing while underwater.

We were picked up by an operation called Dive Makai, which means "to the sea" in Hawaiian. They gave the most in-depth dive briefings that have never been matched to this day by telling us what we'd see and showing us 8"x 10" pictures of each of the critters from their three-ring binder on the boat. Then on the dives, they would actually show us almost every critter they told us about.

They showed me nudibranchs, rockmover juveniles and adults that look totally different from each other, cleaner wrasses, and schools of blue stripe snappers; all things we'd seen pictures of in the briefings. It seems as though as soon as I finished filming something, owner and guide Lisa showed me something different. My battery ran out just before she showed me a white tip reef shark, but at least I'd seen my first shark.

On the second dive, Lisa brought some pieces of squid with her to feed a friendly green moray eel. I took a piece and handed Dave my camera so that he could film me feeding the eel. He got a great shot of me not letting go of the squid fast enough when the eel shot out for the squid, and the eel's tooth on the roof of its mouth sliced through my top knuckle and fingernail as I pulled my hand away. When I held up my finger to the camera, he also got the brown-colored blood oozing into the ocean from the slice made by the eel. Red colors don't show up as red when underwater because when deeper than 15', the water filters out the wavelengths that make red look red.

That evening, I apologized to Dave telling him that I felt as though Lisa was giving me all of her attention and showing me everything so that I could film them. I thought maybe she was ignoring him more than me. The interesting thing was, he told me he was just getting ready to give me the same apology. I dove with Dive Makai years later, and the quality of their dive briefings still ranked among the best ever.

The last island we visited was Maui. We'd again already scheduled our diving with Lahaina Divers who met us at the cruise ship pier with paperwork in the bus. We filled it out as we rode to the boat that would take us to Molokini Crater, which is a partially submerged volcanic crater. Since it was January and peak season for the migration of the Humpback whales, we were told to stop occasionally during our dives, and listen for the whales singing in the background. When I did this, I could clearly hear the whale songs and those songs could even be heard on my video footage.

During the afternoon, according to plan, I met up with an old friend from Cincinnati, John Greene, who was now living in Lahaina selling real estate. We met at Ka'anapali Beach which is best known world-wide for a snorkeling site called Black Rock. We snorkeled Black Rock at the far-right side of Ka'anapali Beach and then returned more towards the middle of the bay where most people were swimming and jumping waves.

While there, I showed John a juvenile eel swimming around everyone's feet as we snorkeled amongst all those who were just standing and waiting for the next big wave to come. He found it amazing that those people would have no idea of the eels, small stingrays, and fish that we saw so close to them. Of course, we knew that those critters wouldn't harm the waders since they weren't really a threat to the critters at the time.

There were plenty of bars and restaurants around so we gathered our snorkel gear and ambled to a beachside bar and ordered some drinks. It was great fun to see John again and talk about the 10 years or so that we'd known each other. I caught him up on our mutual friends that he hadn't seen in a couple of years and he marveled at the diving I was getting into so passionately.

By the end of the vacation, I didn't have to search for words to describe what I was seeing. I carried and used my video rig on every dive in Hawaii to show others what I'd seen, and that's still the case today. Since then, I've told people on my dive boats if they want to see something like a whale shark or a rare blue ring octopus, they could pay me to leave my camera on the boat and the chances of seeing these things would probably greatly improve!

Roger in Hawaii with his first custom-built housing for his video camera.
(Photographer: David Schrichte)

GARDENS OF MEMORIES~ON CRUISE SHIPS

Where excellent meals and beaches abound,
　　This is where memories are sure to be found.
Island to island show such an array,
　　Then back to the ship for another night's stay.
When morning comes, a dive is a must;
　　And hopes are put in the form of a trust.
Most guides are worthy, but some may not be;
　　We all live and learn as we grow from trainee.
Travel on each day with appetite so wet,
　　Dream new horizons will always be met.
Colors of fish and corals so bright,
　　Astound one and all while gracing our sight.
Feeding an eel, but not letting go,
　　Teaches a lesson of critters below.
Turtles are playing and nudibranchs crawl,
　　Life in the oceans forever enthrall.
Listen for whales and their beautiful songs,
　　Through ocean of blue is where it belongs.
Their tunes are carried on waves so free,
　　Gardens of memories, in open sea.

Southern Caribbean Cruise

In early January 1990, I was on another cruise with my roofing supplier, this time in the southern Caribbean. My travel agent friend Dave from our old high school was on this trip again, meaning I'd still have a dive buddy I knew for some of my dives. But sometimes he'd be too busy hosting others on the trip and wouldn't be able make the dive with me.

Our first stop was in Barbados and we had set up a one-tank dive through the cruise director. This was the first time I'd depended on the cruise ship to make my diving plans but Dave told me he thought it would work out fine. A divemaster from Jolly Roger Watersports met us on the pier and drove us to their dive boat.

We carried our gear onboard ourselves. During the dive briefing, we were told we would be diving the Stavrokinita wreck. This was a 361' Greek freighter that had caught fire in 1976 and an ensuing explosion had ruined the radio system causing the ship to flounder for four days before being found and towed back to Barbados, the nearest island.

Since the ship was beyond repair, the Navy salvaged brass and anything else of value, cleaned it well so there was nothing left on the ship that would pollute the environment, then placed 200 lbs. of explosives on her to sink her to the sea floor. On our way to the wreck, I noticed a fish that had jumped a good 10' in the air. The divemaster had seen it as well and told me it was an Atlantic bonito, which is much like a large mackerel.

After mooring, we assembled our gear. When the divemaster turned on his tank, it blew an "O" ring that is used to seal the first stage of the regulator to the tank. He searched the boat high and low for a new one but found none on the boat. There were also no extra tanks on the boat, either. As I pondered this lack of readiness, I dug into my save-a-dive kit and found the right sized O-ring and handed it to him in order to save our morning dive.

The dive itself wasn't all that impressive and seemed to match the way it started. The end of any dive should include a three-minute safety stop at 15' to off-gas excess nitrogen that could cause decompression sickness (the bends). So as usual for boat dives, I went to the anchor line and started my hang.

These safety stops are usually when I look for fish and watch their behaviors. While hanging there this time, I did notice a boobyfish hanging out of the top of a too-small bikini just below me. I'm pretty sure that my camera was recording as it hung from my hand at my side.

The following day we docked in St. Barthelemy. Since Dave wouldn't be diving this time, the cruise director suggested that I visit an operation called Marine Service and arranged a ride for me to get there. When I arrived at their store, it looked like it was more of a salvage company than a dive shop. I asked if it would be possible to do a dive that morning.

A fellow behind the desk told me they really didn't have any dives scheduled for the day but he thought they could arrange something and went into the back room to discuss this with another person. A few minutes later, they both came out and said they'd take me to a wreck in the bay named the "Non-Stop" which was a large yacht that had very recently sunk during Hurricane Hugo. They locked up their store and we walked to their small motorboat on the dock.

We anchored above the wreck, then all three of us geared up and began our descent. Usually, one person remained on a dive boat in case of emergencies, so I already found this a little odd. As I looked below, I saw a large school of barracuda hanging out around the anchor line almost all the way to the bottom. It looked pretty ominous to me but the other two safely drifted down through the school, so I followed in good faith, albeit with some trepidation.

With my video camera running, I safely made it through the school of barracuda and it wasn't long before I could see the whitish-colored yacht on the seafloor. I wasn't able to see the entire boat as the visibility wasn't all that good around the wreck due to currents in the bay we were diving. But I did learn that my camera would pick up things clearer than I could see, so I just kept filming.

I could see the anchor chains still attached to the boat and stretched out in different directions across the seafloor that was littered with debris from the yacht. There were tables and lounge chairs as well as kitchenware and clothes everywhere. The story goes that when Hugo neared, the captain anchored the yacht and sent his crew ashore. He planned on weathering the storm on the boat with the motors running in case there was something he could do to ride out the storm and keep the boat afloat during the hurricane. Unfortunately, he couldn't and lost his life when the boat sank.

As soon as the first guy got to the wreck, he disappeared without even looking back and I was still 20' up from the wreck. The other guy waited for me to get to the yacht like a normal guide would do. He led me around the aft deck and then along the leeward perimeter of the boat. It wasn't long before I realized we were pretty much just swimming around a boat for this dive.

With the visibility not being all that good, I tried to follow the guide as closely as possible. At one point swimming along the gunnel outside of the cabin, we passed a large window of the yacht so I peeked inside. Inside looked a lot like the seafloor looked outside with tables upside down and strewn with debris. There was also a lone barracuda guarding the room I looked into which was probably a family room/kitchen area.

When I turned back to look for the guide, he seemed to be gone. As I looked ahead, I noticed a second large window next to me that was open. Silt and sand were streaming out of it like a volcano, being carried by a current coming from the other side of the yacht. I went through that mess but once on the other side of it, there was still no sign of my guide and there were even more open windows spewing silt and sand ahead.

According to my training, if I were to get separated from my dive buddy, I should wait a minute or two while doing a 360° pan around, then look up and down. If my buddy still wasn't found, I should do a safe ascent to the surface including my safety stop and wait there. I wasn't all that pleased with the thought of ascending through that school of barracuda alone so I waited longer than a couple of minutes.

I'd guess more than five minutes had passed before my guide came swimming into view with his eyes agape, then he seemed to show a smile of relief knowing he had found me and asked if I was OK with a hand signal. I returned the OK sign and he signaled it was time to surface. At this point, I confidently ascended through that school of barracuda with my video camera rolling to document my bravery.

Once we were back on the motorboat, my guide told me he thought he had lost me and couldn't find me anywhere. He asked if I'd panicked due to the silt-up and I told him no. He looked quite surprised at this.

I explained that the limestone quarries I dive in have the same level of visibility so I just waited at the place where we separated until he returned. After getting certified, I had done a couple camping trips with my dive shop to the quarries for more practice and had been silted out more than once by someone's careless finning near the bottom. I guess people who don't normally dive in low visibility get more panicked about it than those who have that experience.

That afternoon, I met everyone from my group at the beach. We were near the airport and what an airport it was! Any planes landing had to approach the airport, then immediately drop hundreds of feet over a steep cliff to the tarmac. Upon touching down, the pilot had to hit the brakes hard or end up in the ocean that was at the end of the short runway. The tarmac must have had two inches of solid rubber built up where the planes touch down. Obviously, take-offs were towards the water and not the vertical cliff.

Dave would again join me on my last dive of the trip the next day. We were on our way back to Miami and stopped in St. Thomas. Many of the roofers' group signed up for the snorkeling excursion and the cruise director arranged a wall dive for Dave and I, so we paid him the money for the dive excursion.

Since the snorkeling tour began an hour before the dive, Dave and I went with the snorkelers and I spent some time filming them snorkeling using my underwater rig. This would be something new on the trip tape I produced for the group that year. These memento trip tapes that I gave to each couple were just another way I could pay back my supplier for his allowing me to trade labor for these vacations.

When the dive tanks and weights showed up, Dave and I assembled ours and readied for our wall dive. The guide told us and four other divers to go out to the buoy over there and wait until he got there, then he'd take us on the dive. There wasn't enough room for everyone to hang on the buoy at the surface, so I dropped down to the sand at 10' and sat there breathing from my regulator. We waited 20 minutes or more before the guide finally showed up and began to lead us across a shallow expanse of sand that was less than 15' deep.

We saw a searobin that had very pretty pectoral fins exposed as it swam, so I started following it and filming it, keeping the group in view. After a minute or two, I rejoined the group on our swim to wherever the wall might be. We were still in 15' of water or less, so I was hoping to see the crest of a wall soon as we'd been swimming for a good 20 minutes already and my air was depleting. The more I thought about it, I sensed that we had been swimming parallel to the beach where we had gotten our gear and I would have thought a wall would have been more out away from and perpendicular the beach.

Finally, I saw the guide point to a wall rising UP in front of us. Dave and I looked at each other and only being in 11' of water, I motioned for us to go to the surface. When we got to the surface, Dave and I were flabbergasted. We were still only 20 yards from the beach just further away from the buoy.

The guide came up with a worried look on his face and asked us if we were having a problem since we went to the surface. I asked when we might get to the wall. He said that's what he was pointing at while we were underwater and told us that we should drop back down and stay with the group.

Dave and I both just turned around and swam towards the beach where we left their tanks on the tarp and took our gear to wait for the ride back to the ship. Once back on the cruise ship, we went to the cruise director and relayed our story that this was NOT a wall dive, but a swim under 15' of water along the beach with little to nothing to see but sand. I also told him about the Jolly Roger guide's unpreparedness and about the two salvagers who spent more time inside the wreck looking for something to salvage than guiding me on a good dive that I'd paid for.

He finally told us he'd give us our money back for this wall dive since we'd paid him for this dive. I said that was fine, but I'd rather have my mornings back so I could have scheduled real dives with more reputable operations. That would be the last time I'd depend on a cruise ship to arrange my diving. Live and learn!

When in a school of Barracuda, they always split away from divers.

GARDENS OF MEMORIES~ON THE BARRACUDA

A 'cuda with snaggleteeth inward bound;
 This is where memories are sure to be found.
Curiosity prevails as it sidles in close.
 Unnerving? Maybe; but just a small dose.
At first it had stripes, but now silver-gray,
 Showing its teeth that can cause such a fray.
Deciding I'd not be its next meal,
It slides out of sight, but still there I could feel.
While descending the line, a few more appear,
 And I hope at the time there is nothing to fear.
They're just sentries at guard o'er the wreck below;
 No interest in me or my buddy in tow.
Some silversides glisten from sunlight above,
 Then part for a 'cuda, but not out of love.
He travels inside to be hidden from view,
 Some snacks he may take, but only a few.
Then out in the blue there's a spiraling school,
 With hundreds of 'cuda awaiting this fool.
With camera, I join them, but they ignore me,
 Shooting gardens of memories in open sea.

Curacao

In February 1991, I went to Curacao with my local dive shop. I was looking forward to going with an instructor named Richie Smith who had a Navy background. I envied his three-foot thick dive log with over 400 dives in it. I only had 60 dives logged at the time. Plus, Richie's knowledge of marine creatures was very impressive and I always listened intently when he explained various marine behaviors and interactions he'd have with the marine life.

Tom and Sharon were a cute couple from Indiana. Tom didn't have a dive computer so he would always be found just above us knowing if we were OK with our dive profiles on our personal dive computers, he would be safer since he was shallower.

Dive computers were fairly new then and allowed divers to know their safe limits immediately instead of having to compute their safe limits by hand from charts based on the Navy dive tables. One's dive profile takes into account the depths and time underwater before one becomes more susceptible to decompression sickness (DCS), otherwise known as the bends. Deeper and/or longer than what's recommended via computer or the "tables" would lead to DCS.

Theoretically, I understood Tom's reasoning, but I still wasn't sure depending on other people's computers was the safest way to dive. But it worked for him for the entire week and Richie was OK with this as well.

On the second dive, I wrote in my logbook that Richie had shown us a "tarantula" next to an anemone. I still hadn't gotten to know all the marine creatures by sight and wouldn't know what they were until I pulled out my ID books. I'm guessing this "tarantula" might have been a hairy decorator crab.

On one of our night dives, we found a total of nine lobsters, a squid that ended up swimming into the dome port of my camera, a two-foot long octopus that exhibited many color and texture changes, and plenty of bioluminescent plankton that would glow in the water as one waved their hand past it. Most of our night dives went this way with lots to see and film so I could later share.

The next morning, we saw something I'd never seen before or since. It was about six inches in diameter, four feet long, and looked like a beaded, lavender-colored slinky. When I went to turn on my camera, I realized I'd not changed the battery from the night before and I had no power left to film it!

Someone later told me it might have been a sea salp, which is a string of tunicates. But since it had a more beaded, hollow, cylindrical look rather than just a string of things linked together, I'm thinking it may have been some sort of egg case free-floating in the water. Whatever it was, I still wish I had video of it so I could have had it identified.

Somewhere around the middle of our week's trip, we did a day trip to Klein Curacao on a bigger dive boat than we'd usually used. Our first dive site was called The Cavern. The divemaster told us in our dive briefing that there would be a current coming towards the island that split as it hit the island.

He said that when we first drop in the water, we had to stay together and swim a certain direction remaining close to the divemaster. As long as we did this the current would carry us to the cavern. We were specifically told that if we missed the group, we needed to abort our dive immediately and the captain would pick us up.

Our group from my dive shop dropped in and easily stayed together as suggested. We got to the cavern which was not much more than a hole in the side of the island with very little inside of it. The divemaster swam us around inside the cavern for a while, then a little more along the vertical reef above the cavern before we did our safety stops and got back on the boat. We were fairly disappointed with the dive.

As the crew counted heads, they ascertained that two divers were missing. A young girl stated that it was her parents but not to worry because they had just become dive instructors the week before. When the three of them hit the water, her mother realized she didn't have her weight belt and told the girl to descend with and follow the group while she and her father went to retrieve her weight belt from the boat.

We could tell this story wasn't making the captain very happy as he hadn't noticed them come back up in the beginning or he would have told them they couldn't make the dive. We were told that if they missed the proper current at the split, the other current could take them out to sea.

We searched for a couple of hours going back and forth from the mooring to the dive site and back and then to a point where we could see the other side of the island and back. The waves were beginning to grow on our leeward side of the island and when we scanned the other side, the waves were crashing against the huge rocks and boulders up to 10' in the air.

On our third trip to that side of the island, we finally saw them beached on a very rocky shore. The captain carefully maneuvered the boat as close as he could to the island keeping it as leeward as possible, then one of the divemasters swam to shore and walked across the extremely rocky terrain to the stranded couple as we brought the boat around a bit closer to them. The divemaster wanted to make sure the couple weren't injured.

Fortunately, they were OK but the three of them still had to walk back over the rough terrain then negotiate the rough water and huge boulders until they got to deeper water where the boat could get in closer to pick them up. We were glad to have found them alive, especially since the clouds were thickening and storms were about to move in. We didn't get our second scheduled dive that day.

The next morning, the weather was still cloudy and a bit rough on the water but the captain/divemaster took us out in the small, open dive boat anyway. He anchored the boat, then geared up with us and went in to lead us on a shallow reef dive. About 45 minutes into the dive, I noticed we had been circling a certain area and the divemaster began to look concerned as his head bobbed back and forth.

Then I saw him look at Richie and he gave a "boat" signal by holding his hands together with the sides of his hands touching at the bottom and open at the top, making his hands look like a boat. Then he shrugged and Richie shrugged.

He motioned for everyone to do our three-minute safety stop then surface. When we surfaced, we saw the boat about a half mile away. It seems as though the wind and currents had dragged the boat and anchor far from where the captain had anchored.

The captain swam after the boat while we floated on the surface, staying together as a group. Once he caught up with the boat, he weighed anchor and returned to get us just in time. A big storm had just moved in again and our ride back to the hotel was very wet and cold. We never did figure out why he didn't have a second person with him to remain on the boat for this very reason. It's usually common practice to always have someone on the boat when divers are in the water.

On one dive, I started noticing some silt being stirred up at the base of a brown barrel sponge so I went to it to see what might be causing the disturbance. Maybe it would be a fish hunting for food like a goatfish that stirs up the sand with its barbels. Barbels are whisker-like sensory organs near their mouth like cat whiskers. Or it could be a couple of critters fighting over something. But when I got there, there was no sign of life around, yet the cloud was still thickening.

I looked around to see if I could find Richie and noticed the same type of cloud forming around another brown barrel sponge nearby. When I finally saw Richie, I motioned him over to show him, then shrugged as if to tell him I had no idea what this was. He only shrugged back.

But then I pointed at all the barrel sponges around us on the reef and all of them were now "smoking." I wrote on my dive slate, "Reproductive spores?" His eyes got big and he nodded in agreement. This was pretty cool as this only occurs at certain times of the year.

On other dives, I noticed that every so often, Richie would pick up a little sand in his hands then rub his fingers together. After a while, I realized each time he did this, he was getting ready to interact with a marine creature. He'd rub the sand between his fingers then let bristle worms crawl onto his palms or carefully caress the sides of scorpionfish causing them to slowly raise their colorful dorsal fins and spread their pectoral fins as well.

Bristleworms have toxins in their bristles that can burn the skin like a million little needles. Scorpionfish have toxins in their spines that can cause great discomfort and/or harm to divers if touched. I learned from Richie how to carefully approach many different marine creatures. His way was to do it slowly and respectfully allowing the critter to see you. If it doesn't swim away, it may allow you to touch or hold it.

On one dive, I watched Richie grab some sand then rub his fingers together as he was looking at something over a sand dune. He always rubbed his hands with sand when he was getting ready to interact with a critter so I followed him towards the crest of that hill to see what he might be peering at.

As we approached the top of the hill, the only animal I saw was a four-foot long barracuda! Was he really going to pet a barracuda? He ended up only getting close to it and that was probably the only time I saw him rub his hands with sand and not touch the critter.

I can honestly say that I still haven't let a bristle worm crawl onto my palms or caressed a scorpionfish, but I do still use things I learned from Richie about respecting the marine creatures and knowing their comfort levels in order to interact with them.

After that trip, I started doing my own interactions letting cleaner gobies and cleaner shrimp jump onto my hand. Now I also adore establishing enough of a trusting relationship with an octopus for it to allow me to pet it between its eyes or allow a stingray in the sand to watch me carefully approach then slowly slide my hand towards it until I can caress its pectoral fin. Once I even petted an electric ray once, but that story will have to wait.

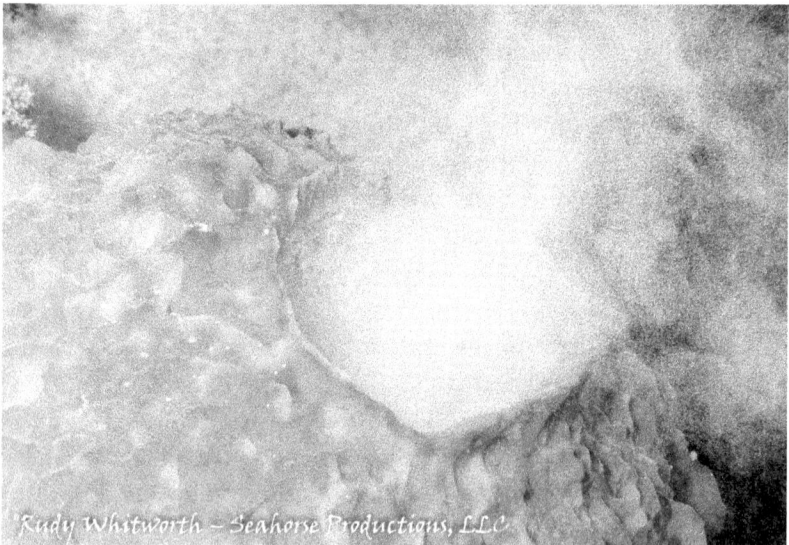

Sponges give off their reproductive spores at certain times of the year.

GARDENS OF MEMORIES~ON SPONGE SPAWNING

At the base of a sponge, a small cloud appears round,
    And this is where memories are sure to be found.
Surely something exotic has darted away;
    Here's a challenge to learn why it chose not to stay!
But upon keen inspection, no movements stand out,
    So, whatever it was, it's quite hidden its snout.
Then a puff of sand shows up at another;
    Maybe the critter's just jumped to the other.
Again, it's not there, but the cloud seems to grow;
    Maybe just current, but how do you know?
'Tis dusty around the base of those sponges
    With no sign of anything making great lunges.
A smoldering fire may come into mind,
    But in water, two sponges of similar kind?
Not likely, you say, as you search for a clue
    Along the whole wall with background of blue.
Now, all of the sponges beginning to smoke
    Causes the brain new thoughts to invoke.
'Tis time to release their spores to be free;
    New gardens of memories in open sea.

One Hour

In July 1991, I was diving in Nassau, Bahamas at Stuart Cove's Dive Bahamas. I'd gone there mostly for the shark dives he was famous for running. Each morning, if possible, I'd sign up for the shark dive where everyone would circle up and fold their arms together. Then a bait box would be brought into the middle of the circle and the divemaster would use a four-foot long stainless-steel shaft to spear pieces of bait from the box and carefully hold it out while the sharks took turns sliding the bait off the spear.

While diving at Stuart Cove's, I met a couple of chaps from New Jersey. At the beginning of each dive, the two of them would dive as deep as the dive site would let them, past normal recreational safe diving limits of 110', and then meet back up with me while I was filming the typical marine creatures like trumpetfish, jacks and white spotted moray eels. Rich and Steve explained that they were Jersey wreck divers and were used to going deep.

One of our dives was a dive site called the Lost Blue Hole. When we arrived near the rim of the blue hole, sharks began filing out as if they were troops marching one behind the other. Rich and Steve immediately dropped down into that abyss while I remained around the perimeter of the hole for shooting my video in better sunlight. When they returned, Rich showed me his depth gauge that had stopped working at something like 175'.

On another of our dives, a fellow joined us by the name of Kent who was staying at the same hotel we were. As Rich and Steve looked for the deepest place to descend, Kent and I enjoyed the critters we could find. At one point, I did notice that the sky seemed to get darker during the beginning part of this dive, affecting my video shots somewhat. But it didn't take long to clear up again.

Later that day, Kent came up to us while we were sitting on the beach and told us his wife was watching the dive boat while we were diving that morning and a waterspout had formed right next to the boat! Before the week was over, Kent brought us a copy of that water-spout picture his wife had developed. No wonder it got darker!

Rich and Steve dove with me the rest of the week and I filmed them and their antics as often as they were around me. After returning home I put together a tape of my dives and things we saw, then sent them each a copy. As soon as they watched the tape Rich called me and told me how much they loved the tape and that they had a deal for me that I couldn't pass up.

He said that his uncle had a time share in Bonaire that he and Steve were going to use soon. If I'd go with them to Bonaire in two weeks and film their trip, they'd give me a place to stay for nothing. That sounded like a pretty good deal to me so I accepted the offer and made my flight arrangements. I would fly to Atlanta and meet them there for the flight to Bonaire.

I arrived in Atlanta a couple of hours before they were to arrive, which gave me enough time to finally consider the fact that they might have been playing a prank on me and I became concerned that maybe they really weren't planning on going to Bonaire at all. They had done a lot of joking around when we were together in Nassau and at this point, I wouldn't have put it past that Jersey duo to do this. With a wife and four children at home, did I make an irresponsible decision to trust these guys?

Needless to say, the next couple of hours probably added a gray hair or two wondering if I should even make the trip to Bonaire alone without having made any other arrangements in Bonaire, or should I just fly back home. Then I figured I was smart enough to make it on my own in Bonaire if necessary. At about the time they should be showing up, I finally heard two boisterous, Jersey accents echoing down the airport hallway. It was in fact Rich and Steve and our trip would be on!

On the flight to Bonaire, I let Rich know that I still wasn't having anything to do with their deep dives, but like in Nassau, I'd hang around the area where they headed for deep water until they returned. I explained that I enjoy my bottom time for filming over any deep dive that would limit me from getting around an hour's bottom time on each dive. That's when Rich said he wasn't going to do any deep bounces like before and we'd both wait for Steve to come up if Steve still wanted to do these deep dives.

We checked into the Divi Flamingo Resort and asked for a third bed to be delivered to our room. We pushed the two existing beds closer together and when delivered, we would leave the third bed closest to the door. Rich chose the bed closest to the outdoor patio and I said I would take the extra bed, leaving Steve in the middle.

We rented a van for our shore diving and I'd brought along a book called the Guide to the Bonaire Marine Park which describes 44 dive sites in Bonaire. It tells how to get to them and what one might see at each of them. Included in the book were also topographical maps showing the layout and depths of each dive site.

All of the dive sites are named and numbered in the book. An easy drive along the main road could be made until you came upon some rocks piled up with a number painted on them which corresponded to the number of the named dive site in the book. After a turn into the parking lot, you could gear up, lock the jeep, and do a shore dive knowing a lot about the site before ever having dived it.

We'd each take two tanks with us in the morning for our morning dives and check our names off from a board that let the dive staff know that we are diving. After our first two dives of the day, we would come back for lunch, and then we'd sign out two more tanks for our afternoon dives. After dinner, we'd do a night dive off the resort's pier. It was much less expensive to do this than it would have been to do boat dives, which many times just go to the same dive sites we were diving anyway.

As soon as we waded into the water, Steve would be off looking for the deepest hole he could find then join us later. Rich was beginning to really enjoy the reef creatures and the behavior explanations that I was teaching him in between dives. He also admitted that he'd never had dives that lasted an hour and liked the extra things he could see in that extra time. Steve would join us after his deep excursion for as long as his air lasted, then head back to shore by himself to wait for us to finish our dives.

One night, we did a boat dive to Klein Bonaire, which is a small island off the mainland. I'd found an octopus and slowly approached it to get some footage before it swam away. While I was filming, Steve moved his head in closer to try to get in the picture.

That's when the octopus jumped onto Steve's head and mask, blocking his entire view. Steve kept trying to remove it, but we couldn't help him at first because we were laughing too hard. Then I reached over and lightly touched the octopus allowing it to grab my hand with its tentacles, then I slowly pulled my hand away with the octopus still holding on to me while letting go of Steve. I have the video, of course!

Each night after visiting the casino for a while after our night dives, we'd sit in our beds and discuss the critters we were seeing using the Paul Humann ID books that I'd brought with me. Rich would ask me what was that fish that darted in and ate something from underneath the gorgonian that Steve had uprooted from the sand and I'd tell him it was a Spanish Hogfish. Then I'd pass the ID book with the Spanish Hogfish picture to Steve who would look at it then pass the book to Rich.

Steve asked me what were those two fish that he'd chased and then caught on the last dive. I looked up the Smooth Trunkfish and showed him the picture in the book. Then, I chastised Steve for pulling up the gorgonian which kills it, then for chasing and catching the trunkfishes. I also mentioned his catching a pufferfish the day before and making it puff up by rubbing its sides was not conservational-minded. All of his actions can cause undue stress on those fish and the reef in general.

Steve then asked me the difference between my letting a cleaner goby or shrimp jump on my hand versus his actions that I'd brought up. I told him I don't grab the cleaners, but I let them make the choice to jump on my hand. Since they made their own choice to go to my hand, I didn't cause stress to them. He finally understood and promised to not do those things again. Luckily, he kept his word.

Each night that we passed the book back and forth, Steve would study the critter we are talking about as the book went between me and Rich. Sometimes we even talked about the behavior we'd seen from those critters. I could see Steve's interest growing somewhat, but each, he would again do his deep bounce dive before experiencing the reef and its creatures.

Before a dive at Balabas Reef, I suggested to Rich that we pick a pretty spot and sit still to see what shows up. He was up for this, so while Steve did his deep dive, we settled into an area of the sand near where he went deeper so he could find us when he returned. I made sure I had a place where the sunlight was coming over my shoulder for the best light possible.

We sat for about 15 minutes and watched a parade of fish meander past us including a Queen Triggerfish, Princess Parrotfish, Trumpetfish, and even a Spanish Hogfish hunting, capturing and eating a brittle star right in front of us. Later that night, while we were sharing the ID book, Steve was becoming even more interested in our reef dives and critter interactions, especially when he learned we sat in one place for so long and still saw so much.

The next morning was to be my 100th dive, but my ear was hurting and I was having trouble equalizing. I told the guys that I didn't think I'd be able to dive that day, but they should go ahead without me. They both said no way, so we decided to spend the day sightseeing around the entire island. Our goal was to make it to the other side of the island and visit Washington Slagbaai National Park.

On our drive, we stopped in a local grocery store in Rincon, a village in the middle of the island and picked up some groceries for lunch. We planned to eat while we marveled at the pink flamingoes wading in shallow water in the park. On our drive to the park, we were seeing wild donkeys roaming the "prairies full of cacti," looking at prehistoric drawings left on rocks above seawater, and saving a whiptail lizard's life by freeing it from the bottom of an empty 55-gallon. drum used for garbage. After lunch, we even spotted a cute gal sunning topless on a beach nearby.

The road around the island was a normal road in pretty good shape, but some of the roads in the park were hilly, rough dirt roads winding through the park. Occasionally, I'd shoot some video of the road and surrounding trees while we bounced around in the Jeep. During one of these times when I was filming, Steve said some bad words. While I continued to shoot, I reminded him that my camera was on and my wife and family would be seeing and hearing this video. He quickly said, "Sorry, Honey!"

The next day would be our last day of diving. Fortunately, my ear felt better so we decided we would dive the house reef and did our first giant stride of the day off the pier. Steve told us he wasn't going to go deep anymore and he hung out with us for as long as his air lasted. He was pretty much an "air-sucking dog," so even though he wasn't doing a deep dive, he would still leave us early and then we'd expect to see him on the pier as always when we returned.

On our final dive of the trip, we played with an octopus in a shallower area of the house reef for about 10 minutes. It really seemed to like our attention. It would shoot from one coral head to another then wait for us to follow it before moving on to the next coral head where it might balloon out over top of what it hoped would be some type of prey. At one point when we finally turned to leave, it shot in front of us and settled down in the sand as if to say, "Let's play some more!"

Steve's air was running low so he motioned to us he was going back to the pier while we played more with the octopus. We nodded and I went back to filming the antics of the octopus. After another 10 minutes with the octopus, we decided to call it a day and headed back towards the pier ourselves.

As we got closer to the pier, I pointed ahead to where Steve was lying face down on the seafloor. He was breathing because I could see his bubbles. Rich and I looked at each other and shrugged having no idea what was going on. When we got next to him, I gave him an OK signal to see if he was OK and he returned it as he continued to hug a round chunk of coral sticking out of the sand. Then he showed us his gauges so we could see his bottom time. He had 59 minutes of bottom time and was going to do his very first hour-long dive!

ROGER ROTH

GARDENS OF MEMORIES~ON BLUE HOLES

Clear water, white sand with a hole quite round,
This is where memories are sure to be found.
From the sky, this hole is a dark azure blue,
While below, this hole can beckon to you.
The rim is coloured with corals and spongin,
But its middle drops down like a path to a dungeon.
A sinkhole it is, amidst a calm sea,
With stingrays around soaring so free.
As you enter its depths, just to explore,
Schools of sharks leave its dark floor.
Crabs on the walls strike a still pose,
In hopes of avoiding your curious nose.
Bivalves like oysters clam themselves shut
And an eel peeks out of a very small cut.
Rocks on the walls create many a home
For animals, there with no need to roam.
As you follow your bubbles, towards the surface you go,
Only then sharks return to cool water below.
Gorgonian branches wave goodbye like a tree;
Gardens of memories in open sea.

Pirate's Lady

In September 1992, I boarded my first liveaboard dive boat for a three-day trip around the Bimini Islands in the Bahamas. By the end of those three days, I had gained a sincere appreciation for liveaboard life. I wouldn't have to carry my heavy gear and camera rig from my room through a hotel then across a common ground or a sandy beach to a dock where I'd hand my gear over the gunnel to a deckhand on board the dive boat. I could just wake up, don my gear and go diving!

The "Pirate's Lady" belonged to a fleet of boats run by Blackbeard's Cruises. Captain Wojo greeted us all as we stepped on the boat and he helped with any heavy gear. Linda was the cook and she was quick to offer us a fruit punch to remind us that we were on a tropical vacation.

Leaving our luggage on the main deck, we went below deck to the main salon which was a room with a large, long picnic table in the middle and over/under bunks with curtains around the perimeter. Everyone gathered around the table to fill out all of the disclaimer forms with which divers are so familiar. Basically, these forms state that if anything happens to any diver, no one can be held responsible for any reason under any circumstances, and all responsibility reverts to the diver. Period.

After the paperwork was completed, Wojo explained a display board that we would use to check out and back in as we left the boat to dive and returned to the boat safely. This would help the crew keep track of all divers. We had to do the same thing while shore diving in Bonaire.

After handing over the disclaimer forms, everyone returned to the main deck to assemble our scuba gear and stow our masks, fins, booties, snorkels, etc. into our personal plastic crates. Then we took the rest of our belongings to stow in one of the three- by six-foot curtained bunks downstairs that would be our "rooms" for the trip. Once unpacked, empty suitcases were gathered up by the crew and stowed elsewhere to maximize our living spaces as much as possible.

I was traveling with my local dive shop and Richie Smith was our trip leader again. Janine was dating another instructor from the shop, Mark, who was with us also. Judy and Jeanne were sisters, but I'd never been diving with them before. There were others on the boat I'd not met before but everyone got along fine.

Our first dive had about five feet of visibility and didn't make this trip look very promising to us. We saw some large permits and hogfish swimming by, but the limited visibility affected the quality of my video so I knew I needed to concentrate on the smaller, macro subjects that would minimize the backscatter in my shots. I did find a juvenile spotted drum about the size of a pea and could get close enough to eliminate the amount of suspended matter in the water between the drum and my camera for some more acceptable video.

The visibility slightly improved to 15 or 20' on the second and third dives of the day. This still wasn't great for any wide-angle video shots. I did find three lobsters in a crevice, but I couldn't figure out how to get them out so I could get a better, clear shot of them. Mark noticed my dilemma and placed his extra regulator (called an octopus) underneath that crevice and purged it releasing a large amount of air. The bubbles caused the lobsters to jump out further towards me, waving their antennae and claws. Now I could finally get good shots of them before they ducked away again.

That afternoon, Linda made some jalapeno and cream cheese roll-ups in tortillas and cut them into bite-sized pieces as an hors d'oeuvre. Then for dinner she made some hamburgers that she called her "Big Macs." I got Linda's recipe for the hors-d'oeuvres and still make those jalapeno roll-ups for tailgating at football games and family get-togethers, but I never did find out what made the meat in her Big Macs taste so good.

The next day, Wojo moved the boat to a different area and our visibility improved immensely, ranging between 60 and 100'. I was glad for this as I was able to follow a couple of scrawled filefish that were playing together as well as a white-spotted filefish. Both species have very nice markings that show up well on video if the visibility and sunlight is good. The same was true for the honeycomb cowfish I filmed.

On the last dive of the day, a three-foot long Juvenile lemon shark swam straight towards me, then bumped my video light. I'm not sure if it was curious or just didn't see my light because as soon as it hit the light, it took off quickly as if it was startled. This was only the second shark I'd seen in the 110 dives I'd done thus far, but it didn't surprise me as Dr. Sam Gruber's research lab is located in Bimini and most of his research is with lemon sharks.

Since we were in the middle of the ocean, during some of our surface intervals when all divers were out of the water, Wojo brought out his AK-47 to play with. He would blow up balloons, tie them closed, then release them into the water allowing the current or wind to take them farther away. Then he would aim and shoot at them.

On the last dive of the trip, we found a three-foot long pufferfish tucked back in a crevice of the reef. There was no way to get it out, but it surely was the largest puffer I'd seen so far, as most pufferfish might be 10-12" long. All in all, Bimini isn't someplace I'd return for diving, and I knew I'd have a difficult time putting together a respectable trip video. But I was sure that the friendships I formed would be ones that would lead to more dive trips together. As a matter of fact, I'd be joining Richie, Jeanne, and Judy on a trip to San Salvadore a month later.

This diver has found a very nice reef setting with the Vase Sponge and Seafan.

45

GARDENS OF MEMORIES~ON CURTAINED BUNKS

A private bed only covered with gown,
    This is where memories are sure to be found.
A Pirate's Lady is known as a wench,
    Her rooms surround only one long bench.
Clothes are stored where all will sleep,
    While dives are made in water that deep.
Three lobsters hide in crevice so tight,
    Then bubbles create a will to fight.
You do what you do to get the shot,
    Only later to think about the plot.
A cook on board that serves good food,
    Keeps divers going and in a good mood.
Good visibility adds to a dive,
    And to the quality to which we strive.
A shark is a shark whether large or small,
    And turns a bad dive into a ball.
Guns are fired at air-filled balloons,
    Not much smaller than divers' rooms.
A room on the boat only six by three;
    Gardens of memories, in open sea.

San Salvadore

On our way from Miami to the Riding Rock Inn in San Salvadore, Bahamas, the pilot of our small plane with half of our group told us that we'd need to make a quick stop on Cat Island before we got to San Salvadore. He didn't have enough fuel to return to Miami from San Sal and there was no fuel to be had on San Salvadore Island. By law, he had to have enough fuel to return to Miami from San Sal. When we landed on Cat Island, we were directed to taxi towards the customs office before refueling.

As we neared the office, we saw another small plane parked there with luggage and gear sitting on the tarmac everywhere. Our pilot told us that plane had been unloaded and searched from cockpit to tail and there was probably more stuff piled inside the customs office. We were ordered to deplane and go into the open-air lobby and wait for the customs officers to meet with us. When we got in the lobby, we saw three large tables full of cases of beer, pop, some bottles of liquor and cartons of cigarettes and cigars, along with a sundry of other items.

While we waited, a customs officer with his rifle across his chest came up and asked us if any of us were carrying cigarettes, liquor, or any illegal drugs. I told him I had seven packs of cigarettes for my week of vacation, but nothing else. No one in my group had any of this either. That's when the pilot of the other plane came out of the customs office, grabbed a case of beer, a case of pop, and a couple of bottles of liquor and took it back into the office.

I looked at our pilot and asked if this guy must be somewhat bribing the customs officer to let him get on his way. The pilot nodded and added he was sure there was probably money involved as well. He said there is a new customs officer in charge on the island trying to make himself look good. This delay had already taken a half hour of our time and if we had to unpack our plane, it would be another hour or two wasted.

What no one else on this trip knew was the fact that I'd brought along a few marijuana joints with me and they were packed away in my luggage. From the time we deplaned and walked to the open-air lobby, I was a basket case thinking I would be busted and possibly spend years in some low-rent jail. I hoped that no one else on the plane would be punished for my own selfishness. One can only imagine the scary thoughts I came up with during that hour with customs.

As the other pilot left the office and began loading up the stuff that was left on the tables and heading for his plane, the customs officer in charge came out and asked us where we were going, why did we stop on the island, and a lot of other questions. The pilot told him his passengers were on vacation and he only stopped for fuel before finishing the flight to San Sal then on back to Miami. Whatever answers we gave him seemed to be acceptable as he finally told us we could go refuel and finish our flight to San Salvadore without having to empty everything from the plane.

I can honestly say that I NEVER traveled with marijuana again!

The other half of our group were on a different plane and must have had enough fuel for the entire trip as they were already in their rooms and unpacked before we arrived at Riding Rock Inn. Richie, Jeanne, and Judy were again on this dive trip with me. We all got along and dove together well. To my delight, not only was Richie a great spotter to find interesting marine creatures, Jeanne and Judy were also.

Manny was another instructor on the trip and Tom and Jill were new to the dive shop with which I usually associated, so I hadn't met them yet. Everyone got to know each other at dinner and it looked like this would be a good group of people. After dinner, most of us went to the bar and had a few beers before turning in. The bar had a list of exotic tropical drinks on a chalkboard with some sort of dare to try them all while visiting Riding Rock Inn. Manny ordered one and stated maybe he'd try to drink them all before the end of our week there.

Captain Tony greeted us at the boat the next morning. He went over the rules of the boat as we made our way to the first dive site. On our first dive, we saw three three-foot barracudas and the third one I found was hanging in the water with its mouth wide open. I thought maybe it was getting cleaned so I inched myself closer and started filming.

I couldn't see a cleaner in its mouth or gills but kept inching closer, getting within about five or six feet. I noticed Richie watching me when all of a sudden, the barracuda lunged at me with lightning speed. I was ready to bump it with my camera but as quickly as it lunged, it stopped on a dime, just short of me.

I guessed it must have been some kind of warning and I surely heeded it by leaving that area quickly. Since she went back to hanging exactly where I'd seen her first, I think she might have been guarding her nest and I'd gotten just a tad too close so she gave me a warning, knowing she could have eaten me for a snack.

Other than the barracuda, the first couple of dives were pretty uneventful but we did see numerous yellow stingrays as well as conchs everywhere. We found some cleaning stations with cleaner shrimp open for business, and also saw a few butterflyfish and a lot of small blue chromis. We also noticed that there were a couple of 14" long groupers that seemed to be almost following us throughout the dives. One of the groupers had what I called a blonde forelock on the front of its dorsal fin.

We went back to Riding Rock for lunch and weren't surprised to see conch chowder and conch fritters on the menu due to the large population of conchs we had seen on our dives. We ordered some of each along with a sandwich or burger. The conch chowder is probably still the best conch chowder I've ever eaten. I ended up getting it every day for lunch, spicing it up with some Frank's red-hot sauce that was always on the tables.

Around mid-afternoon we met Tony back on the boat for our last dive of the day. As soon as we hit the water, it seemed as though the same groupers were there waiting for us even though we were at a differently named dive area than our morning dives. Blondie was there as well, and came up to me right away.

When Blondie just sat in front of me not moving, I reached out to see if it would let me touch it. It didn't move away, so I started to pet it along its side and it seemed to like it! After everyone gathered together, Tony led us through a sand chute and Blondie continued to follow us. At around 45 minutes, Tony was trying to get us all back on the boat, but we were all used to at least an hour underwater so we dawdled around and found more critters. After about 65 minutes, we returned to the boat.

After our third dive of the day, we returned to our rooms, showered, then walked into town to see what might be there. We passed a large sign mounted on a shack that stated, "Elect Sheriff Roth," so I had to have my picture taken next to it. Then we ambled down an alley and into a local bar where the men were playing dominoes. At first, we got some pretty questioning looks, but after ordering a beer and watching the games, the guys in the bar seemed to accept us being there.

When they played a domino, they would loudly slam it on the table seemingly making some kind of definitive statement. These seemed like pretty rough natives at first. When finally asked if we wanted to play the next winner, we said sure, putting a domino tile on a table to reserve a place for the next game.

Richie played first and did a good job of slamming his dominoes after a couple of tries, but he lost the game. Then Manny tried with the same results. When my turn to play came around, I tried like heck to slam the dominoes, but each time it either flew out of my hand as I was coming down to the table with it, or it just didn't slam at all. I finally just placed my dominoes on the game table quietly, but I did win one game.

The next morning, Richie had taken some sausage from breakfast and put it in his pocket thinking maybe he would try to feed the groupers if they were around on these next dives. They were predictably there again (I think they follow the sound of the boat's motor), but as Richie held out the food, the grouper that he was trying to feed just stared at him and wouldn't take it. We couldn't figure out whether this stand-off was because the grouper didn't trust Richie or the sausage wasn't something it wanted to eat, probably the latter.

After lunch, Judy announced that the next dive would give her 100 hours underwater. I only had 115, so we were pretty equal in our diving experience. The highlight of the dive was when Judy pointed to a spotted eagleray off in the distance swimming towards us. Tom was next to me at the time and got so excited, he accidentally pulled the regulator out of my mouth.

That night Manny had two or three more of those exotic drinks like Sex on the Beach, Bahama Mama, Hurricane, Painkiller, Bushwhacker and Lava Flow. It didn't seem like he would be able to make it through the list of about 40 drinks by the end of the week, but he was having fun trying each one. I don't think he had a drink he didn't care for the whole time we were there.

In the bar area, there were dart boards and steel rings on the end of strings that were hung from the ceiling and hanging on hooks mounted to the wall. This was a game to extend the string straight then try to swing the ring in a way to catch itself on the wall hook. Some people made it look easy and others like me rarely got the ring to land on the hook. I guess I was better at dominoes.

The next morning, Blondie was in the water to meet us as soon as we hit the water, and again seemed to be following me and no one else. As I was swimming horizontally in the water, Blondie tried to swim between me and my camera, seemingly wanting to look into my viewfinder. Just for fun, I turned on my camera and held it below me pointing forward as I swam. Believe it or not, Blondie rushed directly behind my viewfinder and kept swimming with me with its nose right behind the viewfinder. I looked around hoping someone nearby had a camera but no one did. At least I was glad Manny, Tom and Jill were there to see this phenomenon. What a hoot!

On the next dive, I saw a yellow ray and thought I'd try to pet it. I set my housing down in the sand and slowly inched my hand towards the ray allowing it to see me coming. It didn't move away and finally I was close enough to start caressing the top of its pectoral fin. Tom saw this happening, picked up my camera and started filming the interaction for me. I noticed Blondie looking over Tom's shoulder towards the viewfinder and started giggling about my groupie grouper videographer.

After that, we saw a three- to four-foot dog snapper which is just about as large as they get, and I filmed a honeycomb cowfish changing colors as well as a Nassau grouper changing from white to spotted. These color changes are purposely made by the fish for camouflage reasons and always entertain me, especially when I can capture it on video. After an hour or so, we all started making our way back to the boat, ending with a total of another 64 minutes of bottom time.

On our third dive, Manny was standing in the sand and happened to be face to face with one of the groupers. The two of them had somewhat of a stare-down for 30 seconds or so, then the grouper started lightly pecking at Manny's nose while Manny stood still for it. It was hilarious and a shot that I did get on tape. These kinds of memories were great to watch after I assembled a trip tape for everyone on the trip.

Richie found a snowflake eel, started rubbing his fingers and hands together, then offered his knuckles to the eel to see if it would come close enough to pet. I guess he thought the eel would be less apt to bite a knuckle than it would a finger. Then he found an anemone and touched it with his finger, showing us how the anemone tries to hang on as he pulled his finger away. That's how an anemone would normally hold a small fish it captured for food.

After 70 minutes, we got back on the boat and Jill said she saw two harlequin basses having sex. We teased her relentlessly about being a voyeur, and asked her how she knew that's what they were doing anyway. She said they smoked a cigarette when there were finished. I liked her sense of humor.

On the first dive the next morning, two other fellows on the trip said they saw a hammerhead, but no one else saw it. The most outstanding thing I experienced on that dive was watching a honeycomb cowfish sprinting back and forth between two tall gorgonians. Cowfish usually slowly flutter when they swim. There was nothing chasing this one so I couldn't figure out what it was doing. But it made those fast laps seven or eight times back and forth as if it were training for the San Salvadore Olympics. No one seemed to have an explanation about this behavior, but I'll never forget seeing it. Maybe it was a courting dance for Cowfish?

The second dive didn't produce much for anyone other than petting Blondie. We had spread out over "Snapshot Reef," thinking we'd be finding some really cool stuff, but the reef didn't live up to its name. After 80 minutes, we started gathering in the sand under the boat and started looking for small, macro critters to no avail.

That's when I looked over and saw Manny holding his fins in his arms that were crossed in front of him. He was standing barefoot in the sand watching Jeanne and Judy play with a conch. Since he hadn't seen me yet, I set my housing down in the sand and slowly crept up behind him and tickled the tops of his toes. He bolted so fast I thought he might hit the surface like a submarine-launched ballistic missile! Richie, Tom and Jill had watched me creeping up and we all couldn't stop laughing, including Manny who must have thought he was being attacked by a Manny-eating toefish.

Once we were on the boat, we could see that Tony wasn't happy with our long bottom times, but that didn't faze any of us. We were there to dive and as long as we had air in our tanks, we had bottom time to accumulate. We talked more about this at lunch over our conch chowders and agreed to keep diving the way we had been.

Our third dive was at a dive site named Hamlet Holes but I renamed it San Sal Quarry because it had such poor visibility. I did find a three-foot long green sea turtle and filmed it for a while. I learned that if you ignore a turtle and don't chase it, sometimes they get curious as to why you didn't chase it and approach closer. This worked on that dive and I got some pretty good close-up shots of it.

I think Tony was taking us to poorer dive sites on purpose in hopes we'd cut our dives shorter, but we already knew that wasn't going to happen even if we just sat in a circle in the sand and played a game of cards. Once back on the boat we did spot a pilot whale on the surface about 20 yards away. Too bad it hadn't shown up while we were still in the water!

When we got to the boat the next morning, Tony asked us if we wanted to try to see hammerheads. Of course, we all said definitely so he took us to a dive site called, "Great Cut." This was a cut in the reef that became a tunnel which, according to Tony, finally opened up at 110' deep on a wall. Tony said the hammerheads would be that deep because of the cooler water at that depth.

He told us once we were in the water, we should wait for him to join the group and he'd take us to the cut. I was usually first in the water and while I was waiting, I started filming two cowfish ascending and twirling around each other, then they would separate and drift downwards some. Then they would ascend together and twirl around each other again.

As I began thinking this might be a courting dance or a pre-cursor to their mating, Tony was rounding up everyone to head down to the cut. I wondered whether I should stay with the cowfish since I knew something was going on and I could continue to film it, or should I follow the group and maybe get footage of a hammerhead or two. Hoping I wouldn't regret my decision, I left the sure-thing and went with the group.

We followed him down and came out of the tunnel at 130' with no hammerheads in sight. Now, it was obvious to most of us that he was trying to again limit our bottom time because the deeper one goes, the more air one would deplete, plus it puts one closer to decompression limits, thus limiting bottom time. It was no problem for us though, as we safely eased ourselves back up the wall and found shallower areas in which to play until we finally got safely back on the boat within no-decompression limits after 64 minutes of bottom time.

Tony told us our last dive of the week would be on a dive site called Tony's Reef. He moved the boat to an area where we had just seen a cruise ship leave. This was looking very suspicious to us again, and once we hit the water our suspicions were confirmed. The cruise ship had stirred up so much sand, visibility was no more than 5-10 feet. We all just shrugged and began looking for macro critters again like small shrimp and crabs, and gobies and blennies. He was very perturbed when we came back up after 70 minutes. We figured he must have had a hot date, but no one could figure out what difference our extra 10 minutes of bottom time would make.

When I assembled the trip tape, I named each dive site and showed what we saw there. Instead of Tony's Reef, I titled this last dive site, "Tony's Reef-enge."

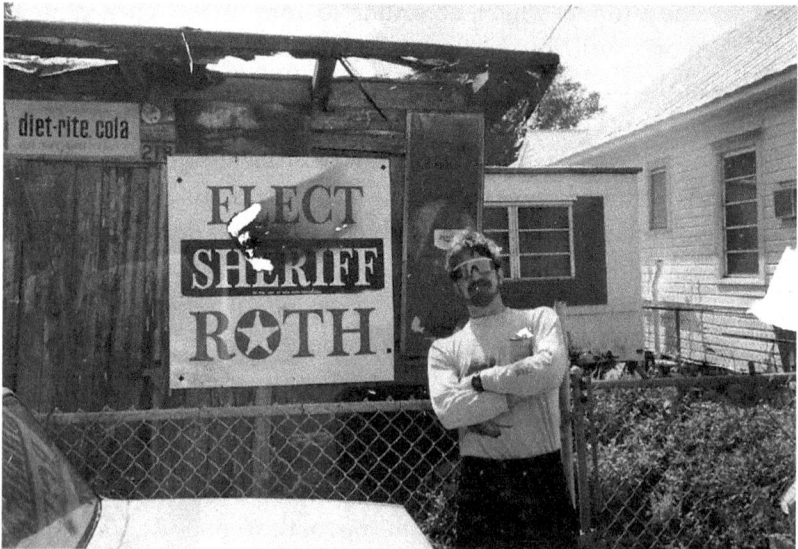

While exploring San Salvadore, we came across this perfect photo op!

GARDENS OF MEMORIES~ON CONCHS

Reefs and sand with conchs all around,
This is where memories are sure to be found.
Visibility low and little to find,
We're having fun and really don't mind.
No matter to us, an hour we'll get,
While you sit on the boat with your own little fret.
'Cuda attacks, but not all the way,
Hints are respected while moving away.
Conch chowder and fritters and hot sauce combined,
Meeting for lunch, we all are aligned.
Groupers want petted not fed on a dive,
Toefish assuring you're still alive.
Viewfinder for Blondie to see what's ahead;
Into Great Cut with lies we were led.
Honeycomb cowfish race to and fro.
That's a behavior we'd like to know.
Ignoring turtles to get them in close.
Then watch a grouper peck at a nose.
Drinks galore being served to Manny,
Gardens of memories, in open sea.

The Florida Keys

On a whim in January 1993, I entered a short video production entitled "Camouflage Beneath the Sea" into the international underwater photo & video competition at a national dive show in New York called Beneath the Sea. The video was a short three-minute piece that included shots of a flounder swimming then landing on the sand only to seemingly disappear as it blended in with its background just like another shot of a trumpetfish blending in with nearby gorgonians. Mating cowfish from my San Salvadore trip with lighter undersides makes them more difficult to see when looking up at them and their darker bodies make them more difficult to see when looking down at them. This is a camouflage phenomenon called countershading.

I anxiously awaited any word from the competition director as to how I might have fared competing against other underwater videographers. Each day I opened the mailbox I hoped I'd find a letter from them. Finally, in April I was delighted to receive a letter from their judges telling me that I'd earned first place in their video category and I would be getting a certificate good for a trip for two to Cozumel including diving and accommodations. This was my first ever competition entry and I was tickled and honored that someone else other than my family thought I did a good job of filming and editing!

This was enough of a reason for me to consider upgrading my 8-mm video camera so I finally broke down and bought what I thought was the latest and greatest at the time (you know how technology goes). I spent $3500 on the Sony VX-3, which was a 3-chip, Hi-8 mm camcorder.

Then I sent the camera to Ikelight to again build a custom housing for it for an additional $1500. I had been pleased with my first housing from them so it made sense to have Ike do another one for me. I also asked Ike to install a built-in red filter that could be placed in front of my lens or moved away from it as necessary.

A red filter is used to add red to whatever it was I was filming. As one descends deeper in the water, red wavelengths are filtered out by the water at around 15', then as one goes deeper oranges disappear at around 25', yellows are filtered out between 35-45', and greens are lost at 70-75'.

Up till now, I had to put the red filter on my camera lens before putting my camera in the waterproof housing and the filter would have to remain on for the entire dive, obviously since I couldn't open my housing underwater and remove it. If I was in shallow water less than 30' or so, the red filter would make my video way too red. Since this was my second custom housing from Ike, he didn't charge me for the new red filter he mounted inside the housing and the lever that went through the housing for me to move the filter on or off as necessary.

My dive shop was running a three-day trip to Looe Key Reef on Big Pine Key in the Florida Keys in July, so I went down with them taking my new rig to practice using the new system before I went to Cozumel in November. This trip would include diving with a couple of other dive operators in the southern Florida Keys. Mark was the instructor from our dive shop who served as our trip leader. My friend Judy who I met on Pirate's Lady and dove with in San Salvadore was also with us. If I wasn't diving solo, I would buddy up with Judy.

After four dives at Looe Key Reef the first day there, we decided to go to Key West for a couple of morning dives the next day then return to Looe Key for our night dive. We had an early breakfast and made the short drive to Southpoint Divers in Key West. Our first dive would be on the Cayman Salvager, AKA Cayman Salvor.

This 187' ship was built in 1937 and had served as a buoy tender for the Coast Guard, a cable layer, a mine planter and a freighter, then sold. During the 1980 Mariel Boat Lift, she ferried 5,000 Cubans to Key West. It was seized by the US Government for illegally transporting these Cubans and towed to Key West where it accidentally sunk while docked. It was raised, cleaned and prepped as an artificial reef structure and towed seven miles southeast of Key West and sunk in 90' of water, settling on her side. Hurricane Kate nicely righted her in 1985.

Judy and I buddied up on this dive. As we were descending to the wreck, I noticed someone had done a free dive down to the dive-master and took a breath of air from his regulator. When I looked at my depth gauge, I realized that he had come down to 75', a feat I still couldn't do if my life depended on it!

Once we got on the wreck, we started looking for whatever marine life we could find. Blue and French angelfish were abundant and schools of creole and bluehead wrasses circled the wreck. The most impressive schools were the silversides that flowed around the wreck like ever-changing clouds. One blue angel swam right up to the dome port of my camera and looked in as if it were a mirror making for a cute video shot.

Our next dive was a mile away at a dive site named Nine-foot Stake. There's a nine-foot long telephone pole there, but no one knows how or why it got there and even if that's how this dive site got its name. The dive is a fairly shallow one, which was good since our first dive had been so deep and long. Shallow dives allow for better nitrogen off-gassing.

There were schools of sergeant majors and yellowtail snappers, a couple conchs I played with as well as a couple of hermit crabs. Judy found a high hat that I'd never seen before and had to look up before I knew what it was. We also saw four different species of parrotfish in abundant numbers. These were Queen, Red Band, Midnight and Stoplight parrotfish.

On the night dive at Looe Key Reef, I found a Princess parrotfish sleeping in a cocoon and filmed it for the first time ever. I had found these cocoons rolling on the sand during morning dives, but I had not seen a parrotfish sleeping in their cocoon until now. I'd learned that when parrotfish sleep, they form a cocoon around them possibly to camouflage their beautiful colors or possibly conceal their scent at night from their predators. Another theory presented in 2010 by marine researchers from the University of Queensland was that the cocoon protected the parrotfish from blood-sucking predators/parasites like isopods.

But the highlight of this night dive were the dozens of lobsters out crawling around the reef. I'd never seen that many lobsters on one dive. I kept thinking that it was too bad it wasn't currently lobster season.

The next morning, we did the same early breakfast like the day before, then made the drive north to Marathon Key to do a couple of dives with Tilden's Dive Shop. We would dive the 188' long Thunderbolt, another cable layer that sat upright in 115' of water. She was purposely sunk in 1986 as part of the Florida Keys Artificial Reef

Association project.

While we waited to load our gear onto the dive boat, we were hanging out near a small canal. When I looked into the water, I noticed hundreds of lobsters nestled under a ledge about 30' long which reminded me of our last night dive. It also made me wonder if they are still there during lobster season, because if they were, it wouldn't be fair to them but a boon for lobster hunters.

We started our dive on the Thunderbolt at the deepest point which was to visit her two bronze propellers at the sand, then worked our way up to her deck where the huge cable laying spool stood proudly. The spool looked much like a wagon wheel from an old covered wagon mounted horizontally to the deck.

Hundreds of gorgonians growing on the deck made it look more like a forest. Barracudas and silversides swarmed above the gorgonians. We saw a triggerfish seeking protection inside of a large barrel sponge before we headed into the wheelhouse.

There was a beautiful Queen Angelfish sitting pretty in the middle of a porthole which made for some great video footage. Then Judy pointed out a large dolphin fish swimming by another window. After we did our three-minute safety stop at 15', we went to the ladder and saw a large turtle resting on the surface. All in all, this ended up being one of the prettiest dives of the trip.

Our second dive was again a shallow reef dive where we spotted a green moray eel sitting with four high hats together! That was pretty much the best part of the dive until the divemaster signaled to me to sit on the bottom while the group ascended. I wasn't sure why but then I started hearing Elvis singing "Love Me Tender" underwater. I later found out that the captain had put an underwater speaker in the water for us. Then the divemaster organized the rest of the group in a big circle and they slowly ascended holding hands while I shot if from below.

After returning to the dock, we realized that we might be able to get back to Looe Key Reef in time to catch the boat for the two afternoon dives, so we called them and asked if they would make a couple of sandwiches for us and told them we would be there in less than a half hour. We made it back to Looe Key Reef in time to grab our lunches and eat them on the way to do our last two dives, which I'd do solo.

GARDENS OF MEMORIES~ON THE FLOUNDER

A spot with two eyes and a mouth in a frown;
 This is where memories are sure to be found.
At first glance, this spot of coral seems dead,
 But a flounder rests flat on a coral head.
Upon close inspection, a fin fringe appears,
 And the shape of a fish soon becomes clear.
With a closer approach, and hopes it will freeze,
 The flounder takes off like a flag in the breeze.
Its markings and colors display drastic changes;
 This fish matches backgrounds of many ranges.
Bright circles to match deep water of blue,
 When it takes to flight away from you.
Like paper, it ripples and curls o'er the reef,
 Then lands in dark sand as soft as a leaf.
Blue disappears before touching down,
 And then it appears many shades of brown.
But once there, the flounder blends in so well,
 It needs double checked to really tell.
With little effort, it glides away from me,
 Gardens of memories in open sea.

The Attack of the Yellow Tail Snappers

Looe Key National Marine Sanctuary is about 200 yards wide and 800 yards long but is not a large reef, per se. It is what's called a groove and spur reef that parallels the Atlantic side of the Florida Keys. The grooves are the sand chutes and the spurs are the long "islands" of coral reef structures in between the sand chutes. The grooves and spurs are each about 15-20' wide.

On the first dive of our last day, I found an octopus on my own for the first time. I was beginning to feel a sense of oneness with the ocean due to a better awareness of what was around me. And my comfort level in the water was increasing.

On the second dive, I was lying in the sand filming some cleaner shrimp around a corkscrew anemone when all of a sudden something nipped at the leg of my wetsuit. I turned around but didn't see anything like an eel or barracuda that might have nipped at me. Since I couldn't figure out what it might have been, I went back to filming and concentrating on the close-up shot.

Just as I started recording, I again felt a couple more nips at my legs. It startled me just as it had the first time and I quickly turned around only to see some yellowtail snappers swimming around above me but nothing else that might have been nipping at me. There were still no stingrays or giant monster fish that might have done it. I even lifted myself up off the sand to look underneath me to see if I might have been lying on top of some sort of nest. But there was nothing under me either.

As I went back to filming the cleaner shrimp, I felt a nip on my arm and when I quickly looked over, I saw a yellowtail snapper getting ready to nip again. I wasn't sure why these snappers might be nipping at me but I was now aggravated enough with them to just turn off my camera and leave to look for something else to shoot somewhere else. As I left, I happened to turn around and noticed that this school of about a dozen snappers was following me.

As aggravated as I was with the snappers, the picture of them following me was comical enough for me to turn on my camera, turn it around to face me, and at least do a selfie video showing this posse of yellowtails shadowing behind me. I'd swam over two of the small reef spurs, but the snappers were still hot on my fins. I swam around and shot a barracuda hanging in the water and a hogfish swimming by. As long as I was moving, the yellowtails didn't bother me, but they were still around.

But as soon as I stopped swimming and settled in for any close-up shots, they would move in closer and begin nipping at me again. Since this diving was so shallow, I slowly went up to the boat and asked Captain Dan about these rogue yellowtails. I explained that they were beginning to really tick me off.

He laughed at my story then asked if I'd been feeding them. I told him no, then asked him how I could stop them from following me. He suggested that I go five or six sand chutes over and they'd probably not follow me. I did that and they in fact did not follow me, so the rest of my dive in that area was good. I decided that I wouldn't want to dive on Buoy #15 again. (Remember, each dive site is named according to a buoy number only.)

That night at the Tiki bar, Dan again asked me if I'd been feeding them since that's really the only times he's ever heard of the yellowtails nipping at people because they want more food to eat. I assured him that I had not been feeding them. But then I remembered that I had filmed a couple of guys feeding yellowtails on my first day there and went back to my room to look at the tape.

I put that tape in my camera and fast forwarded it until I got to my shot of this feeding frenzy. One fellow was feeding fresh fish from a baggie to this huge school of yellowtails that almost hid him from view. His buddy was filming the process. To my surprise, the videographer not only had a clear acrylic Ikelite housing with a bright red base identical to mine, he was also wearing a black wetsuit with a blue stripe and a blue US Divers BC, all identical to mine!

I went back to the Tiki Bar and relayed this to the captain. He verified that it is quite possible the snappers remembered those color combinations and therefore they thought that I had been the one feeding them the day before. Who would have thought snappers were that smart?

While practicing with my new rig for those few days, I'd gotten to know the crew, staff, and hotel manager, Madeline, pretty well. When we got back to the dive shop that afternoon, they invited me to stay longer than the group from the dive shop so that I could keep practicing. I told them I appreciated the offer but I really couldn't afford to stay longer and I also had some roofing contracts that I needed to fulfill back home in Cincinnati, Ohio.

They said that they would comp my room and diving if that helped afford staying, but I reminded them that I still had those roofing jobs to complete. That's when they told me the offer would stand even if I wanted to come back another time. I told them I'd like that and would see how my roofing jobs went in the next couple of months.

In less than two months later, I returned to Looe Key Reef for another eight days of practice with my new rig and new-found friends in crew and staff.

Rudy Whitworth – Seahorse Productions, LLC

Imagine a half dozen of these guys pecking at me!

GARDENS OF MEMORIES~ON YELLOWTAIL SNAPPERS

Yellowtail snappers swarming around,
  This is where memories are sure to be found.
Wreck dives and reef dives to shake it up,
  Then visit the Tiki to empty a cup.
Divers feed fish to give them their fill,
  And shoot the video to prove their thrill.
Right place, right time to shoot that scene,
  Till baggie is empty and oh so clean.
Then off to film whatever to find,
  Keeping that shot in the back of my mind.
A nip here, a nip there that makes for jumps,
  And heartbeat so fast to feel the thumps.
No eel or 'cuda nor monster fish,
  To know what it was, the only wish.
Nothing around and nothing beneath,
  Nothing was showing a mouthful of teeth.
Yellowtails remember from days before,
  The camera and suit those divers wore.
Then never expecting that rogue posse;
  Gardens of memories, in open sea.

More Florida Keys

In early September I contacted Madeline, the manager at Looe Key Reef, and asked her if the offer still stood for me to return and practice more with my rig before my trip to Cozumel. She remembered me right away and confirmed their previous offer to comp my room and diving. I remembered the nicknames the staff gave her as well. They called her the Dragon Lady and Madam Dragon, but I never did find out why.

A couple of days later, I returned to Looe Key Reef for another eight days of diving and fun with their staff. Many times, after the last dive of the day, they would invite me to their homes for a barbecue, steak dinner, or fresh fish they'd caught on their days off. This really helped a lot as far as not having to buy my dinners for those evenings.

My first dive was coincidentally at Buoy #15, the same dive site where the yellowtail snappers were constantly nipping at me wanting food. Two months had passed and I was interested in testing the snappers' memories. There were plenty of yellowtails swimming around, but none seemed any more interested in me than any other fish were, even when I was lying in the sand and zooming in on smaller creatures. I guess the short-term memories of yellowtail snappers are better than their long-term memories.

I did find quite a few damselfish nests on that dive. It must have been mating season for them. The damselfish will guard their nest with vigor from any intruders as well as keep their eggs aerated using their fins to wave water over the nest. I did find one nest that was being invaded by other fish eating the eggs. There were also damsels pecking at the eggs as well. Once a damselfish loses control of its nest there's not much it can do but join in the feast.

My second dive was on Buoy #2 where I saw a few large snook and tarpon, both of which I hadn't seen on my first trip to Looe Key Reef. These fish average one and a half to four feet long. I also saw a barracuda that I remembered from my last visit because it had a short fishing leader hooked onto the left side of its mouth.

That evening, I was driven to Captain Cary's house to meet up with some of the crew for a steak grill-out. Everyone was treating me like royalty even to the point of having Rolling Rock beer for me, which is the beer I liked at the time. During our conversations, I was noticing that I was teaching them about marine creature behaviors as much as they were teaching me about their reefs. At the end of the evening, Madeline drove me back to the hotel since she lived there as the manager.

The next day, and many other days, the crew would buddy me up with a diver who wasn't necessarily diving with their own buddy, or with a couple who were fairly newer divers and probably shouldn't be left to themselves. I didn't mind since I was being comped. Each time I was paired with someone new, I told them I shoot a lot of video footage but I'd keep an eye on them if they wanted to meander around where I was shooting. Or they could watch what I was filming and it may entertain them since I like filming marine behaviors, that I'd explain to them during our surface intervals.

Besides seeing the typical pufferfish, angelfish, grunts, parrotfish and filefish, I spotted a four- to five-foot nurse shark as well as a whitetip shark. I'd follow the sharks for a while to get my shots, then return to my assigned buddies if they weren't following along with me. One couple that didn't follow me behind one of the sharks, told me they thought I was crazy to get so close to a shark, so I explained to them that the sharks had no interest in eating us as we were bigger than anything they normally eat. Like most newer divers, I'm not sure they believed me.

We ate at Captain Dan's house the following night. He had been spearfishing the day before and grilled up some hogfish and snappers for dinner. Madeline brought some fresh shrimp and shrimp cocktail and Capt. Cary brought the beer. They asked if I minded being paired with these other divers and I explained to them I was grateful for being comped and I enjoyed showing and teaching them things about the critters we were finding anyway. Cary said he heard my discussion about sharks and thought I'd done a great job of trying to allay that couple's fears of sharks.

Since the boat went out for two dives in the morning and two more in the afternoon, many times I'd be paired with the same person or people in the mornings and different ones in the afternoons. For example, Paula from Atlanta was traveling alone and liked the morning dives for the few days she was diving with Looe Key Divers. Owen was from Wichita, Kansas and had morning work meetings with Boeing, but had afternoons off which he used for his diving excursions with me. Paula and Owen both enjoyed watching what I was filming and always had questions after our dives.

I'd shown them how to get cleaner gobies on their hands and how I pet stingrays. I looked and looked for an octopus, but didn't find one for them. All I could find were piles of shells that I'd been taught will mark the place an octopus was feeding on various crustaceans which may also be its home. Christmas tree feather duster worms were common. Paula had already known that if you get too close to them, they close up and disappear into their tubes. But I did convince her to wait with me until the worms emerged from their tubes so I could film that process. She told me she'd never even thought about waiting and it was a beautiful thing once she saw how they re-emerge!

While diving with Owen that afternoon, I noticed a damselfish nest of eggs being raided by many fish. As I pointed it out to him and signaled that I'd describe what was happening later, a large grouper shot in and gulped down a damselfish that was still trying to defend its nest. I had been so busy showing Owen the nest, I hadn't even had my video camera turned on yet and unfortunately missed that predator-prey shot.

After a few days of diving the groove and spur system for as many days as I'd dived them, I asked Dan if there was something different. When looking away from the groove and spur reefs all I could see was nothing but sand. He told me there were patch reefs 60-100 yards south through that sandy expanse I was seeing. On my next dive, I decided to do a solo dive and navigate in that direction to try to find the patch reefs he was talking about.

Once I got out there, I was glad to see a really nice patch reef; like a real reef! After swimming around it to familiarize myself, I chose a pretty area and kneeled in the sand. During the next 20 minutes I had a barracuda come in close to hang in the water and just watch me. A large hogfish came close then just sat there watching me the same way. A hermit crab crawled towards me, then started feeding as if I weren't there. There was a yellow-cheek jawfish in its burrow about eight feet away that would swim out of its burrow towards me, then return to its burrow only to do it again and again.

Out of nowhere, I noticed a snorkeler with a very elaborate still camera system who started doing surface dives down to this patch reef area. He would take pictures of many of the critters around me. For him to have swum this far from the groove and spur system and the mooring buoys, I figured he was surely aware of these patch reefs and how good they are. I was really beginning to enjoy how curious all of these marine creatures were on this patch reef and pondered the thought that maybe the critters out this far aren't chased by divers as much as the critters might be at the buoy dive sites.

On one of my dives out there, I was sure I was hearing whale songs in the distance. It reminded me of my dives in Hawaii during whale migration season. I was able to hear those songs when I played back my footage from that dive at Looe Key just like I did in my tapes from my dives in Hawaii.

At lunch, Madeline told me she would be hosting dinner at the hotel's Tiki Bar that evening. I asked her if she could get some things from the grocery for me and I'd make some jalapeno roll-ups like the ones Linda made on Pirate's Lady, when I finished diving for the day. After eating the roll-ups, everyone wanted the recipe, which was no surprise to me. Madeline had made shish kebabs with chicken, mushrooms, onions, green peppers and small red potatoes. She also had key lime pie for dessert.

The next morning, I was paired with Jeff and Mary from Knoxville, Tennessee. Once Mary found out that I was a videographer, she was excited to tell me how she would be able to get schools of yellowtail snappers together and showed me some muffins she'd brought with her to feed the yellowtails. I laughed and told her my experience with yellowtails from my last trip. I knew I would just have to be aware of what buoy numbers I dived after she ran out of muffins.

Besides the yellowtails, translucent moon jellyfish about six to eight inches in diameter seemed to be everywhere that morning. I filmed quite a few of them, practicing to see which angles might give the best results in relation to the sun. My best shots were ones where

I had the sun coming from over my shoulder while I was filming up at the jellies with the blue sky and puffy clouds in the background. I ended up with some other pretty neat shots accidentally as well, including one where I was filming a jellyfish three feet in front of me. As it pulsated and spread out, I could see divers behind it through its translucent membrane!

That afternoon, I was paired with a newlywed couple, Glen and Karen, who were staying in Key West for their honeymoon. Our first dive was at Buoy #29. I found and petted a yellow ray for them at the beginning of the dive. Then I began seeing orange encrusting sponges giving off their reproductive spores everywhere, similar to the brown barrel sponges of San Salvadore, and showed Glen and Karen the gametes.

Once back on the boat, I explained what was happening and they said they'd never heard of this before. The orange spores about the size of a pencil eraser were still being released at Buoy #3 on our second dive, so I later explained to them this is a day and time of year thing and is reef-wide for this species of sponge.

The next morning, brown tube sponges were giving off their reproductive spores which were brown and about the size of a BB. Only remnants of the orange encrusting spores were visible, having been caught up by gorgonians or other corals as they floated by. I was paired with Steve and Omar, who was a divemaster from Columbus, Ohio. At first, I thought this might be a fun time since they were experienced. I offered to take them out to the patch reefs explaining that they were more interesting than the groove and spur system everyone else would be diving, and they said they liked that idea.

As we started our dive, they were following me, but as I got about half way out to the reefs, I looked back and they were gone. I went all the way back to get them at the spur and groove system and they began following again. This time I got three quarters of the way out, only to find them missing again. I gave up trying to show them the patch reefs and attempted to stay with them wherever they wanted to go. Omar kept leaving so many times on his own, Steve ended up staying with me for the remainder of that dive and the next one.

That afternoon I was paired with the nicest couple of the week. Krysia and Brian were from London and were thrilled with everything

I showed them. At first, I showed them the remnants of the brown tube sponge spores that had been released that morning. I also pointed out a dog snapper protecting its fry (babies) from hungry and persistent chubs and blue tangs. During our surface interval, I explained more about the orange sponge spores from the day before as well as the different sponge species' spores that we just saw together.

On the second dive, I petted a yellow ray and got cleaner gobies to jump on my hand, filming both by setting my housing in the sand and positioning it properly. Brian always ran out of air sooner than Krysia, so we'd take him back to the boat when he was getting low on air, then do more diving until our air got low. On the return boat ride, they invited to buy my dinner at the Tiki Bar so we could talk more. I graciously accepted and shared more of my experiences, including the story about the yellowtails that they thoroughly enjoyed.

Rusty was one of the divemasters and joined our table for drinks after dinner. He and I traded stories of our travels while Krysia and Brian listened intently and laughed heartily. They added their two cents every once in a while. They didn't do any diving around London because the water was too cold, so their dives were mostly at tropical destinations like the Florida Keys and nearby Caribbean islands.

After the couple left, Rusty told me he was off work the next day and asked if I wanted to go spearfishing with him and another fellow off of Marathon Key. I accepted and he brought his boat with Ed to the dock to pick me up after the dive boat pulled out. Ed was a friend of Madeline's from Provincetown, Massachusetts. He was president of the Chamber of Commerce and the Crustacean Society there and was here on vacation.

I did more filming than spearfishing, obviously. On the second dive, Rusty shot a mutton snapper, but it was getting away so he dropped his game bag and archer bow he was using and went after the fish, so I followed, still filming. Once he caught up with the mutton snapper, he lost his fin while trying to grab the spear, but the snapper got away, with the spear. He retrieved his fin, but couldn't remember where he'd dropped his game bag and archer bow. Neither did I as I wasn't familiar with this reef at all and was concentrating more on getting the video shot of him shooting and chasing the fish. We searched for the rest of the dive with no luck finding his expensive gear.

Once we got back on the boat, I told him I could show him the video where he'd dropped those items and he was tickled with the idea that we might be able to still find them. I took my camera out of the housing during our surface interval and rewound the tape until I got to where he was dropping things and leaving to chase after the snapper and spear. He studied the footage closely, including before and after dropping his gear, and thought he might know where that was.

We did our next dive in the same area and due to my footage, our search and rescue mission was successful fairly quickly! He started hunting again and speared a hogfish. Before he could take the fish off the spear, he saw another larger one, so he used that same spear to get the second one as well. What a fun video shot that was with two fish on the same spear!

After he put those fish in his game bag, Rusty offered his bow to me to use and showed me how to use it. After two to three tries, I finally speared my first hogfish. Dinner that night was at Rusty's house with many of the same staff people and friends showing up. Cary brought the beer again and Madeline brought her famous key lime pie.

I dove solo on my last day of diving. While lying in the sand shooting two hermit crabs, I happened to look sideways and was surprised to see a five-foot green moray eel lying in the sand next to me. I wasn't sure if it was watching me or the hermit crabs but it didn't attack any of us. I guess I was becoming one with the reef so well, the reef creatures were accepting me as one of them!

That evening at the Tiki Bar, I noticed a gal sitting with a few friends in a booth across the room who looked familiar. She looked like a gal by the name of Lisa who was a good friend of the girl I was living with at the time when I was in college at Miami University, 20 years previous. Lisa lived with her boyfriend Tom in the same house with us, but I hadn't seen her in almost 20 years.

When she got up to visit the restroom, I gathered up enough nerve to go to the booth and ask her friends if she might have gone to college at Miami University. But everyone just looked at me and no one seemed to want to answer. That's when she returned to the booth.

I apologized for the intrusion and told her she looked familiar and

2

that I'd asked her friends if she had gone to Miami but they hadn't answered me. She studied my face intensely until I told her my name. That's when a huge smile grew on her face and she stood up to give me a big hug. We spent an hour or more sharing stories with her friends, like when we went camping on a party island in Lake Erie called Put-In-Bay.

Lisa went on to tell me, after we graduated in 1973, she and Tom moved to Cleveland and had a baby boy who was now 22 years old with a 16-month-old baby. But she broke up with Tom after the baby was born and did some traveling with a big drug dealer of hash oil that he was buying from the Mafia. He'd gotten busted in 1985, so she left him and her past behind to move to the Keys. I guess that answered why her friends were still protecting her identity.

Damselfish will chase away much larger fish and even divers to protect their nests.

GARDENS OF MEMORIES~ON DAMSELFISH

To intruders, Damselfish stand their ground,
 And this is where memories are sure to be found.
Their warnings are quick to instill a fear,
 And Damsels will nip if approached too near.
They guard their domain with discerning eyes,
 Protecting themselves from any disguise.
Quick to jump out to remind of their den,
 E'en their own image is threat to them.
The males take charge of protecting egg nests,
 But join in the feed if they fail their test.
Some also tend beds of algae nearby,
 Which grazers delight in taking a try.
Damsels maintain tiny worlds of their own,
 And with passion, impart a very clear tone.
But if their attention is distracted,
 Another fish might become quite active.
It's Nature's way whether on sea or land;
 Predator and prey, swirling clouds of sand.
With mouthful and grin the fish looks at me;
 Gardens of memories in open sea.

Don't Drink the Water

In November 1993, I took an instructor friend of mine from my dive shop to Cozumel with me to dive for the week. This was the prize I'd earned from the Beneath the Sea competition. Mark had dived with me on Pirate's Lady around Bimini and on my first trip to the Florida Keys. Mark was actually the third person I'd invited on this free trip (without airfare) after the first two said they couldn't make it due to their work schedules. We would be staying at and diving with Del Mar Aquatics. The hotel was only a short walk to their dock across the street and also close to many restaurants in town.

Cozumel is known for its healthy reefs due to the constant currents that help keep silt from settling on and choking the corals and sponges. This meant that most of our boat dives would be drift dives. We'd roll into the water as a group and the guide would hold a large tethered buoy that would stay on the surface to show the captain of the boat where we were so that he could follow us and be ready to pick up any divers running low on air.

Some of our drift dives were pretty mellow slow drifts and others were in currents that felt like we were covering miles every few minutes. I remember one fellow pretending like he was superman flying through the air over a pure white sandy bottom in front of the group. That definitely made for an interesting video shot. Too bad he wasn't wearing a cape!

On one dive, the guide told us there would be a small cavern under part of the reef that we could swim through. As he led the group into the swim-through, I remained on top of the reef since there usually wasn't much I liked to shoot in those caverns, and there wasn't much ambient light in there anyway. I found it interesting that I could follow the progress of the group from the top of the reef by watching their bubbles rising through the reef then appearing in front of me. I stayed above them the whole time they were in the swim-through and met them as they emerged from it with my camera rolling.

On another dive, the divemaster told us we'd be visiting a tame green moray eel that he feeds every time he dives with it. As we got to the eel, it came out of his den and went straight to the divemaster who handed him a piece of fish from a zip-lock baggie he kept in his pocket. The divemaster was smiling and sort of posing for photographers who were getting the shot of the feeding.

As I was still filming everything, I noticed that the eel was circling around the divemaster who was just beginning to look for the eel again. As the divemaster turned to his right, all he could see was the eel's tail, so he kept turning and looking. By that time, I guess the eel got perturbed that it wasn't getting more food yet, and nipped the divemaster under his left armpit, making the divemaster jump. It wasn't a serious bite, but the divemaster quickly fed the eel more pieces of fish.

Knowing enough to not drink the Mexican tap water in our room, each morning we'd brush our teeth using bottled water from the store then we'd walk down the street looking for any good breakfast specials before our two morning boat dives. After those dives, we'd find someplace for lunch before grabbing tanks for one or two afternoon shore dives. We got to know the shore dive sites very well and it was the first time I realized how beneficial it is to become so familiar with a dive site.

We could return to the same coral head each day and feel confident that we'd find the same Sergeant Major damselfish guarding its nest of eggs. If we got too close, the damselfish would fly up at us in an attack mode until we backed off to a certain distance. These little guys seem to have no fear of things larger than themselves when it comes to guarding their nests or their gardens of algae that they maintain for food.

We could also go to another large coral head where a spotted moray eel always hung out. The first day that we found this eel, it seemed to have something caught in its throat as it had its mouth wide open and kept shaking its head like it was trying to swallow something. I followed him with my video camera rolling until it ducked into a nook in the coral head.

As we looked around that area to see where it went, the eel came up over the coral head from the other side until we noticed it. Then we would follow it towards another coral head at which time it would disappear again. It was almost as if the eel was playing a game of hide and seek with us. This was one of our daily routines with that eel at that specific dive site and it never changed.

We even visited the eel on a night dive one evening. We found it hunting for its prey so I followed it quite a while in hopes that I might capture a shot of the eel getting its dinner. That's when I saw a blue tang sitting tight next to a small piece of coral and I noticed the eel stalking the blue tang by slithering closer and closer. I had my bright video lights on and my camera recording in anticipation of the strike. I really wanted that shot of the eel capturing its prey.

The eel lunged at the blue tang but missed it by a fraction of an inch. At that point, the eel turned towards me and started lunging at my camera as if it was my fault that it missed its prey. I kept the camera in between the eel and myself and the end shot was spectacular as it went straight for my wide-angle dome port and hit it before retreating into the darkness!

On our last day in Cozumel, we decided to do a couple of shallow shore dives that morning. Half way through the last dive I began hearing some heavy-duty engines beginning to fire up. In no time at all the noise increased to what seemed a million times louder and we could feel the vibration in our chests. We'd heard that there were cruise ships tying up at a dock in town but I couldn't imagine one of those ships coming as close to shore as we were at the time. But I'll have to admit, it sure sounded and felt like they were going to run over us at any second.

Being in only 25' of water I decided to go to the surface slowly to make sure a ship wasn't heading our way. To my surprise the nearest cruise ship was in fact a mile or two away at the town pier, but it sure still sounded like it was on top of us. I had no idea how loud ships like that sounded underwater and it made me consider what marine animals of all kinds must think of this audio disruption to their underwater realm.

As a matter of fact, it has been found that ship noise does affect whales and other cetaceans. Scientific studies have found that the low frequency rumble of ships can cause whales to be distressed, lost or unable to hunt. Some whales use echolocation to hunt for their prey like dolphins do by sending out clicks then waiting for the return echo to figure out where the prey might be and how far away it is. The ship noise also interferes with their ability to communicate in much the same way.

After cleaning up, we decided to find a good Mexican restaurant for dinner and a couple of beers. The one we chose had a large menu as well as specials for two people. We decided on getting one of those specials and splitting it. I ordered a beer and Mark ordered a bottle of water first then got a beer later. After dinner, we went back to our room to finish packing for our trip home the next day and watch some TV before turning in. That's when Mark started feeling pretty ill. He quickly began vomiting then the diarrhea set in. There were times when he couldn't figure out which to do first. Montezuma's revenge had hit him, and hit him hard. His bathroom visits went on most of the night.

Fortunately, our flight home wasn't until early afternoon, giving him time to recuperate. Being the son of a doctor, I had all the right medicines. I'd given him some diarrhea medicine and something to calm his stomach as well. At breakfast, he didn't eat much, but we discussed his ailment and went through everything he ate and drank the night before.

Since we had shared the same meal, the only thing we could think of that he had and I hadn't eaten or drank was the bottled water. That's when a fellow next to us apologized for listening in but told us many of the restaurants take their water bottles out back into the alley and refill them with their own tap water, but would still charge for bottled water. He said not only does he not eat salads or order mixed drinks with ice in Mexico, he will also bring in his own bottled water to a restaurant purchased from a grocery store.

GARDENS OF MEMORIES~ON THE SPOTTED EEL

Watch spotted eel bay like a hound;
This is where memories are sure to be found.
Out on the sand, with its head up high;
Middle of the day, bright sun in the sky.
It looked as though it was singing a song;
I listened intently, but must have been wrong.
I heard nothing more than my bubbles escape;
No tunes from the deep, and no song to tape.
What might have caused this display I witness?
Swallowing its prey, I'd venture to guess.
Now, night has fallen, it uses its snout,
Searching the reef for its carryout.
With poor sight, it follows its smell appeal,
As nooks and crannies are combed for a meal.
A blue tang is spotted out of its crevice;
The eel stalks and strikes, but alas, a miss.
Bright video lights may have come into play;
It continues to strike, coming my way!
Good shots are caught with more lessons for me;
Gardens of memories, in open sea.

The Big Matt Attack

In mid-July 1994, I went on a trip to the Exuma Islands with friends from a local dive shop. The Exumas are in the middle of the Bahamas islands and just south of Nassau. We would be living on the Cat Ppalu for a week, which was a comfortable catamaran with a good crew I knew. The Cat Ppalu was another Blackbeard's Cruises vessel like Pirate's Lady.

We flew out of Miami on a small two-engine prop plane. I got to sit in the co-pilot's seat up front while everyone else was packed in the rear. The pilot was very friendly and told me about each island we flew over as we made our way right through the chain of Bahamian islands. When we passed over Cat Island, I told him my story about the newer customs agent and he said he'd met that guy in a similar situation.

I was glad to see Captain Wojo greeting us as we arrived at the Cat. I'd traveled with him before and he was very adept at his job. This would also mean Linda would be our cook and she was great. The group found our assigned rooms to unpack then met in the main room for our initial briefing as the Cat was beginning to make its way out to sea. Capt. Wojo was a fun bloke to travel with and I remembered how much he enjoyed bringing out his AK-47 in between dives and shooting at floating balloons on the surface.

Late one afternoon as we geared up for the fourth dive of the day, I was having trouble equalizing so I didn't go in with the group. I went back to my cabin and used some Afrin nasal spray in hopes my sinuses would clear up quicker since the Sudafed I'd been using was beginning to not work for me. 15 minutes or so later I was able to equalize and checked with Wojo to make sure it would be OK for me to dive solo assuring him I'd stay close to the boat. He said my solo diving was no problem.

I made my giant stride into the water and descended 40' to the seafloor and began just looking around. The sun was bright and at a perfect angle illuminating the reef's colors quite nicely. Since I wasn't planning on cruising around the entire dive site, I decided to find a very pretty area to settle into and just sit and breathe air to see what critters might get curious enough about me to appear.

Once I set myself up with the sun coming over my shoulder nicely, I looked around at all of the two- to four-foot tall coral heads nearby and all the nooks and crannies they held. I didn't see any fish nearby at first, but knew I just had to be patient and they would show up. I shot some video of the seemingly lifeless reef then one small tobaccofish popped itself out from behind one of the coral heads while I was shooting so I followed it to the sand where a small goby jumped into the picture.

It took less than five minutes for a dozen or more critters to become comfortable with my presence. I noticed a hermit crab about six feet away and began filming it as it literally crawled up to my knees with another one not far behind. This was becoming a very enjoyable dive and I didn't have to go anywhere.

30 minutes into my dive, the rest of the group was beginning to return to the Cat and hang around under the boat then make their safety stops. Some of them hovered nearby watching whatever it was that I was filming making sure they weren't shadowing my shots. As each climbed the ladder to the dive deck, I contemplated whether I should go up with the group or at least get in a 50 to 60-minute dive.

As the last diver climbed aboard, I noticed a very colorful barred hamlet a few feet away just hovering over the reef so I started filming it. I wasn't even sure what kind of fish this was at the time. I thought to myself how beautiful of a shot this was with the sun hitting the bluish hamlet perfectly causing its colors to bounce through the water to my camera.

As I watched my viewfinder, I noticed the hamlet had started quivering on and off quickly. Then in an instant another barred hamlet shot up to it from underneath, they clasped together for about a second and a half, and then separated in a flash. The first one stayed in mid water and the second one slowly drifted back down to the reef in what seemed to be a dreamy stupor.

Being an ardent student of marine behavior now, I pondered this meeting but it didn't take long to realize that this enjoinment was not an act of aggression. Could I have in fact captured these two in an amorous moment? Were they procreating? What a coup that would be!

I thought to myself never mind the 50 to 60-minute dive, I wanted to get back on board and ask those who knew more than I about this behavior. Unfortunately, no one in my group could verify mating habits of barred hamlets (I looked the fish up in Paul Humann's Reef Fish ID book as soon as I was dry). But after I showed my footage on the TV near the main table while sharing hors d'oeuvres before dinner, Wojo was confident I had in fact captured them "doing the dirty."

I would later assemble another short production about this dive entitled "One Patch of Coral," and enter it into another international underwater video competition the following year. This production would eventually become the third first-place win for me in the Environmentally Aware Photographic Competition (EPIC) which was an established, highly regarded international competition.

My prize this time was a check for $500. This wasn't a trip worth thousands of dollars like the other first place still photographers got, but it still wasn't bad and I was proud of my accomplishments in video production. The check was definitely better than the $75 attachment for a still camera that I'd received for my fifth first-place underwater video competition.

The next day we were taken to a sandy bottom area for a shark dive. I love shark dives. Ever since my first encounters with Caribbean reef sharks while diving with Stuart Cove in Nassau on the same trip I'd met Rich and Steve, I've had a penchant for diving with these unpredictable "puppy dogs," as I've called them. My anticipation was high as the crew loaded a milk crate full of bait, tied another crate atop as a lid and lowered the bait to the seafloor to attract the sharks as we readied for our dive.

Each dive pair was given a bump stick. I was odd man out and turned down a stick knowing I had my housing for protection if necessary; and anyway, I'd never seen the need for a bump stick before so I wasn't that concerned. We did our giant strides into the water and descended towards the arena where the bait box was centered at a 40' depth. There was a U-shaped vertical wall on one side and open ocean on the other.

Matt was our friendly, fairly good-sized divemaster and once everyone was settled near the wall, he swam towards the bait box about 20' away and waved me in closer since I'd already told him I was comfortable with this and had many shark dives in my logbook already.

The Caribbean reef sharks were already circling the bait box sometimes nuzzling at it trying to get to the bait that was tied inside the two crates. At this point, Matt and I were only about six feet away from the bait.

As the sharks continued their circling and swam past me, I noticed that they seemed to be swimming closer to me than any other Caribbean reef sharks had in any of my past encounters. I also noticed that as I looked them in their eyes, they didn't seem to have any desire to back farther away like during my previous shark experiences. The sharks even made a point of swimming close to the other divers who were backed up against the walls. I was beginning to understand why the buddy pairs were given bump sticks. These sharks had no fear of divers like any other Caribbean Reef Sharks I'd seen.

20 minutes or so into the dive, Matt swam towards me and wrote on his dive slate that he was going to open the bait box and take out a piece of bait with his stainless-steel rod to feed the sharks. I shrugged and gave him the OK sign knowing this was the normal procedure for Stuart Cove's shark dives.

I wondered why he would tell me this plan, but I didn't think anything more about it as he swam back to the bait box and began untying the ropes. That's when I began rolling tape of the process. (After the dive, I found out that they'd never fed this school of sharks like this before. They would always just leave all of the bait in the box for the entire dive then feed them the bait after everyone was safely back on board.)

Once he got out a large fish head on the end of the rod, he hid the bait under his fin while he retied the ropes. Then when he saw a couple of sharks getting closer, he began raising the bait into the water column for them to see. KAWHUMP! I felt a huge concussion in my chest as a five-foot long grouper hit that bait in an instant, vacuuming it into its mouth and then shooting away past me in a flash.

My first instinct was to keep following the grouper with my camera but fortunately I decided not to, since that shot would have been too fast and probably not smooth. I kept the camera still focused on Matt allowing the grouper to swim out of my shot. One second later the two sharks I thought would swim past Matt took a sharp 90° turn towards Matt. One zipped under his legs. Matt bent his knees, pulling his legs up and ducked down to watch it go under his legs. As Matt raised his head back up to see what the other shark was doing, the second shark attacked Matt's head!

All I could see in the viewfinder was bubbles coming out of the shark's gills and I could not see Matt's head at all! The bubbles seemed to make the shark uncomfortable and it bolted up and away, but I still couldn't see Matt's head! Crud, being closest and probably the most experienced diver of the group, was I going to have to take a headless body up to the boat? Would the sharks be following me as blood streamed out of a lifeless body? What was I going to do?

By this time, Matt's head seemed to slowly appear like a turtle's head emerging from its shell as he inched his way backwards to a near-by 10' coral head. I'd followed those two sharks with my camera as they swam away and circled back. Then they swam directly in front of Matt while I was still filming and one opened its mouth and unlocked its jaw almost like a slingjaw wrasse or a snake that's getting ready to eat a rabbit. As its jaw unlocked, the shark bared its teeth to Matt. (I later learned from experts that this unlocking of the jaw is meant to be a warning like, "Don't mess with me!")

It was obvious this dive was getting carried away as the other sharks also seemed even more frenzied after the underwater concussion and excitement, so Matt gave the roundup signal and we all began heading back to the boat. Even with the bait still sitting on the seafloor and no one around, the sharks followed us up to the boat. I even have footage of the ladder three feet in front of me while two sharks eyed me as they swam between me and the ladder.

Since I'd been closer to the boat than the others who were on the walls, I was the first up the ladder while Matt waited for everyone else to climb the ladder safely. Wojo was standing there with a concerned look on his face and asked me if everything was OK. He had been watching the divers' bubbles on the mesh trampoline at the bow of the catamaran when, as he described it, a volcano of bubbles erupted above the surface telling him something definitely went awry.

I quickly told him everyone was OK then relayed the story. He asked if I'd gotten the shot thinking that would be too much to ask, but I proudly told him I got the shot. I told him after I dried off, I'd hook it up to the TV before our lunch of Linda's "Big Macs" and fries.

When everyone was gathered around, I rolled the tape. Matt's eyes got bigger than they were underwater and he remarked it looked even more frightening on tape than it seemed in real life! I reminded him that's what we saw the first time around!

After the trip, I assembled a trip tape for the group and called this the "Big Matt Attack" which wasn't lost on anyone who was on the trip since Linda called her hamburgers "Big Macs." I also sent a copy of the tape to the International Oceanographic Foundation (IOF) to get something else identified. It looked like a dryer vent flex duct but I had no idea what it was. A few of weeks later I received a letter from the IOF Programs Director, Kurt Heinonen, suggesting it might have been an egg case of some kind, but he wasn't sure from what creature.

Then he added that he had mentioned this shark attack footage to Dr. Sam Gruber of the University of Miami's Rosenstiel School of Marine and Atmospheric Science. Dr. Gruber is a well-known shark researcher with a lab in Bimini. He requested permission to make a copy of the footage to use in his classes because it illustrated something that he has always taught his students. I sent a letter to Dr. Gruber giving him permission to make a copy for his use and also asked him to interpret the behavior of the one shark opening its mouth then dropping its jaw. I'd never seen that behavior before and wanted to know if it was something recognizable to him.

A week or two later I received a reply from Dr. Gruber. The letter showed his excitement from the beginning stating this was great footage. First, he explained to me that this school of sharks that I had filmed in the Exumas was in fact a renegade school of sharks. They were known to swim closer to divers than most other Caribbean Reef sharks. Their aggressiveness also made them less apt to back away with just a stare. I could surely verify that!

Next, he explained that the jaw drop is a behavior similar to dogs raising the hair on the scruff of their necks; it's an official warning sign. Finally, he addressed the Big Matt Attack directly and explained this was why he wanted to use my footage in his classes.

According to Dr. Gruber, if Caribbean reef sharks attack divers, they usually attack towards the face because they think the regulator might be food hanging out of a diver's mouth. If you've done any shark diving, you may have noticed an occasional shark trying to get the bait out of the mouth of another shark that was just fed a piece of bait. Smaller pilot fish also use this same steal technique as a shark might swim away with the bait.

I answered Dr. Gruber reiterating that he was welcome to use my footage and I thanked him for clarifying and explaining the behaviors in question since I was a former science teacher and loved studying marine behavior. That's when another letter came back to me from him asking me if I'd be interested in running his research lab for a year or so since he was having some issues with cancer and couldn't be available to run the lab. What an opportunity!

I really had to do some difficult thinking about this since I still had four children at home and a roofing & remodeling business with 15 employees to run (and my name wasn't Stan Waterman). In the end, I had to thank him for the wonderful offer, his confidence in me, and the opportunity, but I had to decline. If he gave me that offer today, I'd be there in a shark attack second.

Roger has always loved the excitement of diving with sharks of all species!

GARDENS OF MEMORIES~ON THE GROUPER

Grouper family so large; their numbers abound;
  This is where memories are sure to be found.
The Nassau not found in Nassau alone;
  Black stripe through its eye with white undertone.
The black has fins with margin of yellow,
  And color changes that blend quite mellow.
Red groupers are curious and playful it seems,
  When divers are still and try not to be seen.
Yellowfins named for their pectoral fin;
  A red phase exists to somewhat match kin.
The tiger has teeth it's not wary to bare,
  And stripes on its back that are usually there.
A graysby has spots below dorsal fin,
  But its mouth still tells the family it's in.
The coney has freckles on all given days.
  Red, red-white, yellow; no matter the phase.
A Jewfish as large as a diver is shy,
  And warns with a grunt that you're too nearby.
Feeding concussion felt from chest to your knee;
  Gardens of memories in open sea.

Los Angeles Underwater Photographic Society

When I returned home from my Exumas trip aboard the Cat Ppalu, I had a letter from the Los Angeles Underwater Photographic Society (LAUPS) sitting in my pile of mail notifying me that I'd earned a first place in their very reputable international underwater photo and video competition for a three-minute piece I called, "Expect the Unexpected in the Ocean World." This video showed things like my finger getting bitten by a moray eel while feeding it a piece of squid in Hawaii, a green moray biting a divemaster's underarm in Cozumel, two cowfish courting and mating while I waited for the rest of the group to enter the water in San Salvadore, and ending with a slow motion shot of the spotted moray eel attacking my dome port on that night dive in Cozumel.

This would be my second international first place award to date. Since I sent "Expect the Unexpected" to Beneath the Sea's international competition at the same time, that production would still be eligible for an award from them. It also won first place in their video category later that year and I would get their congratulations letter a couple of months later for my fifth first-place award.

My first international award had been from the Beneath the Sea competition, but they didn't have an awards ceremony. The LAUPS was going to have a film festival and I was invited to attend if I could get myself to Los Angeles. I figured I'd probably never dive in the cold water off California on my own, but this might be a great excuse to attend the film festival as well as dive in the kelp beds off the coast. So, I made arrangements to fly to LA and first attend the film festival, then ferry over to Catalina Island to dive some kelp beds and spend a day shark diving with blue sharks.

My plan was to meet and have dinner with some of the officers of the LAUPS club before the film festival. Since I was about an hour early for dinner after my flight and obtaining a rental car, I stopped in a bar near the restaurant and got a drink. Making conversation, the bartender told me he hadn't seen me in there before and asked if I was from around the area. I told him I was from Cincinnati and was passing through on my way to the Channel Islands for some scuba diving.

He told me that he grew up in Newport, Kentucky (just across the Ohio River from downtown Cincinnati) and asked if I knew a certain person from that town. I told him I'd heard of the fellow since he was a politician there and had quite a bad reputation for allowing nude dancing and other illegal things to go on in Newport. The bartender laughed and told me he was sure I knew who the guy was because I had described him perfectly.

He had worked in one of those girlie bars owned by that fellow years before, but had to leave town when things got hot. I remembered that time to be around the early 1980's and he agreed. After I finished my drink, I paid my bill and headed to the restaurant to meet members of the club for dinner.

As the LAUPS film festival emcee announced winners with their prizes and showed the wining still photos on the large screen at the stage, the audience oohed and aahed and clapped. If any winner was in the audience, they were asked to come up on stage to accept their award and/or certificate after each category was completed. My heart was pumping pretty hard and I think my shirt buttons might also have been popping off as I thought about going up on that stage.

The last category was the video category. The emcee announced and showed the third-place winning video, then the second-place winner, then he showed my video. The emcee knew the 3rd and 2nd place winners were not in attendance but knew I was, so when my video finished, he announced that I was in attendance there from Cincinnati, Ohio and asked me to come up on stage to accept my prize which was a certificate for a trip on the Belize Aggressor. As I walked up onto the stage I turned around and noticed I was getting a standing ovation!

After the emcee handed me my certificate (which I eventually couldn't use due to lack of funds for airfare), he announced to the audience that I represented the last category so he invited all winners in attendance to come back up on stage so that anyone in the audience could come up and talk to any of the winners personally. All the winners present lined up across the stage, then some members of the audience began filing up. As I looked around, each winner may have had one or two people around them, but a line began to form in front of me and kept getting longer.

I was already pretty blown away from the awards ceremony, but then the number of people wanting to congratulate me and ask about my video was even more impressive to me! As I was talking with one fellow I glanced at others in the line and noticed Bonnie Cardonne, editor of *Skin Diver Magazine*, was also in my line about five or six people back! When it was her turn to congratulate me, she told me she had been one of the judges along with Jim Church and Stan Waterman and she told me that the judges felt I'd won unanimously. Wow, what an honor for this little ole landlocked diver from Cincinnati, Ohio!

The next day, I caught a ferry to Catalina Island and walked from the dock to a hotel someone recommended I stay at, wheeling my suitcase and all my dive gear with my huge housing box that was about 20" square balanced on top of my dive bag. I checked in with an older lady at the desk (which was also the bar), then went to the room and took a shower. The shower curtain rod kept falling off the wall and after showering I noticed the heat still had not come on and it was quite chilly in the room. After drying off, I laid my suitcase on the bed and got out some clean clothes, then tried to hook up my video camera to the TV to be sure it would work for reviewing any footage I'd get. But the TV wasn't working at all, even though I'd requested one for this purpose when I made my reservations months earlier.

On my way to get something to eat for lunch, I stopped at the desk and asked the lady if there might be someone who could check out the lack of heat in my room and told her I would also need a TV that worked. As a couple of drinking buddies sat listening nearby with their highballs in front of them, I explained to her that as an underwater videographer and I needed to check my footage each day to make sure everything was working properly so that any necessary changes could be made before the next day's dives.

She told me there was no maintenance person, nor other rooms, nor were any other TV's available. Frowning, I told her I'd already used the shower but would be happier if she was OK with my just leaving to find another room in town. I offered to pay something, but she declined, saying it was fine for me to leave. I went back to my room, packed everything up and walked around town until I found another room available to settle into for a few days. The new room was a much nicer and less expensive room.

I had previously made arrangements to dive with Burnie Ramming who owned a dive boat called the "Catalina Mako." The next day I met Burnie and we did a couple of morning dives in the kelp beds with the sun rays glistening through the kelp blades just as I'd seen in so many wonderful pictures of the kelp beds. There were many colorful fish that I'd never seen before but filmed anyway knowing I'd look up their ID's the first chance I got.

My last day of diving in Catalina would be a single shark dive hoping to attract Blue or Mako sharks. I got to the dock early enough to film Burnie and his first mate bringing the shark cage down the ramp to the dock and hoisting it onto the boat. This would surely be a good introductory shot for a shark diving story. Then they loaded a 55-gallon Rubbermaid container full of bait onto the stern before loading our dive gear and helping me and two others on board.

Burney dumped some seawater into the bait, then untied the ropes while the first mate started the engines and began pulling away from the dock. On the way to the dive site, Burnie explained what was in the chum as he mixed it up and stirred it with a 5-iron golf club. As he talked, he was also displaying a very interesting but sly smile as if he enjoyed this mixing process more than the diving itself. After a while, he started filling a gallon bucket of the chum and dumped it into the Pacific while he called to the sharks as if they were his pets.

Shortly afterwards, the boat stopped and the first mate and Burney lowered the cage over the side until the four top corner buoys kept the cage hanging about 15' below the surface, then tied it off at that depth. Burney attached a large tuna head to an extra line with a float that would hang in the water just below the cage. Now, we'd just wait until some sharks showed up.

It only took less than 30 minutes for three to five blue sharks to begin circling the cage and biting at the tuna head. Everyone geared up. I grabbed my video camera and followed Burney into the water where he held open the door at the top of the cage for me to enter. Then he went back to get the other two divers and bring them down.

I tried to get used to the bouncing up and down of the cage as well as tried to figure out how I'd hold my housing so that it didn't get bumped and scratched by all the cage movement caused by the waves moving the buoys. Burney opened the top door again to let the other two divers in then looked at me and asked if I was OK. I signaled no and motioned that I'd like to shoot from outside of the cage. To my delight, he kept the door open and waved me out.

I held onto the cage with my left hand and my camera with the right, and I was much more comfortable outside of the cage. With good buoyancy, I could comfortably let go of the cage for a second or two to use both hands to turn the camera on record or standby, re-focus, or zoom, etc. Bring on the sharks!

The blue sharks would swim around the cage, then go for the tuna head. After taking a bite of the tuna, they'd swim out of sight while others took their place. We had a constant parade of blue sharks circling us. All of the blues had bright white fluorescent snouts and one had a large dent in its side. That was the only one I could recognize and discern from the others.

I'd gotten pretty good at recognizing various markings and scars on some Caribbean reef sharks I'd dived with just like the grouper Blondie in San Salvadore. But these blues all seemed to look alike to me as they swam past looking into my dome port and/or bumping my fins. After about 40 minutes, Burney opened the top of the cage and led the other two divers safely back to the boat. Then he and I swam the cage closer to the boat so the first mate could secure it until Burney got back up and helped hoist it into the boat.

On the return trip to the dock, Burney explained that the dent in the shark's side was probably made by a dolphin protecting its calf from the voracious blue shark's attack attempt. The bright white fluorescence on their snouts probably indicated that they had been hunting squid the night before. They swim through large schools of fluorescent squid thrashing their snouts back and forth, knocking the squid senseless. Then they swim back through the schools and chow down on the unconscious squid just floating in the water column.

As we were tying up the boat at the dock, a sea lion hopped out of the water onto the dive deck, then made its way into the boat. Not knowing what to do, we three divers backed away. Burney laughed and tossed a piece of leftover bait to the sea lion then tossed another into the water. The sea lion ate the first one, then dove back into the water to get the second one before another sea lion could eat it. Burnie just closed the gate from the dive deck to the boat deck to keep it from returning.

As I flew back to Cincinnati, I had no idea this adventure was not over yet. The first thing my wife asked me when I walked in the front door was, who was the prostitute that called my wife and told her that I'd gone to this lady's place, spent time in her room, laid in and messed up her bed, used her shower, broke the shower rod, then left without paying. I'm thinking that lady and those two rapscallions sitting at the bar are probably still laughing about that phone call to my wife to this day!

© Andrew Sallmon

The Blue Shark is often ranked among the top 10 most dangerous sharks.

GARDENS OF MEMORIES~ON BLUE SHARKS

Cages and bait with no sign of ground;
> This is where memories are sure to be found.

Deep water, cold thoughts, rumbles from bubbles;
> All heighten the feelings of double troubles.

From out of the blue, slender shapes take form,
> With nostrils and fins quite far from the norm.

They each approach with a stealth all their own,
> But the look in their eye has a definite tone.

"What in the sea are you and where are you from?
> Where is the food? I know I sense some!"

With fluorescent noses from last night's squid,
> It's surprising these blue sharks still wish to be fed.

A quick shot from the left and a dip to the right,
> It's got the scent and ready to bite.

Twisting and thrashing and then down under;
> A fish on a rope is torn asunder.

But once bait is gone, and the scent no more,
> These sharks uncover a vanishing door.

Shadows from sun, wave of tail to me...
> Gardens of memories in open sea.

Rescue Diver

Between my original NASDS (the National Association of Scuba Diving Schools) certification in 1988, and 1994, I'd volunteered at my dive shop in Cincinnati, helping instructors with their beginner's certification classes. I figured the more time I spent around diving, the better diver I'd become. It wasn't long before I was considered an assistant instructor doing all of the exercises in the water with the students while the instructor stood poolside watching all of the students and assistants at once. These exercises included what instructors do regularly like mask clearing, regulator clearing, buddy breathing, doff and don, etc.

You have to keep in mind that NASDS didn't really offer an advanced diver certification because we learned basic navigation, wreck penetration, and various other skills in our basic certification class. Another certifying agency named PADI (Professional Association of Diving Instructors) didn't offer these extra skills until one paid for and took another class (hence the nickname, Put Another Dollar In). After the basic certification class, the next PADI class would be advanced diver, then wreck diver, then night diver and so on.

In 1994 my dive shop traded NASDS for PADI...I guess they wanted the extra dollars put in. When I showed up to help with the shop's next certification class, I was told I couldn't help in the water anymore. PADI didn't recognize someone as an assistant instructor until they completed certifications for advanced, divemaster, then rescue diver. Only then could they become an assistant instructor as they worked towards becoming an instructor. It was explained that I was no longer allowed to even touch a student in the water until after becoming a PADI divemaster.

So, I enrolled in the divemaster class. But in the first classroom session, it was explained that once we became divemasters, we'd have to carry liability insurance. The dive shop would cover that insurance as long as we kept volunteering in classes, but the insurance would

94

be on us if we stopped helping out. I decided I didn't want to worry about paying out any more money if I got bored with the responsibility of volunteering and I was in fact already on my way to making a good reputation in the dive industry with my video camera.

After diving almost five years, I decided it would be a good idea to take a rescue diver class. But I was told the rescue diver certification was a PADI certification and in order to take rescue diver, I'd have to take the PADI advanced diver certification first. Even though I'd already been taught everything in the advanced class manual when I was originally certified NASDS, PADI said I had to take the advanced class anyway. I put another dollar in and took the PADI advanced diver class so that I could take the rescue diver class next.

The instructor for the advanced class was Karl. He was my original NASDS instructor and we got along fine during my basic open water certification classes. But Karl was becoming increasingly jealous of my underwater video skills and awards since he started shooting video before I did but had done nothing with it. Through the years this jealousy grew tremendously. But the class went OK and I did get my advanced certification even though he'd ignore me or put me down any chance he could get.

One thing I remember from that class was when I was practicing navigation with my compass in a field with a towel over my head. I would put a towel over my head so that all I could see was my compass. Then I'd walk 20 paces, make a 120° turn, walk 20 more paces, make another 120° turn and take another 20 paces and I should end up at the point from which I started.

But every time I did the triangle, I ended up being exactly five feet away from my starting point. Being a roofing contractor, when I measure roofs, I pace them off three feet at a time since each shingle tab is 1' wide. I've always been very accurate even pacing off three feet on the ground without using the shingles. Therefore, I was confident that my paces were even. But my navigation triangle was so predictably five feet off every time, I took my compass back to the shop and told Karl there had to be something wrong with the compass and I wanted to exchange this one for another one.

He became very aggravated with me and told me it was impossible.

He then grabbed the compass out of my hands, along with a towel and proceeded into the parking lot. He told me to watch him do this perfectly so I'd see there was nothing wrong with my compass. He put the towel over his head and proceeded to pace off his triangle from the rear corner of the dive shop's van. He went out, then over then he headed back to the starting area. I could already tell he was going to be about five feet off, but figured he was peeking anyway so I didn't say anything.

When he got near the starting point, he ran headfirst into the side of the shop's van, exactly five feet away from his starting point. He was furious with me for not telling him he was going to hit the van. I was choking back my karma laugh as much as I could and told him I really thought he would be peeking enough to realize his heading was off, thinking he'd at least see the tires of the van. We went back into the dive shop where he begrudgingly gave me a new compass which worked perfectly every time from then on.

I took my rescue diver class during July and August of 1994. My instructor, Jack, was a big fellow around 6'4, 275 lbs. or better. He used to tell us his favorite things to do with his diving buddies was to loosen someone else's fittings on their gear before a dive or cut each other's hoses underwater while diving.

I'm sure I wasn't ready to do all of that stuff, but I was ready to be more self-sufficient and figured as a certified rescue diver, I'd also learn things about self-rescue, which certainly was the case with Jack. He taught beyond the book and that was OK with me. The more I learned, the more confident I'd be in the water.

The class went well and I learned a lot. My dentist, Terry, was in the class as well as others I'd been an assistant instructor with, and one that I'd even taught years before in her basic certification class. Together, we made a very good team in all the exercises Jack could throw at us, which I guess means we had a good instructor.

During our open water dives in a quarry in northern Ohio, Jack began to show his own personality conflict with me (I'm thinking Karl had given him a head's up from his perspective). When it came time for the tired diver tow and carry, Jack buddied me up with Terry who was about 5'10 and 225 lbs. I was about 5'8, 150 lbs. I performed fine towing him back to shore, but I really struggled carrying him over my shoulders 50 yards across a loose gravel beach. But there was no way I would let Jack find any reason to not pass me in this class, and I finally finished the 50-yard carry.

Then the icing on the cake came when Jack made up the buddy pairs for rescuing the panicked diver in the water. He told everyone else who they would be paired with, then looked at me and told me that it was going to be him and me. Really, I thought, a guy who cuts his friends' air hoses for fun and is twice my size is now going to be my panicked diver?

He proceeded out into the water and feigned being panicked. I went out and did all the right things, but his "panicked" diver was really more like an "I'm going to make you fail no matter what" diver. He tried very hard to steal my mask, my fins, or even grab me and pull me under. At one point, he did steal one of my fins then used it to keep me away from him by slapping me with it (which is something a panicked diver would not do).

I went under him to get behind him (remember I only had one fin) so I could grab his first stage on the top of his tank. He obviously knew what I was doing and kept spinning and grabbing anything he could to force me to go even deeper. He even dropped down a bit and tried to kick my face and mask but I forearmed it off. (Again, a panicked diver would never drop deeper in the water since they want to stay above water to be able to breathe no matter what.)

He and I both knew a panicked diver wouldn't be aware enough to know what I was doing, but I did finally get behind him and was able to tow him back to the dock without him drowning me. He was definitely brutal and definitely tried to flunk me, but I passed and I'm grateful for how hard he made the class for me. To this day, Terry and I laugh about the lessons Jack taught us.

After finishing the rescue diver certification, Jack was happy to have me help out in his subsequent rescue diver classes. I'd show up at the quarry early in the morning after his class started and park on a different beach, then act preoccupied with things. I'd do goofy stuff like get ready to gear up then realize I'd forgotten something in the van. These are all things an unprepared diver might do. Then I'd gear up and jump into the quarry and make a solo dive, which again, is a no-no to newer divers. I'd swim underwater out to the middle of the quarry where I'd surface with flailing arms, yell for help, then descend down into the cabin of a sunken boat and wait for his students to rescue me.

I didn't mind helping these students but I did it less and less and finally stopped, because volunteering like this also meant driving three hours, diving in very cold water (which I don't care for), and then sometimes sitting still in the boat cabin for 15 minutes or more without moving until the "rescuers" found me. Then there was the drive home as well, and I got nothing from Jack or the shop for volunteering to do this.

The rescue diver certification gave me a huge sense of confidence in my diving from that point on. I began doing many more "same day, same ocean" dives with my buddies, meaning we weren't always close enough to save one-another if necessary, but we did know where each other was. Then, I eventually did many more solo dives for filming purposes. But I was also much more acutely aware of my environment and what I'd need to do for any self-rescue situation.

Unlike Roger's solo diving penchant, Signal Gobies are usually found in pairs.

Family Diving

During the last half of 1994, my twin children were 16 and going through their basic open water certifications in Cincinnati. Carmen was the oldest by a couple of minutes and usually took her time to study well and think things out. Cyan, being a boy, was always very willing to just dive into things head first and figure things out later.

I filmed some of their classroom sessions and all of their pool sessions with the thought of producing a story entitled, "Kids Can Scuba Dive, Too!" When it came time for the open water dives that they needed to finish their course, I decided to take the family to Grand Bahama Island for a small January vacation so the twins could do their open waters in warm water like I did. I felt that since I hadn't wanted to do my open waters in the cold, low-vis quarries they shouldn't have to either. I got referral letters from their instructor stating that they'd finished everything for their certification except their open water dives and we took those letters with us.

While waiting at the gate to board our flight with Laker Air to Grand Bahama Island, Cyan showed me out the window of the airport that my camera housing box was sitting on the tarmac at the side of the conveyor belt next to three nice leather suitcases. Once we got on the plane, I asked a stewardess to verify that my housing case was in fact loaded because I'd seen it still on the tarmac even after the tractor had pulled away the empty luggage train. She assured me that it would be loaded, but I insisted she double check for me, telling her I was filming a production underwater and could absolutely NOT land without my camera housing that was in that box.

She came back and told me that it was a good thing I'd mentioned something to her as baggage handlers were in fact beginning to move my wooden housing case and three leather suitcases back to the baggage facility. She said they thought the luggage was on the tarmac due to faulty tags but would now be sure to load it on the plane. I was beginning to sense other reasons but let it go being glad to know my housing had finally been loaded on the plane.

After we settled in at our hotel, we took the referral letters from the dive shop in Cincy to Unexso and scheduled the necessary dives with an instructor there. We decided to begin this series of dives the following day. Upon arrival at the dive center the next morning we were asked to gear up and do a check-out dive in their 18' deep tank before going out into the ocean. The instructor watched the twins as they assembled their gear to make sure they were doing it properly as well as assessing their comfort levels.

Upon completing the check-out dive, we were told that the weather was too windy and the ocean too rough to do any diving that day. I asked if there was any protected area where the kids could do their open water exercises since we'd only be in Grand Bahama for five days and would need all of those days to complete their open waters. The instructor agreed to take us to a shallower area where we could at least be underwater and the twins could do a little diving along with performing the necessary exercises to complete their certification.

I filmed all of their certification dives as we weaved around small coral heads and watched upside down jellyfish pulsate while swimming or sitting on the bottom in the sand. Carmen enjoyed seeing a cute pufferfish the most because of its eyes and how cute they always look. We dove in various lagoon areas each day since the weather didn't really let up until our last day when we finally got to do two real ocean dives.

The kids really enjoyed those dives, especially the last one. We did a dolphin experience dive with Unexso's trained dolphins. The dolphins swam with us throughout the dive. At some point, the divemaster must have done something out of the ordinary with one of the dolphins, because it turned around to her and started aggressively yapping at her in its own way, causing her to cringe and back off. We all learned that even tame and trained dolphins can be dangerous if provoked.

Upon our return to the dock, I suggested the kids get some lunch at the restaurant and wait for me as I had one more dive scheduled for myself which was a shark dive. Cyan quickly asked if he could go reminding me that he was now a certified diver!

I told him he could go if they had room on the boat, then I turned to Carmen to ask her if she wanted to go as well. She calmly told me no, she'd be just fine having lunch at the restaurant and waiting for us to return from this last dive. She knew her comfort level in the water and shark diving didn't sound that comfortable to her as yet. I told her I was proud of her for realizing that.

Before the dive Cyan noticed that the guide was donning a chain mail suit and gloves and he asked me if we'd be wearing one too. I smiled and told him no. We would be at the mercy of the wild sharks. I was hoping to add a small sense of excitement to his dive, but having seen my footage of so many other shark dives I'd done, he knew what to expect and my statement didn't scare him at all.

Needless to say, Cyan's eyes were pretty big throughout the dive, as were his smiles. He thoroughly enjoyed the dive and I got some great video of him smiling at the camera while, unbeknownst to him, sharks were coming from behind him and were swimming directly over his head towards my camera. Had he raised his arm he could have touched many of them.

Sometimes a shark would swim up to the guide and put its snout directly on the guide's stomach. The guide would then reach under the shark and begin rubbing its belly. As she rubbed, the shark relaxed and she turned it belly up while she continued to rub and the shark remained in a tonic immobility state until she stopped. This was the first time I'd seen this occur and in the back of my mind I knew some-day I'd try that.

We met Carmen at the dive center and went back to our room to begin packing for the trip home the following afternoon. Upon dis-embarking Laker Air at the Greater Cincinnati Airport around 11:30 PM, we went to the baggage area to claim our luggage, dive gear, and my camera equipment. After we got most of our luggage, I finally saw my housing box come up the conveyor belt then tumble down to the circle conveyor, then tumble over the wall and completely spill out on the floor of the airport. A nearby red cap had seen what happened and came to help and suggested that I call baggage services to document this accident in case anything was broken.

The lid had totally come unhinged from the box and my video lights, arms and dismantled parts of my housing were everywhere on the floor. As the red cap stood next to me, I called the Laker Air baggage service. But after explaining what had happened the guy on the other end of the line hung up on me. When I immediately called back it rang two or three dozen times or more but yet no one answered.

It was getting past midnight by this time and everyone was tired so I decided I'd call the next morning and explain the situation. Of course, during the call the next day I was told that since I left the airport there was nothing they could do. I told them the red cap's name that saw this happen and they promised to look into it. They asked what the box looked like and I told them it was wooden and about 20" square all the way around to accommodate my large, waterproof housing. I also mentioned that the box looked as if someone had taken a straight claw hammer and beat the box all over before I claimed it at the airport.

A couple of weeks later I called again to see what progress might have been made and the person on the other end of the line informed me that they did in fact verify that the red cap had witnessed this box spill out and therefore they would be sending me a box as comparable as possible for replacement of my damaged one. I reiterated that it needed to be the same size to accommodate my video camera housing. What I received a couple of weeks later was a small jewelry box about six square inches.

When I tried to contact baggage services again, they said it was out of their hands so I wrote a letter to Sir Freddy Laker, the CEO of Laker Air. I relayed the entire story even including the box and leather luggage being seemingly snuck away from the tarmac. I told him how expensive the housing was and asked that he look into a proper replacement for my housing shipping box other than a small jewelry box that would not have even accommodated one of my video lights.

His return letter to me stated that there would be no different replacement. Laker Air had stood by their responsibility by sending me the replacement box. He ended his letter by stating that I should know better than to "put such expensive equipment in the belly of an aeroplane." I'm not sure how he might have thought one should get their equipment to a destination without putting it into the checked luggage since it was too large to carry on but I finally contacted my insurance agent.

I showed my agent the broken pieces and holes that were absolutely identical to ones that would be made with a straight claw hammer. Being a roofing contractor, there was no doubt in my mind what they did after realizing that I'd thwarted their attempt to steal my housing and those three leather suitcases. I also showed my agent the aluminum angle pieces I'd previously installed on every edge and corner of the box to reinforce the strength of the box. Even these had straight claw gashes in them.

My agent told me to find a comparable box worthy of shipping my housing and they'd pay for it. He'd keep these broken pieces to subrogate from Laker Air. I contacted Anvil Cases who make those heavy-duty blue cases that bands and musicians use when touring and I ordered one the proper size for my housing. Laker Air ended up having to reimburse my insurance company $620. I gave the six-inch jewelry box to my youngest daughter.

Rudy Whitworth – Seahorse Productions, LLC

The Balloonfish is one of the most colorful Pufferfish in the oceans!

GARDENS OF MEMORIES~ON THE PUFFERFISH

Watching them swim with darling eyes so round,
This is where memories are sure to be found.
Some will be smooth, and others have spines;
Some even have masks they hide behind.
Slow to attack, but with powerful jaw;
Hard-shelled invertebrates they like to gnaw.
Not in a hurry, and with fins so small,
They sidle around like "Gram" in a mall.
Catch their attention in corals amid,
They'll give you a look you'd expect from a kid.
Nosing to coral, they attempt to hide;
Counting on camouflage seen on their side.
With trust, they'll be curious; close but wise;
Here's hoping you won't see a change in their size.
Stress in their life causes them to inflate;
With water inside, their size becomes great.
Bigger than others; hopes not to be food;
Give them more time and they'll change their mood.
With patience, the puffer may choose not to flee;
Gardens of memories in open sea.

Revisiting Hawaii and Dive Makai

During the summer of 1995, my Gavia Scuba Club held a benefit for a high school student who had become paralyzed after diving into a stream and hitting his head on a rock. He was from a community called Fairfield located north of Cincinnati where we normally held our monthly meetings. I met a fellow by the name of Thane at this benefit who also lived in Fairfield.

Thane told me he was moving to the big island of Hawaii in August. He had worked for a dive shop in Fairfield at the time. We talked about diving in Hawaii since I'd done that and he said he knows many people there and could take me diving any time I wanted. I told him I'd be glad to meet him there after he moved and we could do some diving together and he told me that would be agreeable with him.

I flew to Hawaii and met up with Thane in August as we'd planned. We did a shore dive as a check-out dive in Honaunau Bay opposite the famous Place of Refuge Point. We saw a number of Crown of Thorns sea stars ravaging the corals. The population explosion of these creatures was disheartening since they kill the corals.

But we saw many different species of butterflyfish including at least three that are endemic to Hawaii. Since Hawaii is so isolated, the butterflyfish had developed new species due to interspecies reproductions through eons that eventually created new species. There were also a few different species of triggerfish and surgeonfish. The cross section of fish here was stunning.

The next morning, Thane and I met up with his friend Warren who ran a dive operation called Eco Adventures. Warren seemed like a pretty knowledgeable guy. We would do a couple of morning dives with him on my second day there.

During the first dive, Warren pointed out a lot of different critters, but near the end of the dive, he found an octopus, coaxed it out of its hole, and brought it to us. I'd never seen anyone handle an octopus like this before so I was intrigued. If the octopus tried to swim away, he would put his hand in front of its head so that it couldn't swim away, almost like a big kid keeping a little kid at bay with his hand. At first, the octopus inked, but when that didn't work, it stopped inking but still tried to swim away at times as Warren sat in front of us.

Little by little, the octopus calmed down and just draped itself over Warren's arm. Once it got this calm, Warren handed the octopus to Thane, then to me so we could hold it. This was the first time I'd actually held an octopus, but this experience would become the start of better things to come for me. After the dive, I asked Warren as many questions about octopus's behavior that I could think of and he not only answered them well, but he also suggested that they like being petted and/or caressed between their eyes, saying they like the touch of human skin once they realize there's no danger to them.

Our second dive had just as many different fish and creatures as the first and Warren also found a Triton's Trumpet snail that he pointed out to us. After the dive was over, Warren explained that the Triton's trumpet preys on the Crown of Thorns sea star. I was glad to hear there was something that might be able to control the population explosion of these coral killers.

The next day, Thane took me to another friend's house on the other side of the island to pick him up for another shore dive. Dave Seawater (his real name) was a definite hippie, living in a cabin he built from scratch out in the boondocks on the Hilo side of Hawaii. The windows were open louvers, macramé art hung everywhere, and his guitar sat right next to his chair in the living room.

Dave grabbed his dive gear, loaded it in the car, and we headed to South Point. South Point is the southernmost point of all the United States, including Key West. As we unloaded our gear, I noticed Dave didn't have a wetsuit and mentioned this to him. But he said he never uses one because they're too expensive and the corals tear them up too easily.

The parking lot was about 50' above sea level. We had to carry our gear down a steep, rocky path and gear up at the bottom close to the ocean. Then we sat on a large, flat rock and waited for a wave to come up close to the top of the rock before rolling in. If we didn't wait for the wave, it was a 10' drop to the shallow sea, but when the wave was there, it was a two-foot roll into deeper water that would take us to sea as the wave receded. Then we could safely descend.

Dave led us around the reef for a while, then through a lava tube. I followed him, marveling at the fact that he was diving in his blue jeans and tee shirt. I thought, yep, Dave was surely the proverbial hippie with nothing to prove.

At one point in the dive, he showed me what looked like a cleaner wrasse dancing in what I figured was its cleaning station. On a whim, I put my hand out to see if it would land on my hand and start cleaning it, but Dave grabbed my arm and pulled it back. When I looked at him, he pointed to his temple telling me to remember this. Then he pointed at the wrasse and wagged his finger back and forth.

Cleaning stations are much like the old service stations where you could bring in your car and the serviceman would not only pump your gas, but also check your oil, clean your windshield, and do anything else necessary to get you on your way safely. In some of these cleaning stations, cleaner gobies, wrasses, or shrimp will hang out and dance, advertising their services. The cleaner gobies, wrasses and shrimp clean algae, fungus and debris from larger animals keeping them healthy. The algae, fungus and debris turns out to be food for the cleaners. Thus, this is a perfect example of a mutualistic symbiotic relationship where both participants are benefitted.

We swam around some more and Dave pointed out goldring surgeonfish, a cusk eel, domino damselfish, a pearl wrasse and a beautiful endemic Lei triggerfish. When it came time for us to finish the dive, we did our safety stop then headed towards that same flat rock we'd started from. While at the surface, I watched and filmed as some of the local kids jumped off of a 50' high cliff next to the parking lot and splashed into the water near where we were. I got some great video of them jumping, landing, and then an underwater shot of them swimming back up to the surface. Since the tide had raised during our dive, we could easily walk out close to the base where we originally went in.

When we got out, I asked him about that cleaning station and he said the fish he showed me was an Ewa Blenny, not a cleaner wrasse. The Ewa blenny has similar markings to the cleaner wrasse, but when a fish comes into what they think is a "cleaning station" to get cleaned, the Ewa blenny takes a big bite out of the fish! He might have done the same to me had Dave not pulled my hand away.

Then we did a tour through the Kilauea Caldera on our way back to Dave's house. We stopped at some steam vents on the side of the road and Dave told us sometimes he'll stand by these vents and lean over, making it seem as though he is in a steam bath or sauna. I tried it and saw that his description was spot on.

We dove with Warren the next two days and I learned as much as I did the first day. Each night, Warren planned on visiting the Kona Surf Hotel for a night dive where it was almost guaranteed to see mantas. Huge spotlights had been mounted underwater there that attract plankton, and the mantas come in to dine on this feast. Unfortunately, both nights were a bust with no mantas. The Kona Aggressor was even there the second night with its own bright lights shining in the water, but still no luck. I've told this story to many experienced divers who know about the Kona Surf Hotel and many don't believe the mantas didn't show up.

For the next three days, I scheduled my dives with Dive Makai. Lisa remembered me right away from the last time I was there and introduced me to her husband Tom, also her business co-owner. She told me that as soon as I called them to schedule my dives with them before I left the states, she pulled out some pictures she had taken on the boat of divers when I was there. She immediately remembered a hat I wore with pins mounted on it from all over the world. She explained these pictures are how she remembers anyone who has ever been diving with them.

The dive briefings before each dive were as detailed and magnificent as they were the first time I went diving with them. Once in the water, Lisa would show me things to film, one after another. It reminded me of when I apologized to my friend Dave years before thinking she was giving me all her time and ignoring him. At least this time, she had a second divemaster in the water to take care of the other three divers.

When I noticed that my air was running low on one of the dives, I showed her that my air gauge was down to 500 PSI, a given point at which divers should be thinking about ending their dive. That's when she handed me her octopus and led me around the reef for another 15 minutes showing me more cool stuff to film. I felt like a dog on a leash but was pleased and grateful for the extra attention. Tanks like the one I was using normally start with 3000 PSI.

In that last 15 minutes, she showed me a dragon moray eel, butterflyfish feeding on damselfish eggs, and a rare, shy flame angel. We watched a pair of orangespine surgeonfish AND a pair of domino damselfish courting. I've always said the best stuff happens when it's time to return to the boat. This was true, but Lisa made it so that I didn't have to return to the boat yet!

Finally, we went to the mooring line and began our ascent up. Once we made our way up the line and got to our 15' safety stop, she motioned that she was going to take back her octopus and I reached down to my side, grabbed my regulator that had been dangling there, and put it in my mouth as she retrieved her octopus.

After I got out of the water and on the boat, my mouth started stinging horrendously. I said something to Lisa and she suggested that my regulator had probably rubbed against some hydroids on the mooring line on the way up. She gave me some vinegar to rinse in my mouth and said it would eventually make the stinging go away. I rinsed my mouth a couple of times and also poured some into my regulator.

During that surface interval on the boat, Lisa pulled out a bottle of champagne, poured some into small Dixie cups, then passed them around. This seemed odd to me since drinking and diving shouldn't mix. When she finished pouring, she raised her cup and toasted a lady on the boat in her mid-70's who had just completed her 800th dive!

As our necessary surface interval was winding down, Kendra, who was Lisa and Tom's daughter, did the next dive briefing which was as complete as all the rest. We would be going to Turtle Towers. This was a super dive site where there was an actual turtle cleaning station.

After gearing up, I put my regulator in my mouth and did my giant stride into the ocean. Upon taking my first breath I started choking and couldn't get a breath of fresh air. I spit out my regulator and grabbed my own octopus. It had only taken a split second for me to realize that I had not rinsed the vinegar from my regulator that sat in the hot sun for my hour surface interval. I made the rest of the dive using my octopus, but I'm sure my regulator would have been fine to use after a minute or two rinsing in the salt water. From then on, I always take a breath in and blow out of my regulator before getting in the water.

When we arrived at the "towers," I could watch as turtles soared into the cleaning station, softly landed, then they snuggled themselves into the reef until they were comfortable. That's when a dozen or so damselfish would start picking at the turtle shells to clean them. I filmed this for quite a while, then went off on my own to see what else I might find. That's when I saw an octopus standing tall on its tentacles on top of the reef and it was constantly changing colors. This seemed odd to me so I turned on my camera, wedged myself into a nook in the reef to steady myself and started filming. I might have only been five to six feet away.

The octopus didn't seem too bothered by my presence, and actually wasn't even looking at me. As I studied my viewfinder more, I realized there was another octopus on the other side of this small, 20' wide mesa-like reef and both were going through all kinds of color changes. That's when I realized they were probably courting each other.

I had been sitting there for almost 15 minutes waiting to see if I might be able to catch them mating. I couldn't move much so as to not disturb the one closest to me, but I did need to eventually check my gauges to verify my bottom time and more importantly the amount of air I had left. Finally, I slowly reached for my gauge console but that was enough to make the one closest to me swim away as did the other one.

Since my air was below 500 PSI, I needed to make my way back to the mooring line and I couldn't try to follow them any longer for their possible mating. But I did make a decision to have a back-up computer mounted to my housing that I could always glance at without moving if I ever found myself in this situation again.

On my last dive with them, Tom gave the briefing and would lead the dive. This was probably the only dive briefing that didn't describe everything we would see on the dive. We did see most everything Tom described, as he knew where everything lived and only had to take us to it. What he didn't know was, near the end of the dive, a school of thousands of parrotfish would show up and spread themselves over the entire reef, pecking at the coral. Had I known then what I know now, I might have paid more attention. The next time I'd see that many fish show up and congregate out of the clear blue ocean and inundate the reef like that, I was lucky enough to film an orgy. But again, that story is for another time.

Rudy Whitworth – Seahorse Productions, LLC

This small Cleaner Wrasse will even clean a 2" Damselfish when invited.

GARDENS OF MEMORIES~ON CLEANING STATIONS

A coral arch that has gobies and shrimp by the pound;
  This is where memories are sure to be found.
Underneath, hangs a grouper with mouth open wide,
  And three cleaner gobies are darting inside.
Some Pederson's shrimp are getting their fill,
  When one of the gobies slips out of a gill.
While drifting in closer, I overstep bounds.
  The look in its eye seems reflects a frown.
Then the grouper rapidly purses its mouth,
  Ejecting cleaners on their own water spout.
A wiggle, a jerk, and a twitch of its fin
  Sends the grouper to sea and the cleaners to swim.
Not to worry, I thought; be patient and wait.
  A snapper is serving his turn at the gate.
After him is a blue tang, then a coney strikes pose.
  Next, an eel slithers in and offers its nose.
All these creatures are cleaned; the cleaners are fed.
  Nature's plan is precise when all's done and said.
Then I offer my hand and they all come to me,
  More gardens of memories in open sea.

Hurricane Roxanne

My next dive trip was on the Bay Islands Aggressor in October 1995. My dive shop had scheduled this trip almost 10 months earlier and it wasn't until too late to get my money back that I found out Jack would be leading the trip. He was a good diver and trip leader, but I'd begun to not like his holier than thou attitude.

When we arrived at the dock in Roatan, Honduras where the Aggressor was moored, we were told that since Hurricane Roxanne was getting closer to us by the hour, we'd have to only dive protected bays and lagoons then we'd also have to return to the dock each day for the entire week. As a group, we weren't very happy with this plan since we'd paid to be on a liveaboard boat that takes us out to more virgin reefs away from the over-dived reefs closer to shore. We all asked Jack to discuss this with the captain and try to come up with a different option.

Once we got our gear stored and suitcases emptied in our stateroom drawers, we all began meandering around the boat to become more familiar with things. I happened to go topside to the upper sundeck then walked towards the stern to get a better look at some Honduran kids jumping off the dock while armed guards stood nearby.

When I got to the stern, I happened to look down and noticed Jack and the captain having a discussion on the dive deck below me. It didn't take me long to figure out that they were discussing our diving options. Since I always try to have my video camera at the ready, I quickly ducked down as much as possible to covertly film what became quite a lengthy, heated discussion between the two of them.

Jack was adamantly standing up for the group telling the captain that this group of divers were advanced divers. He stated that we wouldn't be happy with only diving protected bays and lagoons and that the captain had better plan on getting us out to the better dive sites. The captain took this as a threat which led to the two of them beginning to get angrier with the other one.

The captain finally agreed to take us out beyond the protected bays and lagoons to the better dive sites as long as weather permitted and the hurricane didn't jeopardize our safety. But he did say that we would still definitely have to come back to the dock each night since there was no way of knowing where Hurricane Roxanne would turn next. Jack agreed to this on our behalf then came to tell all of us this final decision.

Across the bay from the dock there were living accommodations for the local Hondurans that looked more like a cardboard, plastic, galvanized box-o-rama. Each little six- to eight-square-foot box was actually someone's family home. These huts were thrown together and mounted on piers in the bay. They were all interconnected to the point that family members might have to go through two or three other families' residences before reaching their own. It was the poorest third world country I'd seen so far in all of my travels.

There was also an outhouse at the end of the dock where the Aggressor boat was tied. Armed guards were always on the dock holding their AK-47's. There were also always young kids jumping off the end of the dock, swimming under the outhouse and climbing back up to do it again. You can draw your own conclusion about that picture.

As we left the dock each morning to go out for our diving we'd pass those box-o-rama huts then not more than a mile away, we'd pass some very nice properties and homes. Someone would always be trimming the lawn with machetes or raking up tree debris. The disparity was quite obvious. I could only guess that these nicer homes probably belonged to wealthier government officials.

Each day, once out on the ocean, we fought high seas as the backlashes of Roxanne kept hitting us in waves of wind and rain. The weather radar looked like a spinning pinwheel. While out on the ocean, at one point I even put my video camera in the housing and took it out onto the port side of the boat, held onto the handrail tightly with one hand, and filmed the high seas and driving rain as the waves and rain drenched me and my dome port with every wave. The Aggressor boat was riding out the storm but it was surely a rough ride.

That afternoon, the ride got so bad we had to turn around to head back to dock. Almost everyone on board was turning green and getting sick, including most of the crew members. I was one of only a few who wasn't vomiting but I'll admit at one point the lounge smelled so badly I did have to get some fresh air before that smell caused me to join the others in emptying my stomach.

Much of our diving was still somewhat alee to the storm but many times we'd fight some pretty strong currents. I remember one dive where we jumped into the water and hung onto a drift line until we were ready to swim to a corner on the wall, then cut up into a protected shallower sandy area for the rest of the dive. It took a good five minutes or more to push my housing the length of the boat against the current just to get to that corner, then by that time I was worn out! Of course, at the end of the dive it was much easier allowing the current to take us to the Aggressor's stern being careful to not miss grabbing the ladder, or at least the drift line hanging behind.

The shallow area on that dive had a lot of small coral heads dotting the sand. My buddy, Marc Weiss, started pointing at something for me to see and film, but as much as I stared, I couldn't see anything. I got closer and finally saw a well-camouflaged scorpionfish nestled in the corals. I started to turn on my camera, but before it turned on, the scorpionfish lunged at a passing fish and swallowed it whole. Had the camera already been on, I might have been able to get that attack. But battery power still wasn't what I would have liked so I had to keep the camera turned off until I was ready to take a shot in order to conserve power.

The Bay Islands Aggressor also had an underwater scooter on board that we took turns using. Marc probably enjoyed that scooter more than any paying diver on board since he was a pretty heavy fellow and the scooter made it easier for him to get around. Don't get me wrong, he was a very good diver and would eventually become an excellent instructor sharing the wonders of diving with hundreds of new students. According to my logbook, Jack used the scooter more than anyone, by far, but since he was the trip leader, his trip was free to him.

Half-way through the week, we had heard that another dive boat had spotted a whale shark about 10 miles away from where we were. Captain Dan told everyone that one of the best ways to spot where a whale shark might be, was to look for large schools of sea bird flocks flying circles close to the water. We looked hard enough to have our eyeballs pop out of our heads for the rest of the week, but never did see this phenomenon or any whale sharks for that matter.

Many of the dive sites had flamingo tongue snails everywhere. Other dive sites like Connie's Dream, were inundated with barrel sponges. When we found a dive site that we liked, Capt. Dan would suggest we do a second dive on it which always seemed to yield even more the second time around. That was great with me since I'd already become a fan of multi dives on the same dive site.

Near the end of the week the weather improved and we were able to do some dives without currents. I buddied up with a fellow named Dan on one dive. He seemed to know where he was going so, I just followed him. When we were heading back to the boat, I heard the generator's hum underwater getting louder, so I knew we were getting closer. But then we seemed to pass it as we followed the crest of a wall and the sound of the generator waned.

After a while I decided to swim at around 15' for a few minutes so that I could safely surface and look for the boat. When I surfaced, I realized that we had in fact gone past the boat and Dan was still swimming away from it. We were now a few hundred yards away and low on air. Fortunately, someone on the boat saw us and sent the zodiac to pick us up. Unfortunately, it took a long time for me to live that one down with Jack.

On one of my night dives, the dive started out slow, and I was finding very little to film. Then I found a couple of Caribbean spiny lobsters slowly making their way across the sand instead of quickly seeking cover. Next, I found a Queen Helmet Snail out on the reef. I think helmet snails have some of the prettiest shells of all the sea snails. Near the end of the dive, I also found a Caribbean reef octopus. While slowly inching closer to it, I was eventually able to make it comfortable enough with me to pet it between its eyes without it leaving, just as Warren had taught me when I was last in Hawaii.

On another dive, I followed a trail in the sand that ended at a conch moving itself across the sand. I grabbed the shell and turned it over so that I could see the conch inside and left it in the sand that way. I turned on my camera and waited to see if the conch would turn itself over. After about four to five minutes, it started coming out of its shell. Little by little, its foot came out more and more until it dug its foot into the sand and flipped itself over.

This made for a good, clear educational shot and I was pleased. But knowing there might have been something not right about the shot, I decided to do the shot again. When I reached to grab the conch, it immediately extended its foot while I was still holding it and dug it into the sand enough to begin walking. Since I'd left my camera on "record" accidentally, I pointed the camera at the conch and I filmed the conch take another half dozen steps forward while I held it.

Then I picked up the conch with its foot still out and carried it over to Marc for him to take a picture of it. The foot was still out for Marc's picture, and when I set it down in the sand it started walking again before I let go of it, so I kept holding it as it walked forward. This was when Marc first started considering that shooting video might in fact show more action than shooting still pictures.

© Cricket Manuel

The Devil Scorpionfish has a face only a mother could love!

GARDENS OF MEMORIES~ON THE SCORPIONFISH

A part of the reef moves and it's showing a frown.
    This is where memories are sure to be found.
Master of disguise, a scorpionfish waits
    For its prey to pass by; then it jumps at a taste.
In just a few shakes its hors d'oeuvre is done,
    And it nestles back in for another one.
With a bottomless eye like a pearl glowing gold,
    It looks all around with a stare very cold.
Its eyebrows stand up at least an inch tall,
    Like old rotten trees getting ready to fall.
There's long warts on its nose and prickly skin,
    And there's juniper branches under its chin.
When its dorsal fin rises, more colors appear;
    But its poisonous spines remind not to get near.
Its fins match its body of orange, browns, and tans;
    And it swims with them open like Japanese fans.
It's then that they show like butterfly wings
    Before settling down to see different things.
Then back to its camouflage specialty,
    In gardens of memories in open sea.

The Dolphin Rebreather

In May 1996, I decided to learn how to dive a rebreather since I was told it could help me get closer to marine animals than I can on open circuit scuba. Rebreathers don't give off bubbles like open circuit scuba does, thus much quieter. The instructor was Jack, the same instructor who taught me my rescue diving skills and trip leader in the Bay Islands. I already knew he had it in for me, but I also knew he was knowledgeable and taught more than the book.

My dentist Terry was also in this class, but happily, I wouldn't have to carry him over my shoulders across a rocky beach for this class like I did in my rescue diver class. We had about six or eight in the class including another good friend, Marc Weiss whom I met on the Bay Islands Aggressor. Marc had been using a small point and shoot camera but he was also becoming very interested in my videos and was considering the pros and cons of upgrading to a better still camera or choosing to get a video system instead.

We were training with the Dolphin Rebreather, which I believe was the first recreational rebreather available on the market. The class went well and we all completed everything at the same time. I made reservations to rent a rebreather at Stuart Cove's in Nassau, Bahamas in late June because I knew Stuart had these rebreathers to rent and was knowledgeable about them just in case I needed any extra help.

By mid-June, I contacted Jack and asked him how long it would take to get my rebreather certification card. I knew everyone else had gotten theirs already. Terry and Marc's certification numbers from IANTD were in the 70's. Jack said he looked in his records, and oh, guess what? He forgot to send in my information.

He said he'd get right on it, but I told him I was leaving in a few days and needed at least a letter stating that I'd completed the course. He said he'd write it so I drove the 30 minutes to the dive shop to pick it up. Of course, I had to wait while he wrote the letter after I got there, but at least I got it and did 20 dives with Stuart's rebreather, including a number of shark dives.

Stuart's cousin, Graham, was our divemaster for most of this trip and I'd done a half dozen or more dives with the Dolphin before my first shark dive of that trip. As I was gearing up, Graham suggested that I put a piece of bait in my pocket for the dive. I looked at him like he was crazy, then I asked him are you serious?

He said, of course he was. The sharks would come in closer giving me better footage. I was understandably somewhat cautious about this suggestion, but when he brought me a piece of bait and told me where to put it, I did that. But I also kept looking at him waiting for him to finally stop me from diving with a rebreather on a shark dive with bait in my pocket.

As I walked to the back of the dive deck to grab my camera, I told him I was getting ready to make this dive with bait in my pocket. He just said that's good! Then I told him I was ready to jump in with my rebreather and bait in my pocket and he again said go for it! Then I did a giant stride into the water, but instead of immediately descending, I surfaced and gave him one last chance to tell me he was just kidding. He looked at me and told me I'd enjoy the dive.

I thoroughly enjoyed the dive and carried bait on every subsequent shark dive on that trip. The sharks did come in closer following the scent of the bait, but they never knew where that scent was coming from. Stuart even invited me to film with a Brazilian film crew on a night shark feed using the rebreather. Unfortunately, the sharks weren't interested in the bait in my pocket nor the bait in the milk crates we had. It may have been due to the film crew's bright lights, but the sharks never showed up even though we were at the same arena Stuart uses for all of his shark feeds.

Near the end of this trip, we were on our way to Rose Island to dive a blue hole and hopefully dive with silky sharks when Graham spotted two different pods of pilot whales at the surface. Everyone wanted to try to get in the water with them so Graham told us to get ready and he'd head off one of the groups of whales. When Graham was directly in front of one of the pods, divers got in the water using their normal open circuit scuba tanks with their loud, noisy bubbles, and descended down in hopes of the whales swimming right past them. But the whales circled around the entire group and went on about their way.

Then Graham got in front of the second pod of whales and the snorkelers dropped into the water thinking they were being smarter than the divers since they weren't wearing those noisy open circuit systems. The whales dove under the snorkelers to about 30' then back up and went on about their way.

Finally, Graham dropped me with my rebreather in the water in front of one of the pods. I descended to about 30' as 12 whales slowly swam past me less than 15' away. I filmed them all and also noticed that the bull was closest to me and the calves were farthest away. It was definitely a magical moment! As I ascended to the surface, I also realized that without the rebreather, I would never have known what it looks like when a whale defecates, as I noticed a loose floating mass coming from behind the bull as the pod swam away.

When I returned to Cincinnati, I told Marc about my experiences. He was stoked and suggested we rent rebreathers from the dive shop and take them on another trip together. I told him I'd recently earned my sixth first-place award in Houston's Seaspace international underwater photo/video competition and my prize was a week's diving for one with Parrot's Landing in Grand Cayman. He said we're on! He knew he'd have to pay for his share of everything but that didn't matter; we'd be diving together again, this time with rebreathers.

My winning entry this time was entitled, "Innerspace Romance" and showed courting dances of a couple of species of fish, as well as no less than six different species mating, including the barred Hamlets from the Exumas and the cowfish from San Salvadore. The video also showed the courting orangespine surgeonfish, domino damselfish, and octopi from Hawaii, and the sergeant majors protecting their egg nests from my Cozumel trip.

We rented the Dolphin rebreathers from the dive shop. Jack assured us that he had personally done maintenance on both of them and they'd work perfectly. So, we paid the rental fee for them and headed to Grand Cayman in May of '97. Unfortunately, one or both of us had problems with the rebreathers on just about every dive. We did have our open circuit regulators with us on the dive boat each day, so we'd use them to finish our diving that day, then repack the rebreathers each night, hoping they would work properly the next day.

After three days of the rebreathers not working right, we asked around to see if anyone knew anything about rebreathers. No one at Parrot's Landing had any idea and they even told us there's probably no one on the island who would fill our oxygen. But in our persistent manner, we finally found someone at the oxygen fill company who suggested we go see Nancy Romanica at DiveTech on the other side of the island since he filled her oxygen tanks. (Nancy has long since married Jay Easterbrook and became Nancy Easterbrook.)

Marc and I took our rebreathers to DiveTech, found Nancy and her number one tech and asked them if they had any idea why were we having so many problems. They looked everything over for almost an hour and finally showed us that we had small pinholes in each exhalation bag. I asked if they could think of anything we could do in order to continue using the rebreathers.

Nancy told us it was no problem because they had Dolphin Rebreathers and therefore, exhalation bags we could use. They brought us two exhalation bags from their storage area, so we took theirs and left ours there to reclaim once we brought back the ones belonging to DiveTech. We thought we'd finally resolved our problems and would still have four days of diving with the rebreathers.

To be safer, we decided to use our regulators and tanks for our boat dives and the rebreathers in the afternoons while shore diving so that if we ran into more problems, we wouldn't be inconveniencing other divers on a dive boat and we'd also be close enough to shore so that our bailout pony bottles could get us back if necessary. Unfortunately, my rebreather was still acting up on almost every dive, even to the point that when the soda lime got wet, I was breathing that caustic mixture that tasted awful. I was getting tired of bailing out and losing dives and bottom time.

The last time it happened at depth, I bailed to the pony bottle and motioned to Marc that we'd have to return to the shore and he gave me the OK sign. On our return swim, I noticed an octopus sitting in the sand at about 30' with four groupers facing it on all four sides of the octopus, like north, south, east, and west so I immediately turned on my camera and started filming.

I moved around getting different angles of this phenomenon and making sure the sun was hitting the critters at just the best angles. This was becoming a great shoot! Then all of a sudden, I went to take a breath and there was no air! Drat, in the excitement of this shot I'd forgotten that I was on a small pony bottle only meant to get me back to shore, not to continue an hour dive. I looked around hoping Marc was somewhere close and I was elated to see him two feet behind me holding out his octopus ready for me to grab and breathe.

We laughed all the way back to the dock. Me, because I didn't have to chase him down or make an emergency ascent and Marc because he saw this coming and just waited for me to take my last breath from the pony tank. We decided that was it for the rebreathers and we'd dive open circuit the rest of the week.

On the last day when we weren't diving, we took the rebreathers and exhalation bags back to DiveTech. Nancy and her tech both asked how things went and we told them Marc's worked perfectly, but mine still malfunctioned on every dive. The tech looked mine over even more carefully than before and finally asked me if I'd taken the regulator apart for any reason. I told him I hadn't since I didn't know anything about how they worked and he showed me inside the regulator where a gasket had been installed in a skewed manner on my regulator which would always allow water to slowly seep into the regulator until the soda lime got wet and I got that awful caustic air that would cause me to abort my dives.

Well, we figured out the problem, but it was a week late and now we'd probably be more than a dollar short. I asked Nancy how much we owed her for renting the exhalation bags for the week. We knew she had her hand in our pockets and could have charged us anything she wanted. Her answer was that we owed her nothing! She said we were there to dive and she was there to make our diving better!

Nancy has been a dear friend ever since and I cherish each time I get to see her in Cayman or at DEMA, the Diving Equipment Manufacturer's Association annual convention. I love telling this story about her over and over again. She is truly one of those industry professionals who care more about diving than the almighty dollar.

Once back in Cincinnati, I found my rebreather certification card in the mail. My number is 179 instead of being in the 70's like my classmates. When Marc and I returned our rebreathers to the dive shop and asked Jack about the malfunctions, egotistical Jack denied doing faulty maintenance. Marc and I both knew better. Since I never took the regulator apart, how it was in Cayman when the tech inspected it is exactly how it was when I picked it up from the dive shop. Then Jack tried to charge us for replacement exhalation bags, but Marc and I refused to pay anything more since our rebreathers didn't work properly from day one.

We later found out that the shop had two exhalation bags with holes in them and those bags had been replaced before we rented the rebreathers. So, we obviously ended up with the bad ones and I'm pretty sure Jack knew it and did it purposefully. A couple of years later, I found out that, for some reason left untold, Jack is no longer connected to the diving industry whatsoever.

Using the quieter rebreather allows divers to get closer to Spotted Eaglerays.

GARDENS OF MEMORIES~ON EAGLE RAYS

Beneath the surface with no breathing sounds,
This is where memories are sure to be found.
My rebreather recycles the air that I breathe,
And bubbles don't rumble the water so free.
Not so intrusive, I join eagle rays
Who watch me watch them; we're all amazed.
A diver so quiet is quite new to them;
Curiosity wins as they follow a whim.
The closer they soar, the wider my lens;
'Tis easy to count their spots by the tens.
Eye to eye, we glide together,
Causing a ponderance of "birds of a feather."
Creatures of God, with no evil intent,
We shared the moment to our heart's content.
Patrolling along the crest of the wall,
The grace of their flight portrays Nature's call.
Riding the currents like hawks in the sky,
Their wings hardly move for the speed they can fly.
Cruising the reef for comradery,
Gardens of memories in open sea.

Return to Bonaire

In February 1997, I returned to Bonaire with Rich and Steve to stay at Rich's uncle's condo again at the Divi Flamingo Resort. Because of the easy shore diving, we would again figure on doing four or five dives a day with no one limiting our bottom time like what might happen when boat diving with many dive operations.

We again met in Atlanta and flew to Bonaire. On the flight to Bonaire, I reminded them that I still would not be doing any deep bounce dives and even Steve agreed he wasn't going to do many if any at all. I did however tell Rich and Steve about a deep wreck I'd heard about that sits at almost 200'. I said I'd do a dive like that since there was something to see and film and not just a bounce dive down and up. The Mari Bahn was a 239' long three-masted schooner but her location was a fairly well-kept secret to most people at the time.

In the beginning of the trip, I was getting a tiny bit of water in my Ikelite housing after each dive. I couldn't tell where it was coming from, so after the first dive during our surface interval, I dried it out, greased the O-rings with grease from my save-a-dive kit, and tried again on the next dive. Ikelite housings are mechanical housings which means there is nothing in them that is electronic that can short out if it gets wet, thus they are user-friendly and can be serviced on the spot.

But after the second dive, I was still getting a little water inside, albeit less than the first dive. I used a small crescent wrench to tighten all of the fittings a little more and hoped this would resolve the problem. Fortunately, that fixed the leak and I didn't have any more problems the rest of the trip.

One of my objectives on this trip was to film educational things that I might be able to integrate into a video production that I could use in schools to illustrate some of the wonderful things found in the oceans. Jacques Cousteau once said, "People protect what they love," and I liked trying to instill that love in the hearts of school children, hopefully creating new ambassadors for the seas.

On one dive, I had a mirror with me and put it in front of a bi-color damselfish, but got no reaction from the fish. I'd used a mirror in Nassau once with a Nassau Grouper that seemed to like the mirror and kept swimming back to it and looking into it. The next time I used the mirror in Bonaire, I put it in front of a sergeant major damselfish near its nest. The damsel kept pecking at its own reflection thinking it was an intruding fish that might try to eat the eggs in the nest.

On another dive, I brought along a plastic syringe that I'd filled with a red biodegradable food coloring. I'd set up my camera and start recording as I used the syringe to introduce the food coloring at the base of vase sponges. Within a few seconds, the food coloring would begin flowing out of the top of the vase sponges. This illustrated how quickly vase sponges filter the seawater.

Steve was doing well with not doing his deep dives and he was also respecting the reef and marine creatures much better than our last trip there. On one of our dives, I noticed a large piece of Elkhorn coral broken off and lying on the sand. I turned to Steve and pointed at him then at the chunk of coral. He started waving his arms wildly trying to tell me it wasn't him that broke it. We all laughed as I knew he was behind me anyway.

On that same dive, we found the Grandpa of all lobsters! All three of us were thinking the same thing: what a great meal that would make. It was huge! While at lunch in the restaurant of the resort, we were talking about that lobster and one of the dive staff overheard us. He said we should have bagged it since lobsters were in season. Too bad we didn't know that beforehand. As you might have guessed, we didn't find any more lobsters on that trip.

Before we left the restaurant, I went back to the kitchen to see if they might have some scraps of fish that we could have to feed things underwater. One of the staff cut some up into small pieces and put it in a baggie for me. We took the baggie full of fish scraps on our afternoon dives.

Not only did we feed some of the fish, but I also showed Rich and Steve how an anemone tentacle gloms onto the fish and pulls it away from my hand, then puts the piece of fish in its mouth at the center of the anemone. They'd never seen that before.

I was able to get numerous shots of various fish changing colors which make for good examples of camouflage in my educational production. I also got shots of juveniles of various species that look totally different than the adults of those same species. I made sure to get good shots of the adults as well for comparison.

Some corals had teeth marks on them which I filmed then I made sure I got shots of parrotfish chomping on corals leaving identical teeth marks. I did the same thing with missing chunks of sponges then filming a turtle munching on a sponge leaving the same type of missing chunks. Overall, I was becoming very pleased with the footage I'd gotten on this trip.

One evening at the casino, Steve was winning at first and in a great mood. Then he started losing badly. Not only had he lost what he'd won at first, he lost another $100 or so and was getting very agitated and boisterous; so much so, that we made him leave the casino before he got into trouble.

Back at the room, we tried to calm him down, but not much was working. That's when he told us that sometimes he totally loses control of himself and that's when he usually gets into trouble. Since my oldest son, Cyan, grew up with ADHD, I suggested that Steve check with a doctor after the trip and see what the doc thought. I told Steve that when Cyan took his meds, he was very much in control of his life. Steve said he was an adult and pooh-poohed my suggestion.

I would later find out that since Steve had a wife and kid now, once he got home from this last trip, he did in fact see a doctor about this. The doc tested him and diagnosed him as having ADHD. The doctor prescribed appropriate meds and Steve's life changed for the better. But now, back to our current Bonaire adventure…

One of the most well-known wrecks in Bonaire is the Hilma Hooker. She is a 240' long freighter that was towed to Kralendijk, Bonaire after having engine trouble. A false bulkhead was found to contain 25,000 lbs. of marijuana so the ship was confiscated. For many months, she wasn't maintained; her hull was deteriorating and she was taking on water. She was finally towed out to sea away from the main dock and sunk in 100' of water.

The Hilma Hooker lies on her side and is a five-minute swim

from shore to a buoy directly above the ship. We found that there's plenty to see on her but no penetration was possible. I got some fun shots of Rich standing behind and "steering" her wheel, but since she's on her side, he was sideways in the video. When I turned my camera so that he was vertical in the video, his bubbles went sideways, again making for a fun shot.

All week long we had been asking people about the Mari Bahn, also known as the Windjammer Wreck or the Deep Wreck which sits in almost 200' of water, but everyone we asked seemed to play dumb. This was a very secret shipwreck that was usually only dived by professional tech divers. I was told it might be difficult to find someone to take us to the wreck.

It wasn't until I dropped the name of that famous diver who mapped caves in Florida and said this guy suggested that I dive the wreck, that one of the dive staff finally told me I should talk with Donnie, another staff member. We found Donnie and asked him about the wreck and he promised to take us to the Mari Bahn the next morning.

We spent that evening after dinner making our dive plan and calculating our bottom time and possible deco stops, if necessary. The next morning after breakfast, we met up with Donnie at the oil refinery, geared up and started our descent along a vertical wall. I noticed that Donnie had carried his gear almost all the way down to the wreck before finally putting it on as we left the wall and could see the silhouette of the wreck in the distance.

Once on the wreck I began filming one of the most beautiful wrecks I'd ever seen. It was on its side and the deck was missing. Whip corals inside the hull were hanging everywhere looking like wonderful spider webs. Fish were swimming about like elves dancing at Christmas. My video lights were lighting up everything in sight! I just kept the camera rolling.

When our bottom time ran out according to our calculations (I think it was about 17 minutes), we started back towards the wall for our slow, careful ascent using the wall as a good reference rather than ascending in blue water. This also allowed us to head towards the entry point as well as up. We knew what deco stops we'd need to make if necessary and I'd even written them on the dive slate I have mounted to my camera housing. At 100' everything seemed to be going according to plan as I still had about 1000 PSI left in my tank, which was about one-third of what I started with. I figured this should be plenty of air for my deco stops if necessary.

That's when Rich came over to me and showed me his air gauge sitting at 200 PSI. Crud! So, I turned around to see if maybe Donnie might have enough air to share with Rich. Surely his air consumption was better than all of ours. But the problem was exacerbated when I saw that Steve was already using Donnie's octopus, which meant I'd have to share my air with Rich.

So, I gave Rich my octopus and wrote on my dive slate for him to breathe slowly. My eyes stayed glued to my gauges at that point and I watched my air deplete with each one of our breaths. I wondered what would happen if it got to the point to where there would only be enough air for one of us to finish all deco and safety stops.

Fortunately, that didn't come into play. Donnie had enough air for him and Steve to complete their ascent and Rich used his last 200 PSI on his short two-minute, 15' safety stop. I did a full three-minute safety stop at 15' and still had about 400 PSI left in my tank; Donnie had almost 1000 PSA left.

That afternoon we did a couple shallower shore dives and a night dive after dinner. I'd filmed arrow crabs, corkscrew anemones, cleaner shrimp and various other fish and critters typical to Bonaire. That night after visiting the casino, I checked out my footage from the Mari Bahn. I really didn't see anything in any of my shots like the beauty I had seen while on the dive. That's when I realized I must have been "narced" pretty bad for the first time ever! Nitrogen narcosis causes a loss of mental capacity due to an over-abundance of nitrogen at depth. The narcosis ebbs as one ascends.

A couple of days after I returned home, I got one of my dive magazines in the mail. The cover story was something about the 10 best kept secret wreck dives in the world and how to get to them. The Mari Bahn was one of the wrecks listed. So much for the wreck being a secret anymore, but at least I could say I'd been there, done that!

GARDENS OF MEMORIES~ON SHORE DIVING

Hour-long dives made from the ground,
  This is where memories are sure to be found.
Driving to numbers painted on rocks,
  Pink flamingoes wading as flocks.
Damsels primping in front of a mirror,
  Giant lobsters showing no fear.
Vase sponges filter seawater all day,
  And octopi want to continue to play.
Juveniles looking cute as a buttercup,
  May look totally different when they grow up.
Elkhorn coral on sand that lay broke,
  'Twas not me he said, not this bloke.
Anemone happy for pieces of fish,
  But finding right info may be only a wish.
Make it happen; drop the right name.
  Someone will know of that person's fame.
Beautiful shipwreck at two hundred feet,
  Footage that proved it wasn't so neat.
Nitrogen narcosis is what it must be;
  Gardens of memories, in open sea.

Sycamore Turtle Club

Sycamore Community Schools is the name of the school system in which I grew up from fourth grade until graduation. After four years of college, I returned to teach science and coach sports at the Sycamore Junior High. I was there from 1973 until I left in 1979 enjoying the teaching stint but making more money roofing in three months of the summer than I did in nine months of teaching and coaching put together.

I always stayed in touch with many of the educators in the district since I still lived in the district and my children all went through Sycamore as well. In the summer of 1997, I was contacted by Maggi and Lynn who were fifth and sixth grade teachers at Sycamore Middle School. They ran a turtle club for any interested students and the club had raised and donated enough money to sponsor a couple of satellite tag transmitters for sea turtles.

In August, they would be traveling to the desert of Baja, Mexico where they would be helping a Rhodes Scholar, Wallace "J" Nichols, tag Pacific black sea turtles for satellite telemetry. The teachers invited me to join them and document their two-week experience. I couldn't pass up the opportunity.

This sounded like another great adventure so I packed my scuba gear and underwater video camera rig and flew with the group to San Diego. After checking into a hotel, we visited the San Diego Zoo then overnighted in the hotel before meeting up with J in the morning. The students would be going into the seventh, eighth or ninth grades in a month, so you can get a good idea of their energy levels and excitement in anticipation of this once-in-a-lifetime experience.

While at the zoo, when one of the gals saw the pink flamingoes, she remarked it looked like they had bird legs. DUH. During one of the presentations given by a zoo employee, he asked how a liquid could flow from one side of a membrane to the other, and the same gal answered, "Because it's a peri-semiable membrane," instead

132

of semi-permeable membrane. The kids constantly came up with different malaprops throughout the trip to keep us entertained.

We all met J the next morning in the lobby of the hotel around 5:30 AM and he told us some of what he had in store for us for the next couple of weeks. We'd ride and drive across half of the Baja Peninsula to Bahia de Los Angeles on the east coast of the peninsula along the Sea of Cortez. We'd live in the desert, stow our gear in three-sided palapas and sleep on cots on the beach under the stars each night. He promised to explain more during our trip and after we arrived at Camp Archelon.

We loaded into a Greyhound bus and departed for San Ysisdro, CA where we walked across the border into Tijuana, Mexico. (Back then this wasn't as much of a problem as it would be today.) Once across the border, we loaded onto another Mexican commercial bus and headed south. One student kept mistakenly calling Tijuana, "Talawanda" since he had an older sibling who went to Miami University and Talawanda was the name of the high school in Oxford.

We stopped a number of times to rest or eat and get the feel of this new country and its people. We drove through many poorer areas and were continuously reminded to be careful and stay in groups any time we left the bus. All stops were patrolled by armed Mexican military. At one roadside stop, a student saw a teak carving and asked the seller if he could use a United States traveler's check to buy it, which really wasn't going to happen.

We rode the bus as far south as its route went, then J and I along with the two teachers and seven students piled into a large three-seated vehicle that may have been a Jeep Wagoneer or something similar. J drove us through the desert on winding roads for the next two to three hours. Fortunately, I was in the front passenger seat with J and Maggi and sat next to the passenger window in order to film and document the countryside and towns we passed.

When we approached the crest of a hill later that afternoon, J told us we would finally see the camp after going over the top of the next hill. It was a beautiful sight, to be sure. The Sea of Cortez was a deep blue rimmed with beaches that stretched around the entire bay. We could see three or four stone palapas off in the distance along the beach near a few other small cabins of sorts and a couple of outhouses nearby.

As we unpacked our gear and stowed it in the palapas, we were warned to remember to hang everything from the ceiling and rafters since scorpions were everywhere wanting to snuggle into clothing, bedding and shoes at any chance they got. (One student continuously called the palapa a pablo.) we were told that when we wanted to get clean, we would get wet in the sea, soap up on the beach and rinse off back in the sea. Then we would walk back towards camp near the banjos (outhouses) to rinse off with a minimal amount of fresh water.

The students were beginning to realize that this wasn't a vacation at a Sheraton Hotel. But in their favor, each of them proved to be good students and they were also very passionate about sea turtles.

Once unpacked, we met at the cabin which would serve as the main laboratory for J as well as our main meeting room and dining hall. The first order of business for J was to explain about the camp. There was no electric, thus no air conditioning or refrigerators and no way to cook food, so food and fresh water would be brought by some local Mexican women that helped support J's studies. The only restrooms were the banjos and with no running water, we'd burn the toilet paper in a bucket and keep our hands clean by dipping them in Clorox water to help kill any bacteria.

Everyone brought their own canteen for water knowing we'd be in the desert for two weeks. J explained that dehydration was a serious concern and everyone had to look out for each other, keeping an eye out for any signs of dehydration like dizziness, weakness or even belly-aches. If anyone became dehydrated, they'd have to start drinking a rehydration mixture that was very effective in aiding the rehydration process. This was similar to a very salty Gatorade, so its taste wasn't all that great.

J had a dry erase board in the main meeting room with a list of chores around camp that everyone would sign up for and rotate. These included keeping the main meeting room clean and swept, cleaning the banjos each day, picking up around camp, setting the table for meals and then cleaning the dishes after meals and putting them away. There were also turtle tanks and turtles that needed to be cleaned and fed, as well as turtle nets needed to be checked daily for turtles so they didn't drown, then the nets would be cleaned of algae and debris. Chores could be traded if anyone was truly against any given task but all tasks had to be completed as described.

Before our dinner of tacos, rice and beans, J began telling everyone how our days would go. His first statement was that we would get up at dawn, around 4:30-5 AM. This one statement was followed by almost every student remarking, "No way! I'm not getting up at dawn!" He smiled and said they would and continued briefing us about eating our dry breakfasts like Cheerios or frosted flakes and drinking plenty of water. (Remember there was no electric, thus no refrigeration nor milk.)

After breakfast, everyone would begin their daily chores. The first day, we set shallow turtle nets to be used for the next two weeks and the rest of our mornings we'd be checking those nets to see if any turtles had been caught. If there were no turtles in the nets, we would clean algae and debris along the nets. If there were any turtles, we would free them from the net and bring them back to camp for documentation and care.

When these chores were completed, we would do other fun things like boating past small islands inundated with thousands of sea birds and hundreds of sea lions. Once we went to an estuary where at high tide, water would rush over a bank then cascade down a stream that we could ride down as if surfing in the stream. One island we stopped on had a smelly dead sea lion on the beach that was probably bitten by a shark and on another we found sun-bleached skeletons of various marine creatures that had washed up on the rocky shore. Returning to camp, many times the kids would fall asleep in the panga (boat). One of the students kept saying people were taking a salsa, instead of siesta.

As night fell, we pulled out our cots from the palapas and set them up along the beach. The students had never in their lives seen a sky so full of stars nor ever seen the Milky Way, let alone in such grandeur. There were no city lights anywhere within many miles of our camp to distract from the sparkling stars in the night sky so the students laid on their cots looking up and identified all of the constellations they could see until each fell asleep one by one, to the lullaby of barking sea lions and whales spouting in the distance.

Being an early riser, I was always awake before dawn so I'd grab my video camera and wait for first light to break across the sea. As soon as a single ray of light began to peek over the horizon, I'd notice the kids begin to stir and eventually sit up. Within 10 minutes every student was awake either lying on their cots or standing with me at the shoreline watching me film a flock of birds soaring low over the sparkling sea with a beautiful sunrise in the background. It was never past 5 AM when they awoke.

Each morning, we stowed our cots and poured some dry cereal into a cup for breakfast. Then we grabbed our canteens and began our daily chores. While some of the students loaded into the panga and headed out to the turtle nets, others began cleaning up the main dining area or picking up around the beaches.

Still others were taught how to clean the turtle pools by J's associate, Tony. The turtle pools were plastic heavy-duty wading pools of sorts where the captured turtles are kept. No matter what we were doing during the day, J always enlightened everyone with his extensive knowledge about sea turtles.

I think there was only one person who didn't want to clean the banjos and that chore was traded to someone who didn't want to do dishes. Cleaning the turtle tanks was probably the most fun for the kids as these 20' diameter "above-ground swimming pools" were drained and cleaned with hard-bristle brushes while the turtles were still inside. The turtle shells were also scrubbed to keep algae from growing on them. In the ocean, Nature provides cleaner fish and shrimp for this task but there were no cleaners in these pools.

After lunch, most everyone went snorkeling in the bay where J and I shared more information about the upside-down jellyfish, small eel, baby stingrays and other marine creatures we saw. J would snorkel down and pick up brittle stars or small anemones for the students to hold and I would help identify the fish we were seeing since I'd brought along my ID books. Each afternoon, the students were given time to write in their journals about their daily experiences and what they'd learned, and some even used my ID books for reference as they drew the fish that they'd seen snorkeling.

About half way through the first week we awoke to a very foul odor in the air. As we strolled the beach, we saw dead fish washed up on the beach everywhere. We weren't sure of the cause but guessed it might have been some sort of algal bloom that poisoned the fish. At this point, new chores had to be assigned including collecting the dead fish in buckets and digging holes in the sand away from camp to bury the foul-smelling fish. After a couple of days, the fish stopped washing ashore and the air around us returned to the fresh ocean aroma we experienced when we first arrived.

One morning near the end of the first week, J told us that we'd be cataloging and documenting a couple of Pacific black sea turtles' characteristics before attaching transmitters to the tops of their carapace with a strong epoxy. Later that afternoon, they would be released to ascertain where they might go. It was J's theory that the female turtles would return to the nesting beach at which it they were born. Remember that this was in the '90's and it wasn't proven yet that this occurred, so his research was instrumental in leading to that proof.

Pacific black sea turtles are similar to green sea turtles but have a very dark coloration to the carapace which is tear-drop shaped at the posterior. Full grown black sea turtles can weigh as much as 220 pounds and measure up to 39" long. Their flat underside, or plastron, is usually dark gray or gray-green.

A few of the students did the chores around camp while the rest of us gathered at the turtle tanks and as a team, two turtles were lifted from the tanks and placed in shallow containers that could be carried and loaded into the bed of a pick-up truck. The turtles were driven to a different open outbuilding that J used as a working laboratory. The students were conscientious with keeping the turtles calm and wet for their safety.

J had already attached a metal tag to one of the flippers of the larger one named Xaviera. He had also cut off a piece of the turtle's skin under one of its flippers to study and genetically determine where she may have been born. If the DNA matched that of other turtles known to be from specific nesting beaches, J was sure she would head towards that specific beach for her own nesting and egg-laying.

After scraping barnacles, sanding, then cleaning the carapaces of the turtles with alcohol, we used paint color charts to describe the color of the carapaces and plastrons as close as possible for J's records. Next, we measured various dimensions of them. Then pictures were taken of her while she was being held up with all appropriate information like name, size, and date when caught printed on a poster board and held next to her for the picture. This was all further documentation for J's project.

Once all of the appropriate scientific information had been recorded, J placed the 3"x 6"x 2"-tall transmitter in the middle of the carapace and traced the outline of the transmitter onto the shell with a magic marker. Then, he mixed up an epoxy cement and spread the epoxy inside that rectangle he drew. Next, he affixed the transmitter and spread more epoxy around the base of the transmitter itself to help hold it in place for the long journey to her original nesting beach.

J explained that the transmitter would send a signal to satellites each time the turtle surfaced for air to breathe, thus giving its location. Each location would then be uploaded onto an internet site. Sometimes the transmitters might fall off due to a poor mounting process or it could get caught on an overhang where the turtle may sleep or feed causing the transmitter to come loose and float to the surface. If the transmitter successfully stayed attached, scientists and students all over the world could follow the progress of the turtle on the internet as it gets closer and closer to the nesting beach that matches the DNA of each turtle.

When all of the prep work was finished with both turtles and the epoxy hardened, J, Tony and five strong students carried the 208 lb. Xaviera to a panga and loaded her in, then loaded the second smaller turtle as well. J and the group piled into one panga with the turtles while the teachers and I loaded into another so we could shoot the group as they headed out, then released both turtles. I got shots of the turtles being held over the side of the panga, then once released, lowered my camera and housing into the water to film them swimming away. Some of the students were in the water with their snorkel gear and could see the turtles first-hand as they swam away.

J ascertained that Xaviera was born on a specific nesting beach on the southwestern coast of the mainland of Mexico, near a town by the name of Lazaro Cardenas, northwest of Acapulco. Theoretically, she should return there to begin nesting. She did in fact travel almost 900 miles to return to that beach within less than two months. The other turtle lost its tag within days.

A third turtle that J tagged with a satellite transmitter and released the year before was a loggerhead named Adelita. He determined from her DNA that she had been born on a known nesting beach in Japan. J released Adelita in August, 1996 from Santa Rosaliita, Baja California Sur, Mexico. After almost a year, J finally lost track of her transmitter only 110 miles from that very Japanese nesting beach. J thinks she must have been caught by Japanese fishermen as her last satellite transmission showed her almost 10' above sea level.

Adelita was the first turtle ever tracked across an entire ocean basin using satellite telemetry. Millions of kids followed her migration path on the internet. This helped prove that loggerheads born in Japan cross the Pacific and feed in California and Mexico, before migrating back home to nest in Japan. Adelita reminds us that oceans are connected and that we need to work together to protect sea turtles and their habitat.

© Cricket Manuel

As you can see, this Green Sea Turtle is quite curious of the photographer.

GARDENS OF MEMORIES- ON ENDANGERED SEA TURTLES

Endangered sea turtles in holding tanks round,
  This is where memories are sure to be found.
In the desert of Baja on the Sea of Cortez,
  These turtles are studied from their tails to their heads.
Caught from the bay in turtle nets,
  Scientists track where they will nest.
Sounds in the bay include sea lions bark,
  And whales are heard spouting in Nature's park.
As seabirds fly in formation above,
  The turtles are handled with feelings of love.
Their sizes and shapes are recorded with care,
  And pictures are taken from here to there.
Cleaning and feeding goes on through the week,
  As excitement builds to an enormous peak.
Then flippers are tagged on every one,
  With samples of tissue to tell where they're from.
Satellite tags finally mounted to shells;
  Release will be soon as epoxy gels.
With friendly glances, they know that they're free,
  Gardens of memories in open sea.

Meeting Stan Waterman

In 1997, I earned my seventh first-place international award for underwater video. This time it was from EPIC (the Environmentally Aware Photographic Competition). My video, "Kiss of Extinction" won in their Conservation category. My prize was a week aboard the Fiji Aggressor.

"Kiss of Extinction" was a short production that showed endearing shots of manatees feeding and playing, then one sitting just below the motor and propellor of a john boat that wasn't running. But this manatee had propeller scars running the entire length of its body. Another manatee was missing most of its tail completely. The last shot of the production was a curious manatee slowly approaching my dome port, then actually touching and sniffing it which could be heard on the video as if it were sniffling back its tears.

When I contacted Aggressor, they said the Fiji Aggressor wouldn't be finished and in the water until October, so I made arrangements to visit the first week in November. I'd never been to the deep South Pacific before, so I was looking forward to Fiji being my first experience. I'd only seen pictures of the beautiful soft corals and colorful fish; all different than anything I'd seen in Florida or the Caribbean. Hawaii had beautiful fish and corals, but no colorful, flowing soft corals.

After almost 30 hours of flights and layovers, I landed in Nadi. I gathered my luggage from the carrousel, went through customs, then I expected to see someone representing the Fiji Aggressor holding up my name on a placard. Instead, some old guy came up to me and asked if I was Roth. I told him I was and he pertly stated, "It's about time you got here! We've been here a couple of hours waiting for you to arrive. I'm Jerry B. and that's Cricket Manuel. C'mon, our driver is waiting outside." So, I grabbed all of my luggage and followed them to find the driver who had already loaded their gear.

I wasn't sure who this guy Jerry thought he was, but I was beginning to think if he's on the boat with me, this may end up being a tough guy to be around for a week. We headed to the jitney bus whose seats might well have been wooden boxes for the hour-long drive to the dock where the Fiji Aggressor was tied. Upon arrival around 1 PM or so, we were told the boat wasn't ready and we'd have to stay in a day room until early evening.

We decided that we'd share a day room where we could take a shower then we'd head to the restaurant for something to eat for lunch. It had been quite a while since any of us had eaten. Once we arrived at the restaurant, we saw that it was empty, so we seated ourselves.

It took about 20 minutes or so for a waitress to show up and take our drink orders. Then it took another 20 minutes or so for her to bring our drinks and ask if we were ready to order. We were very ready to order food by that time, so we quickly gave her our orders for cheeseburgers and fries. As she was leaving, Jerry called her back and told her we didn't want to die of old age before we got our food.

I still wasn't sure how to take Jerry, especially after this last remark. In our ensuing discussions, I found out that they both were from Clearwater, Florida. Cricket was Jerry's tennis coach for the last 15-20 years or so and they dived together regularly on his large cabin cruiser.

Cricket was a still photographer and Jerry shot video. Cricket even had one of her pictures published on the back cover of one of the older *Ocean Realm Magazines*. It was a picture of an anemonefish holding one of the anemone tentacles in its mouth. She told me that she and Jerry also enjoyed spearfishing and always ate what they speared.

When we finally got our cheeseburgers, they each had a fried egg on them. We surely didn't expect that, having never heard of putting a fried egg on a cheeseburger. I took the egg off of my cheeseburger to eat it first, then ate the cheeseburger.

After lunch, we all went back to the room and had a couple of cocktails to pass the time. We got to know each other better and I decided Jerry wasn't that bad of a guy after all; just a little gruff at times. I was hoping the rest of the week would go as well as the afternoon did.

Finally, a crew member came to let us know the boat was ready and he escorted us to the boat. As we boarded, there was another older fellow sitting on the upper deck reading a book while smoking a pipe. Looking at him reminded me of my own father smoking his pipe for relaxation while reading medical journals. My father was a general practice family physician.

Within an hour, the boat was bustling with people. Everyone unpacked clothes, set up gear, and slowly got to know each other. I was rooming with a young fellow from Canada by the name of Steve Engo. He was a fairly new diver and we fast became friends.

Dinner was announced, so everyone found a place at the tables. Then, the manager of the Fiji Aggressor, Capt. Tom and his wife, Tinker, entered the room, introduced themselves first, and then Capt. Tom introduced the pipe-smoking gentleman as Stan Waterman. Tom proceeded to tell us that Stan had five Emmy awards and had helped produce movies like, "The Deep" and "Blue Water, White Death," and was also good friends with Peter Benchley who produced the movie, "Jaws." Then he told us that Stan would be entertaining us after dinner with one or two of his own video productions about his personal travels all over the world.

Wow! I was on board with a famous person who was also an underwater filmmaker! I was ecstatic and looked forward to learning as much as I could from this gentleman. I only hoped he'd be down to earth enough to talk with, and that he'd be willing to help an amateur such as myself. Anyone who knows Stan knows he can and will talk with anyone as a peer, and he was in fact very helpful and enjoyable to be around. Since that trip, I've always called him the consummate gentleman.

One of my goals for this trip was to film blue ribbon eels. I'd never seen them before in the water and was looking forward to finding some, not only in their blue phase, but also in their black and yellow phases. Each life stage is represented by a different color. The black phase is a juvenile and always a male. The blue phase is an adult male and the yellow phase is an adult female.

I had told Jerry, Cricket and Steve about my desire to find these eels, so it was now our intention to find some. Surprisingly enough, our guide led us right to one. We noticed that Capt. Tom was trying to get some shots of the blue ribbon eel, so we hung back so as to not interrupt his shot. This is a common courtesy between shooters. We just meandered around the reef looking for other critters to shoot.

About five minutes later, we ambled back to the area where

Capt. Tom was shooting, only to find him still trying to get whatever shots he was looking for. Cricket and I just looked at each other and shrugged. After another 10 minutes, we went back to check to see if Capt. Tom was gone yet.

It looked as though he was just finishing up as he was beginning to ascend from his perch. Unfortunately for us, as Capt. Tom straightened up, he silted up the entire area horribly with his fins as he took off. It was almost as if he did this on purpose as we'd never seen a photographer be that careless.

Once we got back on the boat, we all discussed how rude Capt. Tom was. He'd spent an inordinate amount of time shooting the eel. This would be a long time for any underwater photographer, let alone the general manager of the boat who can visit any time he wants. We decided that since we were diving the same site again, we'd make a beeline straight to the eel and then we'd take turns shooting it as we always did.

Much to our surprise, Capt. Tom was already there shooting the eel again! Since it was the first blue ribbon eel I'd seen, I really wanted to wait around for my turn and Cricket and Jerry agreed. They had already seen and shot/filmed these eels in the Solomon Islands and understood my desire to do the same, so we hung out around the area again. After waiting another 10 minutes or so, Capt. Tom began ascending from his perch and for a second time, totally silted up the area with his fins beyond any visibility to film or shoot stills, so we left, never to return to that eel.

By the end of the second dive, we were cold and decided to see if there was room in the hot tub. Once we got out of our gear and showered, we went to the hot tub. We were delighted to find it empty so we could warm our body cores with the hot water. Cricket said that hot peach pie was being served in the dining room as a snack for everyone, so she was going to go get us three pieces while Jerry and I got in the hot tub.

When Cricket came back, she was carrying only one piece of peach pie. Jerry was quick to remark that she was remiss in her duty by only bringing one piece of pie for three of us to share.

Cricket responded, "You won't believe this. Capt. Tom and Tinker were both eating their own warm piece of peach pie before all the guests were served! This is the only piece left!" The cook had made and sliced enough pieces for all the guests, but we guessed the general manager decided he and his wife deserved it more.

This was not the type of service the Aggressor Fleet was known for, so we all knew that we'd be writing Wayne Hasson to notify him of his need to look into the service on the Fiji Aggressor, even though it was only the third week it was in the water. At first, Wayne denied anything like that could happen, however we did find out soon thereafter, that Capt. Tom and Tinker were let go.

After the first couple of dives, Stan, Jerry, Cricket, Steve and I all realized that we hadn't packed properly for the weather or the water temperatures. I thought it was going to a tropical destination and I packed shorts and t-shirts and a 3-mm jump suit for diving, which turned out to be totally insufficient. Air temperatures and water temperatures both hovered around 72° F or less and I get cold easily, especially after four to five hours in the water each day. This was a mistake I learned from and have never made again, realizing how prudent it is to check these things like weather and water temperatures ahead of time.

Jerry B, Roger & Stan on the Fiji Aggressor.

By the second day, all of us including Stan were pouring hot water down our wetsuits before each dive and quickly taking turns in the hot tub after our dives to help warm our core temperatures. Stan entertained us each evening with his videos and stories told in only the way Stan can tell them. After Stan learned that I'd earned this trip for an underwater video that I'd produced, he asked if I had that production and/or any others with me that I'd be willing to share. I told him of course I did, and delighted in sharing with the group, especially Stan! I showed a few of my three-minute award-winning videos that I'd brought and they were well-received.

I followed Stan as much as I could during our dives, attempting to watch and learn. I was shooting with a 3-chip Hi-8 Sony VX-3 camera in a custom-built Ikelite housing. Stan was shooting with the 3-chip digital Sony VX-1000 in a Light & Motion housing with two HID lights. His better camera came out only months after I'd gotten mine; dratted technology burned me again!

Since I was beginning to earn international awards by the end of '94, I decided I should consider getting a better-quality camera. I'd already waited past two other "improved" video camera models to replace my 8-mm camcorder that was eight years old. I studied Sony's 3-chip, Hi-8 mm VX-3 for only a month or so after it came out before I decided it would be my best choice.

The VX-3 had three CCD chips instead of only one. This was the first video camera ever to have three chips that prismatically split the optics into red, green and blue and processed each individually, preserving quality. All other video cameras had only one chip.

I missed the best by only one new model; the one Stan was using. The 3-chip VX-1000 remained the state-of-the-art video camera for five years, and even then, many thought the VX-1000 was still better for shooting underwater than the VX-2000 that replaced it. My VX-3 was considered top of the line for less than six months and only recorded standard video whereas, the VX-1000 was recording digital video with much better quality.

On one dive that Cricket, Jerry and I buddied up, we were watching Stan as he set up for his shot. He was crowded into a nook of the reef setting up for a shot of a sailfin blenny. His camera housing was resting on top of a coral head and one of his lights was leaning on another coral head. He was wedged against a wall full of soft corals with one foot on top of a coral head and his other fin was dangling onto a vase sponge. This sort of "abuse" of the reef had become a no-no by then, but we figured this was the way he'd dived for almost 50 years, so it wasn't our place to judge him. I did have to film that though, just for posterity. Until now, I've not told anyone about this occurrence.

That night, Stan showed some of the pretty video he'd shot of that sailfin blenny as well as footage of a blue ribbon eel and some sharks we'd seen. Then Stan asked to see what I'd shot. I got my camera and hooked it to the TV and we watched my footage. After my footage ended Stan remarked, "By Jove, Roger, you outshot me indeed! Your colors popped off the TV!" I wasn't sure just how serious he was or wasn't, but I think my head swelled three sizes larger anyway. I wasn't using video lights like Stan was, but after nine years of practice, I had taught myself how to shoot effectively using ambient light during the day.

Throughout the week, I'd ask Stan to make any suggestions he felt would help my learning process and reassured him that I wouldn't take any offense from his constructive criticism. He was very gracious in his willingness to make many positive suggestions to help my shooting. I had just gotten my first two video lights before this trip, but I hadn't learned how to use them yet.

Stan taught me how to use my video lights properly, by describing how and where to point them in regards to the subject being filmed. The beams of the light should be two independent circles that only intersect when they are on the subject. This would illuminate things on either side of the subject while the subject itself got twice as much light. His final advice on using my lights was, "Bang in your lights. Really punch out the color."

Many times, in order to not miss something, I'd start recording my subject as soon as I saw it, then I would work on holding my camera system steady. Stan suggested this was wasting a lot of tape and battery power, and that I should steady my camera first, then start recording. I realized that's what he was doing for so long as he set up his shot of the sailfin blenny, and also why his tape had three very nice shots of it with no mistakes or shakiness like my footage did.

Steve and I buddied up a number of times during the week, and I was showing him a lot of critters on every dive. After the dives, he always asked me about critter identifications and the behaviors I was filming. I was glad to share whatever knowledge I had with him. We both really enjoyed it when the guides placed pieces of bait under corals and then out of the blue, sharks would show up to search for the bait!

On our night dives, he had a battery-powered strobe mounted to the top of his tank that I thought was pretty innovative. He said he had made it himself which impressed me as it looked pretty professional. As it turns out, he was studying to be a mechanical engineer and this was one of his projects. At the end of the trip, he gave it to me as a gift for helping him appreciate so much of the ocean world.

On one of our night dives, Steve found a golden cowrie. I filmed it sitting in the sand for a minute or so, then our divemaster, Fiji Bear, winked at Steve as he put it in his pocket. I'm not sure if the cowrie shell was empty at the time, but at the end of the trip it was empty as well as cleaned and polished when Fiji Bear gave the cowrie back to Steve. It was wrapped in bubble wrap and tucked into a small box that he suggested be taped closed and stashed in a bootie or someplace safe for Steve's entire trip home.

He told Steve that the golden cowrie was a huge status symbol among Fiji rulers, but was prized by shell collectors. He said some thought it possibly even represented Fijian rulers who had passed away. To take a golden cowrie out of Fiji was frowned upon by Fijians which is why he had wrapped it up so well.

Fiji Bear was a good spotter. He told us to just tell him what we wanted to see and he would take us to it. One day, I asked him if he could find a pipefish since I'd never seen or filmed one before. On the next dive, he got me and took me to two of them playing on the reef.

At the end of the week, I mentioned to Stan that I wished I'd waited to buy my latest video rig just two to three more months so that I could have gotten the state-of-the art VX-1000 like he was using. As we discussed our cameras, he told me that I should contact him after the trip because he was getting too old to be traveling with such a large rig. He was in his mid-70's and he might be willing to offer his system to me for an "unbelievably low price!" He needed to check with the sponsors who had let him use their products to make sure that selling me his rig would be something he could do without offending those sponsors. I told him I'd write to him a month or two later to see if he was still willing and able to sell me the system.

I wasn't sure what an "unbelievably low price" might be, but this rig would retail for about $7-9,000 with the HID lights, so I wasn't holding my breath. I put together a short video of our trip and sent that along with a couple of my other productions for Stan's "enjoyment," and mailed them to him with a letter asking him if he'd decided anything about selling me his rig. His return letter highly complimented me on my videos, suggested some things to think about on my next shoots, and told me that he'd sell me the entire VX-1000 system he was using for $2500.

I quickly sent him a check for that amount before he changed his mind and I used that rig for many years. Stan became a great mentor for me and was always gracious enough to view and comment on videos I'd send him, which he'll probably do until he can no longer watch them. We still trade DVD's from time to time.

© Cricket Manuel

Here's the elusive Blue Ribbon Eel finally caught on film!

GARDENS OF MEMORIES~ON STAN WATERMAN

The man who loves sharks just rolled into town,
 And this is where memories are sure to be found.
His pipe and his smile are quite familiar to me,
 As our last dives together were down in Fiji.
After warm greetings and a quick catnap,
 Stan hunkers down for a long judging rap.
Magnificent slides and video shorts
 Stir wonderful stories from starboard to port.
Then comes his Ovaltine and time for respite.
 (I thought it was scotch, but it was late at night.)
Daybreak and Waterman paint his juice and a book,
 While proudly parlaying his antics with the cook.
All of his audience is graced by his grin,
 And new friends or old friends seem the same to him.
He can mesmerize divers for hours on end,
 Then return to his room for more strokes of his pen.
With travels "right on," his tales are "well done!"
 "Good on you," my friend, we owe you a ton!
You're off to more diving weightlessly free,
 And more gardens of memories in open sea.

Meeting Jim Church

The Ohio Council of Skin and Scuba Diving, Inc. (OCSSDI) was formed in 1959 to bring Ohio divers together and share everything about the sport. The OCSSDI is the oldest state council still in existence in the United States. Each year a club somewhere in Ohio would host an annual get-together for OCSSDI. In early 1998 the Gavia Scuba Club to which I belonged agreed to again host Ohio's largest scuba expo. We had done a show in 1994 and were ready to tackle this task again.

In one of our original "ScubaFest" meetings I suggested that, since I had traveled with him, I might be able to get Stan Waterman to be our Keynote speaker thinking this would be a great coup for us. But one of the older members of the club stated he had no idea who Stan What's-his-name was. A couple other board members voiced the same concern thinking if they didn't know who he was, he wouldn't be able to draw a crowd for our expo.

After explaining who Stan was and what he'd done so far for the diving community, the entire board agreed to let me go ahead and see if Stan would be willing to participate and how much he would charge. Having dived with Stan in Fiji a year earlier, I contacted him and asked if he might be interested in being a presenter at our expo in afternoon seminars showing his travel videos, as well as being our keynote speaker for the Saturday Night Banquet Ball. He was more than excited about participating after he heard more about the OCSSDI and the previous Gavia ScubaFest '94 event. He told me he'd charge $2500 plus costs.

I also told Stan that his keynote speaker spot would be shared at the Saturday Night Banquet Ball by the announcement of winners of the non-profit, international Underwater Images Photo/Video Competition that I'd founded and directed since 1995. He said he looked forward to seeing world-class underwater photography and had no problem sharing the stage with me. When I asked if he might be interested in even helping to judge the competition, he was all in. I was always particular about having professionals do the judging of this competition and Stan's assistance would be perfect!

The board felt his fee might be a little steep but I assured them it would be well worth it. I'd seen him do short evening presentations while aboard the Fiji Aggressor that would fit perfectly with our daily hour-long seminars we would offer on Saturday and Sunday of that weekend. And with his Ivy League college education from Dartmouth and his gentlemanly demeanor, he would surely entertain a large group of divers fabulously at our banquet dinner.

Next, I suggested to the board that I might also be able to get Jim Church to come and do a photo workshop for underwater photographers. Jim was a famous underwater still photographer who also wrote monthly "How to Shoot Underwater Video" articles for *Skin Diver Magazine.* I knew Stan and Jim traveled on Aggressor trips together and heard great things about these two on these trips being almost like Laurel and Hardy. It would be great fun to have the two of them together at ScubaFest '98!

Everyone on the board at least knew who Jim Church was and agreed that I should contact him as well. I found Jim's contact information and gave him a call. I explained about our ScubaFest events as well as the history of the OCSSDI. I could tell he was intrigued and possibly interested especially since Stan had agreed to be our keynote speaker.

I asked Jim what he would charge to come and do an underwater photo workshop as well as possibly present an hour-long seminar or two. I explained that we'd be willing to pay his fee if it was within our budget plus give him 50% of the proceeds from his photography workshop and pay his expenses. He asked how big the show was and how big our club was. I told him we'd had about 1700 attendees in '94 and hoped to have more in '98. I added that our club was non-profit, only had about 25-30 members and all of this would be more of our labor of love than it would be a money-making endeavor.

Then Jim asked what we could afford to pay him but I returned my original question, "What do you normally charge?" This went back and forth three times before Jim hesitated a second, then made a suggestion as to what he might be willing to charge as his fee. But he made me promise to never tell anyone outside of the Gavia club's Board about his offer until after he died. It was surely a very gracious offer and I accepted on the spot, even without verifying it with the Board.

At this point, I asked Jim if he might be interested in helping to judge the Underwater Images Competition along with Stan and Wayne Hasson who was the founder and CEO of the Aggressor Fleet at the time. Wayne would also be at the expo representing the Aggressor Fleet and helping with the judging. Wayne is originally from Ohio so it was easy for me to get him to come to the show as well as help with the judging.

We made the necessary reservations and paid for Stan and Jim's flights. Arrangements were made to have Stan picked up at the Dayton International Airport and I'd meet Jim at the Greater Cincinnati Airport and bring him to the expo center. Wayne came to Ohio to visit family, then made his way to Cincinnati for the judging on Friday afternoon.

I'd never met Jim before, but I was sure I could pick him out when he landed since I'd seen his picture in hundreds of *Skin Diver* magazines. When I picked up Jim at the airport, I asked if he was hungry enough to eat some lunch at one of my favorite restaurants and he agreed it was a great idea.

I took him to Montgomery Inn and promised these would be the best barbecued ribs he'd ever eaten. Professional athletes from all over the United States came to Montgomery Inn every time they were in town and the owner would also personally fly 100 orders of ribs to California for events Bob Hope or Frank Sinatra might have since they always visited Montgomery Inn when in Cincinnati and loved the ribs.

While eating, Jim asked if I did underwater photography but I told him I liked shooting video better as it allowed me to capture the marine behaviors I loved to witness and share. I talked a little about the international video competition awards that I'd been earning for the last five years and even mentioned that he'd been a judge in four different competitions that I'd won first place.

This piqued his interest even more and he asked why I thought that might be. I smiled and explained that I'd learned my style of shooting, editing and story-telling by reading every *Skin Diver Mag-*

azine I could get my hands on. More specifically, I read all of his monthly articles on how to shoot underwater video! He rolled his eyes and said, "No wonder!"

We arrived at the expo center and Jim took his bags to his room to unpack and said he'd meet back up soon for the judging. I told him where the judging would occur and went to meet up with Stan and Wayne as well as Kristen Spangenburg who was the curator of the famous Cincinnati Art Museum and her husband, John Gilmore, who was a published nature photographer, both of whom agreed to help with the judging.

The judges all introduced each other and decided that we'd just quickly go through the slide carrousels and if anyone liked the shot all they had to do was to say yes and we'd set that slide aside for further review. The first hour or so was mostly Stan, Jim and Wayne giving their opinions. There was a shot of a shark almost head on and Stan and Jim quickly said no, so I moved on to the next slide. But Wayne suggested we go back because the shark was an oceanic white tip and the photographer was in "grave danger." I went back and all agreed on the merits of the shot so it stayed in the running.

I think Kristen and her husband were a little intimidated by the others and I also think they felt somewhat inexperienced in judging pictures from the underwater realm that they knew nothing about. Nor did they know the difficulty of getting any of the shots they were seeing. When a shot of some flowing red whip corals from Papua New Guinea came up on the screen with a very pretty blue background, Jim and Wayne both said no quickly, so I moved on to the next slide.

That's when Kristen spoke up for the first time and said, "Wait, can we go back? That shot seemed so sensual!" Everyone agreed to go back and when the shot came up on the screen, Stan quickly said, "Indeed! That is a sensual shot! Good on you for recognizing this!" So, this picture remained in the running as well. Kristen and her husband began joining in more of the discussions with their own expertise in composition, and Stan, Jim and Wayne were respecting their input.

At the end of the judging, the oceanic white tip and the flowing whip corals shots both took first place in their respective categories. The only chore left was to pick the Best of Show shot from all the first-place winners. The sensual flowing whip corals taken by Patricia "PJ" Jordan earned the Best of Show honor!

Stan presented about Cocos Island in one of the Saturday morning seminars while Jim practiced for his three-hour workshop that he'd start at 1 PM. We met in the hospitality room for lunch where Gavia club members brought in everything to make sandwiches, as well as snacks, pop, home-made chili, cookies, cakes, and more for any presenter or volunteer to enjoy at any time throughout the weekend.

Stan and Jim both agreed that the hospitality room was a great idea that they'd never experienced before at any show they'd attended. In fact, they enjoyed it immensely because they could sit down and casually discuss anything with all these down-to-earth people instead of having to deal with all the various personalities of the "famous" presenters like they did at other shows.

At the Saturday Night Banquet Ball, I announced the honorable mentions and top three place winners along with the prizes they would receive as the winning shots appeared on the large screen behind me. Then I showed the winning video before relinquishing the stage to Stan. After he was introduced, he told the audience I'd already upstaged him with the world-class photography.

As it turned out, that wasn't even close. His presentation kept everyone on the edges of their seats and was as entertaining as anyone could ever want. He finished to a standing ovation. Anyone who didn't know anything about Stan Waterman before was now a fan of his forever.

The rest of the weekend went very well with Jim and Stan continuing to enjoy the down-home hospitality while our attendees enjoyed them. There are a number of older members of OCSSDI that attend these annual events and both Jim and Stan really enjoyed sitting with these people as much as anything else the weekend had to offer.

By the end of the weekend, Jim had agreed to look at any videos I'd produce if I sent them to him, as long as I was patient for his opinion in case he was out of the country or pressed for time and couldn't get to them right away. I asked him why he would do this for me and he told me that he knew I'd pay it forward. This was huge for me because it meant that I now had two great mentors giving me guidance on filmmaking and more importantly, their input continued to build my confidence that my work was getting pretty good.

Since Jim has unfortunately passed away, I'm free to proudly tell you the very gracious fee he said he'd charge for coming to ScubaFest '98. In our negotiations, he said he would come and do a couple one-hour seminars on his dive travel like Stan would do, and he'd also do the afternoon photography workshop. We would pay his expenses, we would keep 100% of the proceeds from the workshop, and there would be no other fee. He made me promise to not tell anyone until after his death because he didn't want other professionals to think he was undercutting their fee rates, especially when he was only doing it to help a small scuba club have a great dive show. May God Bless you, Jim Church. Rest in peace, my friend!

Wayne Hasson, Roger, Jim Church & Stan Waterman after the many hours of judging of the Underwater Images Competition entries.

GARDENS OF MEMORIES~ON JIM CHURCH

I first meet Jim Church when his plane touches down,
    And this is where memories are sure to be found.
"World-famous ribs and my diet?" he asks,
    But eating them all is not a small task.
While supping, he tells me of judging he's done,
    And I tell him that those were many I'd won.
Good teachers are few, but Jim qualifies
    As one of the best, with no formal ties.
Our pow-wow recedes as his practice is needed.
    Equipment is there; "Practice, practice," is heeded.
With poached eggs his toast must be crispy, just right.
    Then eggs will not fall to the very last bite.
His classes are filled, different levels of learning;
    He'll satisfy each individual's yearning.
Then he'll practice again before turning in;
    More practice tomorrow with a confident grin.
Last sessions go well with new friends that he'll make,
    In hopes of a photo that students will take.
There are thousands of shots he has set up with glee;
    Seeding gardens of memories in open sea.

Meeting Jean-Michel Cousteau

In August 1998, I boarded the Cayman Aggressor III for a week's diving in the Caymans. I was greeted by Wayne Hasson, the CEO of the Aggressor Fleet who would be joining the cruise. Also on board was Charles Stearns who was an accomplished underwater photographer whom I'd heard of via many different international underwater photo & video competitions I'd entered and followed. His name appeared on numerous winners' lists throughout the years.

In the mix of guests, Catherine Leech was a gal from the UK and there were also a couple of other videographers I didn't know yet. One of them was named Bruce who had introduced himself in the Tampa airport while we were waiting at the Cayman Air gate since he had seen my Underwater Video Productions patch on my backpack.

As we unpacked and settled down to meet each other on the sundeck, Wayne announced that Jean-Michel Cousteau would be joining our trip later that evening with a friend Nan and a marine biologist from France, Christine Causse. This news was music to my ears realizing I'd again be diving with another famous industry icon similar to my good fortune when Stan Waterman was aboard the Fiji Aggressor with me the year before. The scuba gods were surely looking down on me.

The next morning our first dive would be at Stingray City which was a good place for a check-out dive. This is a shallow dive site where we would intermingle with southern stingrays and feed them bits of squid as they winged and soared around and past us. For the most part I was concentrating more on shooting video and trying to capture others interacting with the stingrays so I didn't do much feeding, however I did once put some bait in my hand then slowly wave my hand over my head in large circles making a stingray circle over me like a large Mexican sombrero.

Catherine was wearing a very colorful shorty wetsuit so it only made sense that I follow her as much as anyone since we were diving in a shallow, bare sandy area with gray animals. About half-way through the dive while filming Catherine, I noticed a stingray coming up behind her, then it latched onto her elbow like a leech (no pun intended). She jumped a mile and flailed wildly to get that stingray to loosen its suction grip on her shoulder. When stingrays feed, they suck their prey into their mouths.

After the dive, I took more video of the huge six-inch diameter sucker mark on her elbow left by that stingray as if it had been her favorite prom date. This event became the first marine biology lecture Jean-Michel would share with us. As we all sat around and hypothesized why the stingray had so amorously attacked Catherine, Jean-Michel suggested that maybe she had rubbed her shoulder with the scent of squid on her hand. At that point Catherine seemed to remember scratching an itch on her shoulder.

On the next few dives, I buddied up with Charles once and Bruce twice since we were both shooting video. While diving with Charles, I had been able to get very close to a spotted eagle ray that was nosing through the sand to feed. Jean-Michel and Nan joined everyone on the last dive of the day. I remember seeing him vertical in the water while he slowly descended head-first down into the middle of a large six-foot barrel sponge. He kept his arms and hands tight to his sides and never touched the barrel sponge as he inspected the bottom. Then he slowly ascended feet first by just inhaling the air from his tank which makes him more buoyant and able to float up and out of the sponge.

Throughout the week, Jean-Michel and Christine would sit down after lunch and share information about diving, the oceans, marine behavior, conservation and many other interesting topics as we all were gathered around to learn and participate. He would explain how atolls protect islands from the ravaging waves of storms and talk about wars that occur among corals fighting each other for space and sunlight. Some of his information should have been obvious to us all but we'd never really thought about it, and other subjects were things no one had ever considered.

Jean-Michel again joined us the next day on our morning dives. After lunch, he began his marine biology session by asking everyone a question. "Who thinks they had no adverse effect on the marine environment during the morning dives?" A few people raised their hands, but not everyone, including me.

Jean-Michel looked at one diver whose hand was up and reminded that person that his console and gauges were dragging through sponges and gorgonians on both dives. Next, he looked at Charles who had also raised his hand and told Charles that he'd seen him put his hand on different coral heads to steady himself for his photography. Charles admitted that he does this.

Then he looked at a young fellow, Jerrod, and asked him why he thought he had no effect on the reef. Jerrod stated that he was studying for his IED (he was learning to become a scuba instructor) and spent most of the dives practicing his buoyancy in mid-water. I clearly remember him suspended cross-legged and Indian-style in the water column for most of one of our dives. Jean-Michel reminded Jerrod of the time a large grouper swam by him and Jerrod began chasing the grouper thus affecting the "mental state" of the grouper and the peaceful balance of the environment.

Jean-Michel then looked at me and asked me why I hadn't raised my hand since I seemed to have pretty good buoyancy and good control of my gear. I told him I had been lying in the sand shooting a jawfish in its burrow and I could have been lying on other burrows or nests. He smiled and agreed with me, making his point to everyone.

That's when I asked him if lying on the sand to get a good shot could be rationalized by a positive use of the shot. I continued to explain that I put together educational video programs and then share them in schools, senior centers, and more so that non-divers can see and learn about the wonders of the oceans. I reminded him of something I'll always remember that his father, Jacques Cousteau, had once said, "People protect what they love," and I try to instill that love in others by sharing my video productions.

He smiled again and proceeded to totally agree with me. He stated that many people take pictures and video, then allow that media to sit on shelves gathering dust until their children throw it away. But considering the far-reaching benefit of a well-produced and well-shared production, the minimal impact on whatever was under the sand was worth the trade-off. I'll have to admit, I was quite relieved and pleased to hear this answer. The rationalization also made me think of that dive in Fiji with Stan who has more than made up for a little reef abuse.

After dinner on the third day, Jean-Michel pulled me aside and told me that we'd soon be doing a night dive on a Russian Destroyer that was purposely sunk off Cayman Brac as an artificial reef two years previous and that he would be doing his second anniversary survey of this ship to see how it was faring as an artificial reef. He said he'd been watching me use my video camera the last few days and asked if I'd be willing to document his dives on the #356. Being as how there were two other videographers on this trip, my heart jumped. My mind was racing with thoughts like, I should look at my watch and suggest that I'd have to check my schedule, but my mouth quickly stated I'd be honored!

That night I followed Jean-Michel all over the wreck as we listened to Wagner's "Ride of the Valkyries" that Wayne had played through an underwater speaker. Jean-Michel peeked into nooks and crannies of the ship and pointed to nests of marine creatures for Nan to see how life was settling in on this artificial reef. The entire dive was surreal to me, and I still remember it all very fondly.

The next morning, we were told we'd be doing two more dives on the ship which had been renamed the MV Captain Keith Tibbetts in honor of a great Caymanian. There was a definite air of excitement aboard as Jean-Michel posed for pictures with us all after an early breakfast and before the first dive. I even donned a red beanie for one of my pictures with Jean-Michel. This beanie was similar to one Jacques Cousteau often wore.

When it came time to dive, Jean-Michel told me to go in first and set up to capture his and Nan's giant stride entry into the water, so that's what I did. My heart was pounding in anticipation of getting the shot right, not to mention who I was going to be filming in this shot. Then I happened to turn around and glance at the ship behind me.

What I saw literally took my breath away. The sun was hitting the ship perfectly, illuminating all 330' of it as if it was the pot of gold at the end of a rainbow. The visibility was so good, I could see the entire ship clearly. I wanted to turn around right then and there and get that shot but then a horrible thought went through my mind; I needed to turn back around and get Nan and Jean-Michel's entry together or I would have failed my first assignment of the day!

I quickly turned around with camera rolling and steady no less than five seconds before they cut through the surface of the sea. Phew! I hadn't blown that shot! I panned down keeping them in my viewfinder as they headed towards the bow of the Tibbetts. Fortunately, I also took a few seconds to capitalize on the sunlight and visibility by getting a good wide-angle pan of the entire ship before following Nan and Jean-Michel to the bow.

These three dives on the Tibbetts are ones I'll always remember. Being a former science teacher, I tried to integrate shots of Jean-Michel with nests, schools of young fry, small growths, accumulations of schools of fish; all things that would demonstrate this artificial reef was successful in its designed endeavor. I followed Nan and Jean-Michel over and around the ship like the paparazzi.

I had seen Bruce shooting through a ring at the very point of the bow and decided to see what I could do with that shot. As I approached the ring from blue water with my camera running, the ring got larger in my viewfinder with corals hanging towards the middle. Once I got to the ring and shot through it and the middle opening between all the corals, I got a great shot of Jean-Michel and Nan swimming across the bow from starboard to port with the ship's cannons in the background.

Then we went to the wheelhouse and I filmed them swimming through as I remained in place while Jean-Michel studied everything about the wheelhouse. Then we went to an area above the wheelhouse where Jean-Michel was alone and hanging horizontally a few feet above the ceiling of the wheelhouse facing the bow. All of a sudden, he reached out his arms as if presenting the entire ship to someone.

I integrated that shot in my own production to a final "Tada!" moment of the music I'd used. When my kids heard this for the first time, all they could say was, "Synch!" Once we were back on board, Jean-Michel explained to me that the view he was seeing with outstretched arms was what one of his mounted cameras saw as he rode the ship down when it sank.

At the end of the trip, Jean-Michel asked me what it would be worth to me to send him all of my footage for his own use in a short international program after having it bumped to Beta at his cost. We negotiated a price that not-so coincidentally equaled what I'd paid Aggressor for the trip. That's when he added that he had to have this footage with exclusivity.

All of a sudden that wasn't sitting well with me. It would mean I wouldn't be able to use most of my footage of the Tibbetts wreck since he was in most of my shots for the first two dives, not to mention not being able to use footage of diving with him. This would leave me with some shots of Stingray City and other not-so-stunning things to try to salvage a good, educational production from this trip…in other words, a wasted dive trip in regards to what I could use and produce.

I quickly told Jean-Michel I wasn't happy with this part of the deal and if he wanted exclusivity the price would have to go up. Then I explained to him that I was no competition to him or any production he'd make and also that I don't have my productions in markets and video stores. I only produced educational videos that I share in the Midwest for educational purposes and would like to share the wonderful story of Jean-Michel's part in the creation of this artificial reef.

He finally agreed but with the stipulation that I had to send him what I produced to make sure I portrayed him in a good light. If it was done well, then he'd let me use my production, as well as any picture of us together for my DVD cover. We finally had a done deal!

In the next few months, I wrote and edited a 20-minute production about the creation of this artificial reef from how it was obtained from Cuba with Wayne Hasson's help over Cuban rum and cigars with Fidel Castro's brother, to how Jean-Michel sweated in his wetsuit all day in the hot Cayman sun waiting for the ship to start sinking. It was calculated it would begin going down by 9 AM but the calculations were off and it wasn't until 5:30 that afternoon that it began sinking and Jean-Michel rode it down for 17 seconds until it hit the sandy bottom. I was also fortunate enough to find out that a friend of Jerry and Cricket's had taken pictures of the sinking and she gave me permission to use her pictures in my production to augment that part of the story since I wasn't there.

Once I finished my production, I sent a copy to Jean-Michel along with the footage bumped up to beta as he requested. A week or two later, I received a letter from him telling me that he gave me his blessing to use my production as is and promised to send me a copy of the short program he was having produced for international use about the creation of this artificial reef. When I watched his program six or eight months later, I was honored that he'd used some of my production in his own production; word for word, shot for shot. At least I knew he approved of my writing and editing style.

I had also mailed a copy of my production to Stan Waterman and Jim Church since they were both mentors for me and I wanted to get their input. I was proud of how the video turned out, as well. To my delight, Stan sent back a wonderful complimentary letter telling me that I'd done a "bang-up job" of putting together a 20-minute production of an inanimate object (the MV Capt. Keith Tibbetts), because it is normally extremely difficult to keep an audience's attention that long on an inanimate subject.

Jim gave me an A-. When I asked him why the minus, he said he loved the story, but his only critique was that I could/should have used a tripod with my land shots.

Roger and Jean-Michel Cousteau after a week of filming together in Cayman.

GARDENS OF MEMORIES~ON JEAN-MICHEL COUSTEAU

A dive expedition, Jean-Michel around;
 This is where memories are sure to be found.
With a stately grey beard and collar length hair,
 He would catch all our eyes trying not to stare.
A smile, a handshake, then off for a dive;
 We're to study a ship to find what's alive.
While holding Nan's hand, he glides through the blue,
 Down the bow to the sand to check out the view.
Then up over the rail and onto the wreck;
 They could see two big cannons facing the deck.
Next was the wheelhouse where captains did stand,
 Then on to the radar, no longer unmanned.
Some walls in between have collapsed from large storms,
 Exposing the poop deck with seats not so warm.
A peek in the flag bins shows none are left;
 There was a stashed coin for Nan, 'twas a gift.
The dive nears its end, and with batteries low,
 I return to the surface with an obvious glow.
The footage I got, he requested of me;
 More gardens of memories in open sea.

ROGER ROTH

GARDENS OF MEMORIES~ON THE STINGRAY

Two eyes peering from a sand covered mound,
    This is where memories are sure to be found.
A stingray has buried itself in the sand,
    Probably sleeping till bothered by man.
In a huff and a puff, the ray takes to flight,
    A flip of its fins and it soars out of sight.
But soon it emerged from where it had hid,
    For in my palm was some frozen squid.
Enticing approach of my new-found friend,
    It followed the scent of bait to my hand.
Familiar with rhythm of underwater world,
    Over my head the bait I did twirl.
Like a Mexican hat dance, the ray spun above,
    Then tried to enshroud me as tight as a glove.
The ray's underbelly was soft as silk
    And camouflaged as white as milk.
Its mouth and gills pulsed open and closed,
    As it searched for the food it had smelled with its nose.
Then it sucked up my offering quick as can be,
    Gardens of memories in open sea.

Diving Russian Destroyer #356

I didn't know a thing about the Russian Destroyer #356 before diving it. All I knew was that it was purposely sunk as an artificial reef off Cayman Brac. Then my first dive on it was a night dive following Jean-Michel around while he looked at things I could hardly see at times. My first day dive also entailed following Jean-Michel and Nan while he showed Nan things that meant something to him.

When Jean-Michel looked at something, I made sure to find a good angle to film him doing so. After he finished and began to move on to something else, I felt due diligence was for me to film whatever it was he was looking at from a closer perspective even though I didn't know what he was looking at or why. For instance, on our night dive, after he looked in a group of boxes where alphabet letter flags were stored, I got a close-up shot of some of those boxes, even though it would be much later that I learned he had stashed a coin in one of them on the day the ship sank.

I also had no idea that he had his staff mount video cameras in various places on the ship to illustrate what it would look like as the ship sank. The camera he had mounted in the wheelhouse was to show what the captain would see if he went down with the ship. The footage of that on his own production showed a tidal wave of water coming in so fast, the captain would have not had a chance to escape.

My third dive on the ship was a solo dive where I'd hoped to film a little more detail of the ship so that I would have footage that enhanced my story of the ship as well as Jean-Michel's story once I produced it. Since I didn't know any of the history of the ship or Jean-Michelle's story of riding it down, I also didn't know what might be of importance, so I began at the deepest part of the ship and worked my way shallower.

I went to the sand and filmed a long-shot of the keel from a crack in the keel amidships towards the bow. Then I started at the crack in the keel and ascended while I followed the crack up the hull showing how extensive the crack was. Later, Jean-Michel explained the sounds he heard during the 17 seconds it took for the ship to land on the sea-floor. He said the sounds of air rushing out of pockets of the ship was only surpassed by the snap of the aluminum hull that split the living quarters into two sections.

As I panned up the crack, near the top of the crack was an open porthole that just happened to have a school of fry inside. This showed how fish were using the ship for protection of their nests and young. Since I didn't realize the fry were there when I started my shot, it was a lucky shot that worked out perfectly.

I swam along the starboard deck towards the bow as if I were a crewman to show what they would see as they walked that area. In front of me, there was a piece of the steel decking that was peeled up and a couple of divers were coming towards me, just then swimming over that piece of steel. I let them swim past me on the video, then pointed my camera to the opening and swam to it until I could see inside below deck in my viewfinder.

It looked like there were some interesting things down there so I decided to squeeze myself through the opening and go below deck. I knew I shouldn't have been in there since most dangerous areas of the ship were closed off with bars and welded steel plates. Being below deck alone with no one knowing I was there was surely not the safest thing to do, but what I found there completed many parts of the story I would research and learn later.

There was a steel stairway coming down from a room that had a barred window just above the curled deck plate. I decided to not go up there since it was barred off, but the room where I'd entered had dozens of empty slots that once held gauges of all sorts. Some of these slots still had labeled signs written in Russian below them that would have told the sailors what that specific gauge was for. I filmed all of this room carefully and closely before inching out and back on deck safely.

I would later find out that before the ship was sunk, Caymanians were allowed to tour the ship and remove one piece of it to keep as their own souvenir. That day, Caymanian men, women, and children invaded the ship with screwdrivers, hammers and crowbars to get their own gauges, signs, and pieces of history. Going down into that room and filming everything there turned out to be another lucky shot for me that worked into my production brilliantly.

As I swam around the ship, I continuously shot as many different species of fish and marine creatures as I could. Some were just swimming around and others were showing specific behaviors like using parts of the ship for protection, which is the point of an artificial reef. When I later studied Jean-Michel's description of what he saw after the ship settled in the sand, I matched my shots with the creatures he named. This included matching my shot of a spotted eagleray nosing in the sand for food since the spotted eagleray was the first marine creature he mentioned.

In an area where some of the ship had fallen over exposing what had been inside, I took shots of a deteriorating tile floor and a row of open porcelain toilets mounted in the floor with no privacy walls or toilet seats. I would later find out sailors would crouch over these as women might use a regular public toilet without sitting on the seat. These shots were a great lead into my narration about the lack of privacy on the poop deck.

I made sure to get different angles of the cannons as well as inside the rooms where the sailors would be protected while firing the cannons. These shots supplemented the story of how the deal of buying the ship from the Cubans almost fell through. Wayne Hasson thought the deal to buy the ship for $265,000 was final until Fidel's brother put a stipulation that the cannons would be removed before the ship left Cuba. He said the Russians were afraid we might gain some knowledge about their technology.

That's when Wayne told him, "No deal. Without the cannons, the ship lost a lot of its character as a Russian destroyer and we aren't interested." They negotiated further for a month or so, and for another $10,000, the cannons could remain on the ship.

I also got a shot of Wayne swimming along the side of the ship with his camera in hand. As I was editing my footage, I noticed that "MV Capt. Keith Tibbetts" was printed on the wall behind him. After learning that the Russian Destroyer #356 was later renamed the MV Capt. Keith Tibbetts after a great Caymanian, even that shot ended up working perfectly as I narrated that part of the story.

I'd like to think my great planning was why my production worked out so well, but as you can see, there was as much luck involved as there was planning!

GARDENS OF MEMORIES~ON THE #356

Diving a wreck, cannon pointing down,
　　This is where memories are sure to be found.
A Russian Frigate, number three fifty-six;
　　Re-christened MV Captain Keith Tibbetts.
Undressed to her hull, she was led to the floor,
　　Where she settled in peace to fire no more.
Now, she's attracting new friends every day,
　　From fish to coral sprouts to divers that play.
On side deck, steel plates cracked like a table;
　　Peek down inside reveals Russian labels.
Somewhere amidships, some superstructures collapsed,
　　Having lost a war with strong currents, perhaps.
I passed alphabet bins and doors barred from entry
　　And stairways that lead to an empty sentry.
From beneath the turret, new life will emerge,
　　As long as the Majors protect from all scourge.
Resident fish scour her hull for a meal,
　　And a crack can be found from the deck to her keel.
Deeply snuggled in sand at one fifteen feet,
　　Gardens of memories, in open sea.

The Underwater Images Photo/Video Competition

During the early and mid '90's when I was entering many of the international underwater video competitions, the rules of each competition varied tremendously. Some were for amateurs only while others allowed industry professionals to compete in the same categories as amateurs. The competitions were designed to promote underwater imaging, but many times the playing field wasn't very level for everyone.

After earning a first place in one of the reputable international competitions in the late '90's, I received a letter from them not long after learning of my honor. The letter stated that their competition was for amateurs only and they deemed I was a professional videographer and my prize would be rescinded. When I asked how and why they ascertained I was a professional, I was told that they learned that I had sold a trip tape to a friend on one of my trips for $10.

I was really taken aback by this ruling. Granted, I had been earning first, second, and third places numerous times in various competitions for four years, but that didn't make me a professional. I wasn't making any money with my video productions. $10 mostly paid for the blank VHS tape and mailing costs. That's when I decided to look into somehow standardizing rules between these reputable competitions.

I'd always been taught by my parents that if I wanted to change things, I shouldn't do that from the outside looking in. I needed to get involved, then I could work on changing things from within a system. I figured the best way to standardize rules would be for me to establish a new and reputable competition, then work with the directors of all the other contests to see if they might want to be on board with standardizing the rules.

It was then that I consulted with the directors of EPIC, the Environmentally Aware Photographic Competition, to see if they might help me in this endeavor. EPIC was one of the top international competitions and had the best environmentally sound rules of all the contests. I told Gayle and Richard that I wanted to launch a non-profit, international competition of my own, then work with all of the other directors to make the rules clear and fair for all contestants.

My first step was to get their permission to copy and use their set of environmentally sound rules in my newly formed contest. I assured them that I would also give EPIC credit for the rules every time they were printed and used. They gave me their blessing to do this and were very supportive of my efforts, even to the extent that they shared their mailing list with me to help me get started. It would only be a year or two more until the Los Angeles Underwater Photographic Society (LAUPS) also merged their mailing list with ours in support of underwater imaging.

EPIC's basic conservation rules disqualified any entrant that displayed any of the following in their photographs or videos:

1. Divers with gear dragging or visibly damaging the environment.
2. Divers kicking up sand.
3. Animals showing signs of stress.
4. Animals viewed in an unnatural environment or location.
5. Animals being fed.
6. Marine life being touched.
7. Divers exhibiting poor buoyancy control.

My next step was to solicit prize sponsors. I decided to look through the dive magazines and contact some of the larger advertisers thinking that if they had an advertising budget, they might also be willing to support my new contest as long as I did things that had a good enough return for them. I assured them that every penny that came in would go out to non-profit marine conservation, preservation and/or educational purposes. I also told them our website would advertise their participation in as many ways and web pages as possible.

The only other person I had to help me with this competition was Mark Beatty from the Gavia Scuba Club who created and maintained our website. He was a still photographer and an excellent web designer. Within the first three years, he had developed the most comprehensive website for underwater photographers in the world, which was even written up as such in an article by Stephen Frink in a popular diving magazine.

Once I had enough sponsors willing to participate, I gathered their logos and sent them to Mark for posting on our website. Then I print-ed up rules and entry forms and mailed them out to the same list of people EPIC shared with me. That first year, I received more than 600 entries from around 200 entrants from all over the world, competing for 30 prizes in 10 categories.

Next, I needed a venue to announce the winners over and above just posting them on our website. The Ohio Council of Skin and Scu-ba Diving, Inc. (OCSSDI) held an annual get-together every year for local divers in Ohio and nearby states. My local Gavia Scuba Club hosted this event a few times and we called it "ScubaFest." Therefore, the first few years from 1998, I was director of the new contest, I called it the "ScubaFest Images Competition," and announced the winners at the annual OCSSDI events, similar to the festival I attended in '94, where the LAUPS announced their winners.

Once the ScubaFest Images Competition proved its value with a good reputation, I arranged to meet with as many directors of the oth-er international competitions as I could while we attended the annual DEMA expos (the Diving Equipment Manufacturer's Association). We had meetings together to discuss standardization and clarification of rules. By the end of our second year of meetings, everyone was on board to use EPIC's ecologically-friendly set of rules. In those meet-ings, we also discussed dividing the categories into amateur and open categories so that amateurs didn't have to compete with more accom-plished underwater image makers unless they chose to do so.

These international competitions were great fun for entrants want-ing to find out if their deftness and artistry of underwater imaging showed any promise. The anticipation of waiting for the announce-ment of winners might only be surpassed by notification of placing or winning for any given shot or short video. Many of the entrants have gone on to become world renowned for their skills as photojournalists and book publishers.

After the Gavia Scuba Club hosted the 2000 OCSSDI Banquet Ball with Georgienne Bradley and Jay Ireland as keynote speakers and Jim Church doing more photography workshops, the Southern Ohio Scuba Club offered to host the 2001 event in Portsmouth, Ohio. But with only a month or two before the date, that club was unable to find a keynote speaker as well as gather exhibitors to any great extent.

Since I was the OCSSDI Chairman of the Board at the time, and had experience on the Gavia ScubaFest boards, I started contacting exhibitors I thought might be interested in attending as well as contacting Mark Bernardi from Colorado to see if he would be the keynote speaker. Mark ran a dive travel agency at the time and I'd known him since 1993 when we both upgraded to the Sony VX-3 camera when it first came out, and we both had Ikelite create custom housings for that camera. He agreed to be our keynote speaker ultimately, we saved the ScubaFest expo that year.

On Sunday mornings of the expo weekends, the OCSSDI meets as one of our four meetings each year. As Chairman of the Board, I proposed and convinced the group that it may be time for OCSSDI to take over the annual event rather than passing it to various volunteer scuba clubs around the state. With the onset of email and such, this undertaking could be accomplished from anywhere in the state by a constant committee instead of any given Ohio scuba club re-inventing the wheel each year with little experience on how to run an annual event such as these.

This proposal seemed to make sense to everyone and a motion was made and passed to do this. With permission from the Gavia club, "ScubaFest" became the OCSSDI moniker. To differentiate from the OCSSDI event, I opted to change the name of the contest to the Underwater Images Photo/Video Competition which remained until after 2010. That's when I finally wore out from hundreds of hours of work I did alone each year in organizing, obtaining sponsors and professional judges, mailing out entry forms, hosting the judging then creating the show to announce the winners, then mailing out congratulations and thank you letters.

Since Mark Beatty and I did not receive any pay for our labors of love in keeping this reputable international competition going, we were able to raise and donate almost $93,000 in the 12 years we maintained the contest. Some of the smaller non-profit beneficiaries included an OCSSDI memorial fund honoring OCSSDI members who had passed away, an OCSSDI Scholarship fund for up-and-coming marine biologists and researchers, and the Maritime Archaeological Survey Team (MAST) that documents shipwrecks in the Great Lakes.

Roger and Stan celebrating successful presentations at ScubaFest.

The bulk of our donations each year supported the Mahonia Na Dari (MND) program in Papua New Guinea and Grupo Tortuguero (Turtle Group) in Baja, Mexico. I'd followed the MND program since 2000 and watched that program grow from 12-15 kids to an educational outreach program in PNG that had expanded to touch the lives of over 150,000 students and teachers. Of course, Max and Cecilie Benjamin of Walindi Plantation not only founded MND, but they were also the Best of Show sponsors for UW Images all 15 years I directed the competition, so it only made sense to give back.

Grupo Tortuguero was founded by Dr. Wallace "J." Nichols in the late '90's in order to gather Mexican sea turtle fishermen together and teach them about sea turtle conservation and monitoring the ecosystems the turtles depend on. These annual meetings started with about a half dozen sea turtle fishermen meeting with "J' in Loreto, Mexico in '98 learning things like sea turtles can carry heavy metals such as mercury in their meat. Then these men took this information back to their cities and towns to share how dangerous it can be to feed this contaminated turtle meat to their families, thus beginning to curtail the sea turtle harvesting that had gone on for generations.

As the years went on, this program grew to 45 the following year and 350 by 2006. Attendees came together each year to share their individual conservation programs, policies, and successes. This would give others more ideas on how to help preserve sea turtles and their nesting sites that were always being robbed of eggs by poachers. Many of the sea turtle fishermen even brought their families, and the children began to be offered fun, educational programs to attend while the parents were in the larger meetings. Attendees now come from throughout the Caribbean and farther.

In the end, I'd directed the competition for 15 years through 2010 and raised almost $93,000. Every penny of that was donated back to marine conservation, preservation and educational purposes. I couldn't have done it without Mark's awesome help with our website.

Red Sea Aggressor

Around 5 AM on April 9, 1999, an F4 tornado ripped through my neighborhood and nearby communities leveling homes and killing four people. My home was spared due to a 25' tall, solid concrete sound barrier wall along the expressway that's behind the backyard of the house across the street from me. The wall caused the tornado to jump that 25' as it traveled easterly, shearing the tops of three blue spruce trees in my side yard, and then touching back down a few hundred yards later.

Being a roofing contractor by trade I became quite busy with repairs, but it was to become a very emotional task as days passed. As I attended to calls for repairs, the sound of chain saws seemed never ending for many days until it was gradually replaced by the din of generators and circular saws. Contractors of all kinds were everywhere sometimes leaving the closest parking a half block or more away from my repairs.

Clothes and plastic bags were hanging in every tree still standing. Tarps were on every other roof. At times I was carrying a bundle of shingles through yards stepping over splintered wood and plaster, toothbrushes, teddy bears, men's and women's underwear, golf clubs and anything else that reminded me of the disaster.

One repair I had to make was to a five-foot diameter hole in a roof. When I climbed onto the roof and looked into that hole, I realized the hole was caused by a baby crib that had blown in, as it didn't belong to the family for whom I was doing the repair. It's possible that this could be the same crib in which a baby had been sleeping before the tornado picked the baby up and set her down unhurt 50 yards away from her home.

Three weeks of dealing with this every day, all-day heartbreak was beginning to take its toll on me. A strong depression was setting in and my days of work were also filled with tears that wouldn't stop flowing. Having caught up with most of the repairs I'd been asked to complete, I knew I needed to get far away from this devastation and all of its reminders. I contacted Wayne Hasson, the CEO of the Aggressor Fleet and asked if he had any trips scheduled soon. Any destination would be fine with me as I just needed to get away.

He invited me to join him on a boat in the northern Red Sea the following week that could become an Aggressor approved vessel if the boat and crew met Aggressor standards. The MV Excel was owned and captained by Ramy Refaat and the first mate was Karim Eric. Upon our arrival, Wayne told all of the guests that at the end of the week, he would ask our opinion as to whether we felt this boat was good enough to become part of the Aggressor fleet. Everyone aboard had numerous previous experiences with Aggressor trips so this would definitely give Wayne some good insight since we all had a good idea of Aggressor standards.

Jim and Lois Blumenthal lived in Grand Cayman and brought their children David and Janice. Kat and Bill Smith were from Houma, LA and I'd recognized Kat's name from winners' lists of many international underwater photo competitions; Bill was her model, almost always with a dive light in his hand. A. Scott Johnson from Murfreesboro, TN had also earned similar awards and he was becoming an accomplished photojournalist world-wide. Others on the trip included Wayne's sister-in-law Caroline from AL, David from Toronto, and Nathania and Patrick from WI.

I enjoyed diving with Kat and Bill as they were great models for me as I just filmed Kat perfecting her photography with Bill as her model. Many times, Scott would have a very large wide angle dome port that would reflect what he was shooting and seeing that reflection made for some nice video shots. The Blumenthal's all wore hoods with shark fins on them.

This trip would be my first trip to use Stan Waterman's rig that I'd purchased from him the year before. After our first day of diving, I was exhausted. Bedtime couldn't seem to come soon enough, however after about an hour and a half of sleep I was wide awake. I tossed and turned for a while then decided to go to the lounge and maybe catalog some of the day's video footage at the table until I got tired again. Karim was in the lounge so we talked and began to get to know each other until almost dawn. That's when he laid down on the couch in the salon and I went back to my cabin for an hour's nap.

After that short nap, Scott and I buddied up so to speak; it was that "same day, same ocean" type of buddy diving. We basically knew where each other was and would share subjects once we finished shooting them. But if there had been an out of air emergency, we may have been too far away to help the other one.

Capt. Ramy started our diving around Ras Muhammed, a well-known reef near the southern tip of the Sinai Peninsula. This is where a popular tourist city, Sharm el Sheikh was located. To me, Red Sea diving was even more beautiful than Hawaii because of the beautiful soft corals that aren't found in Hawaii and the water was warmer than the water in Fiji.

After four dives on the reefs in this area, we did a night dive at a dive site named Temple. I thoroughly enjoyed this dive as I was always followed by beautiful lionfish wherever I went. I was able to get close enough to an octopus to film myself petting it between its eyes. One of the grandest shots I got was of Scott getting a picture of a giant green moray eel tucked back in a nook of the large coral head that was shaped like a Temple (hence the name of the dive site). As I looked in my viewfinder, I realized that the eel's head was larger than Scott's! Since Scott was closer to me, his head would normally look larger, but that wasn't the case.

The Excel worked its way around the southern tip of the Sinai Peninsula westward towards the Straits of Gubal at the southern end of the Gulf of Suez. This is where there are many shipwrecks that we would be diving.

One of the wrecks we dove was the Kingston shipwreck. In 1881 the ship had plowed directly into the top of a bommie (an underwater mountain of sorts) whose crest was hidden under only a couple of feet of water. The large propeller was still intact at 60' in the sand and up around the tiller on the stern of the ship was a virtual aquarium teeming with colorful anthias and surgeonfish. The wooden deck planking is missing exposing the steel I-beams and the bottom of her hull which was filled with corals, anemones and plenty of other marine life including the giant green moray eel that lived in the bow.

Inside, I'd found some Red Sea anemonefish aerating their eggs and while filming that, I noticed a beautiful Chromodoris nudibranch just inches away, making for a better shot once I included it with the anemonefish and eggs. After I'd finished shooting, I found Scott just outside of the hull and got his attention to show him this colorful combination. Once he saw what I was showing him, I left to go find what he had been shooting at the crow's nest of a fallen mast on the reef floor.

No sooner than I had settled in for a close-up shot, I heard a loud CLUNG echoing in the water. I looked around but most of the other divers had already begun to make their way away from the wreck so I went back inside the hull to see one of the I-beams of the Kingston resting on Scott's tank pinning him to the bottom. He must have leaned against the I-beam and dislodged it. I dropped my camera out of the way and put my hand in front of his face giving an OK sign which he returned. I was glad to see that he was responsive and seemingly unhurt.

I wedged my feet against something sturdy and got a good grip on the I-beam in order to try to lift it off of Scott's tank. I wasn't sure how heavy it would be but hoped being underwater would make it doable for me or else I'd have to find help. With a strong tug, I barely lifted the beam with one hand and yanked his first stage on top of his tank just enough to let him know which way to go. He slowly moved along the bottom until he was totally out from under the beam at which time I dropped it. He gave me an OK sign then we picked up our cameras and proceeded to continue our dives as if nothing had happened.

I had been pretty tired all day from the lack of sleep the night before. But as much as I wanted to take a nap, I figured if I stayed awake, maybe I'd sleep better this time. I struggled to remain awake until about 9:30 at which time I went to my cabin hoping for a good night's sleep. Unfortunately, by 11:00 I awoke not feeling tired anymore, so I made my way back to the lounge finding Karim cleaning up and straightening.

We again started talking about our lives and experiences, which this time included my tornado stories. This lasted until about 3 AM at which point I went back to my cabin to try to fall asleep. By 5 AM, I was still wide awake so tip-toed past Karim sleeping on the couch in the salon and went out on the sundeck to wait for the sunrise. At dawn, Karim came outside realizing I had still not adapted to the six-hour time zone change.

I began to realize that each day around dawn is when I would start getting very sleepy. This would be about midnight at home: a time I would normally find to be past my bedtime. At least now it was beginning to make a little sense, but not really helping anything. I decided to work at staying awake all day as before without taking a nap and maybe I'd soon be able to get a good night's sleep.

The next few days' diving was as spectacular as all previous days; however, I was still never able to get more than one or one and a half hours sleep at any given time. And each night Karim and I would become closer and closer as friends.

On our second to last day, we dove Jackson Reef in the Strait of Tiran. This was on the east side of Sharm el Sheikh at the southern end of the Gulf of Aqaba. I noticed three Red Sea Bannerfish together along the wall when they usually only travel in mated pairs. I quickly turned on my camera and began filming. As I watched, it seemed that two of them were fighting each other, possibly two males fighting over a female.

One male seemed to be the dominant one continually chasing off the other one while the female just hung around and watched. Once the dominant male seemed to be sure the other one wasn't coming back again, the remaining two bannerfishes paired up and swam off together. This made for a very cute anthropomorphic video story about bannerfish jealousy!

On our last day of diving, we did two morning dives. After the first one, Scott mentioned that he'd seen a large five- to six-foot long Napoleon Wrasse just as he was finishing his safety stop and asked me if I wanted to join him to try to find it again if we would be allowed. I agreed it sounded like a great idea as I found these large fish strikingly beautiful as well as somewhat odd-looking with the hump on their foreheads. Scott asked Karim if it would be possible for the two of us to be dropped back at the same spot of the last dive and Karim said that would be no problem as the group would be taken to another dive site not far away for their last dives.

When our surface interval was long enough, we got into a zodiac and the driver dropped us exactly where we had surfaced on the previous dive. It took less than five minutes to find that beautiful whale of a fish. We each slowly approached it from different sides trying to not alarm it.

He slowly swam along a small ridge while Scott and I got our shots. Sometimes we'd keep each other in our shots to give a nice perspective of the size of this fish and at other times we'd take turns dropping out of the other's shots allowing each of us to get shots of the Napoleon without a diver in the picture. One of my shots with Scott somewhat in the picture was of him behind the wrasse with only his fins visible, and Scott is about 6'3 tall! There were obviously plenty of other things to shoot when we dropped out of the other's shots.

I'd found two giant green moray eels together and shot them for a while. Then they rose up into the water column and coiled around each other. I wasn't sure what they were doing but I was getting the shot and would figure out what they were doing later, which turned out to be the beginning of their mating process. But all of a sudden, a gal from another boat came down and poked at them with her camera's strobe causing them to part and ruined my video shot of them mating.

At one point, since neither one of us were shooting the wrasse, it approached us as if to ask us why we had left. This made us appreciate the relationship that had been formed and thus we played with it some more. When Scott dropped off, I noticed the Napoleon had slipped behind a large, 12' diameter coral head, so I swam to the other side anticipating that it would appear over there. When it didn't come out, I swam further around to catch it with its mouth wide open and cleaner gobies swimming in and out of its mouth and gills. It let me stay there filming it while it got cleaned instead of leaving quickly as many fish do.

After spending over an hour with our friend, we decided to call it a day and began our ascent to 15' and our safety stop. The Napoleon just watched as we left and I can only imagine it had a tear in its eye. I know Scott and I both did, thinking about the new friendship we had formed with this beautiful behemoth.

That evening Karim led the group into Sharm el Sheikh to do some souvenir shopping. After he told everyone where things could be found, he asked me what I might want to get. When I told him a couple of ideas I had, he took me to a shop and told me to go in and look but don't buy anything. He would go back in for me and barter on the price on my behalf while I waited outside. He explained that Egyptians can barter better than Americans who are actually patsies when it comes to bartering, especially when in Egypt.

Karim came out with everything I'd picked out and it only cost about one third of what the items were marked at. With my shopping complete we just stood around and did some people watching. To my surprise, Karim would point to a couple and tell me they were Italians, then point to another and tell me they were French, then point to another and tell me they were Dutch.

I asked him how he thought he knew and he began to describe the behaviors, haircuts, clothes, purses, etc. that were good indicators of their individual cultures. After listening to him describe these characteristics for a while longer, I began to make guesses and he'd tell me if I was right or not. I'd never thought about these things before and I was tickled to learn something new like this about various cultures.

After everyone returned to the boat, Wayne gathered the group together in the lounge and asked us our opinion of the boat and crew and if we thought it could match the quality that he wanted for an Aggressor vessel. Our opinion was unanimously in favor of this. The next day, the MV Excel became the newest member of the Aggressor Fleet. After returning home, I would produce the first promotional video for the Excel about our adventures on that trip.

Later that morning, Wayne and the rest of our group took the hour-long flight to Cairo to spend a few days sightseeing there. We started with the great pyramids of Giza and the Sphynx followed by a camel caravan ride into the desert behind the pyramids for a couple of hours. I'd ride ahead and try to get on top of sand dunes to film the group riding by.

When we stopped to look at the pyramids from the desert, sand was blowing and we felt like we were in the middle of no man's land with absolutely no sign of civilization. While reveling in this thought, I suddenly saw a fellow jogging over the top of a nearby sand dune wearing his nylon shorts and tank top, passing us by and heading towards the pyramids! That really ruined my visualization, but surely not the experience.

After returning to our hotel that afternoon and a nice, hot shower, I decided it was time for a good alcoholic drink. I hadn't had a good drink for over a week and was ready for one, so I ordered a long island iced tea from the waiter in the bar area. He came back a few minutes later and said with his Egyptian accent what I heard to be, "I'm sorry sir, but that would be $19. Do you still want it?"

I thought about that for a second, but then realized that even though a regular long island might be $8-10, I'd spent upwards of $13-15 in a nice restaurant, so even though $19 was a little on the expensive side, I told him I did still want one. A few minutes later he brought my drink and it was by far the strongest long island iced tea I'd ever had. The bartender must have actually used a full shot of each of the five clear liquors that make up this drink; rum, vodka; gin, triple sec, and tequila. Most bartenders might normally use partial shots of these liquors then water it down with a sweet and sour mix.

As I was finishing my drink feeling sated and probably a little tipsy, the waiter brought my check. I looked at the total of $90 and asked him what that would be in US dollars. He gave me a funny look and proceeded to tell me that was in US dollars.

I quickly asked if there was a manager I could speak with and he led me to an office in a hallway nearby. I knocked on the door and was told to enter. I introduced myself and told the gentleman the story. I reiterated that I'd heard (or in this case mis-heard) the waiter say $19 not $90 and asked if there was any way to lower my bill since I would never have order a single drink for $90.

He told me that the duty on alcohol was very large in Egypt and there really wasn't much leeway. I explained that I had been on a live-aboard dive boat the past week determining whether that boat would become a permanent member of a high-quality fleet of dive boats world-wide and the captain of this boat had recommended this hotel for its guests when they visit Cairo. If I had a poor encounter at this hotel, I'd have to report this and it could mean the hotel recommendation might go to another competitor.

I knew I was drawing at straws here, but had nothing else up my sleeve. Happily, he told me that he would cut the bill in half but that's all he could do. I cut my losses, paid the $45 tab and headed to the restaurant for dinner with the group.

The next day we visited the Cairo Museum and other famous pyramids. Our lunch that day was to be at a certain restaurant that served real Egyptian foods. As we neared an intersection our driver told us the restaurant was on the right a half block away but traffic only went from right to left so everyone needed to duck down so he could see.

Not understanding why, we all still ducked down. He explained that if he drove the correct way, it would take us another 20 minutes to go around and then end up at the restaurant, but he knew a quicker way to get there. That's when he turned left, drove across four lanes of traffic, then looked back and backed up against traffic for a half city block with horns honking at us the whole way.

On our last day in Cairo, we were free to do whatever we wanted. Kat, Bill, Scott and I got a taxi and did some more souvenir shopping. Our driver agreed to wait for us each time we stopped. Once we decided we were finished shopping he asked us if we were in a hurry because if we weren't he would drive us around and show us more things in Cairo that we may not have seen. We all agreed this sounded like another good adventure so took him up on his offer.

One place he took us was to Sadat's Tomb. As we got out of the taxi he led us up the sidewalk to the tomb and gave us a tremendous amount of history as we walked towards the cordoned-off, above-ground tomb. When we arrived next to the tomb, he pointed to a long glass building across the street and told us that there were armed guards in many of those windows with their guns trained on us. Then he lifted the ropes so we could get closer for our pictures and told us since he was with us, those guards would allow us to get closer.

After taking us to more places and giving us more history lessons, he finally said he'd have to take us back to the hotel since he had a wedding to get ready for. Supposedly his daughter was getting married and having her wedding reception in the lobby of our hotel later that evening. Then he asked us if anyone had used or planned on using our passports to buy duty-free liquor.

When we all answered no, he asked if we minded if he stopped at a duty-free shop and used our passports to get liquor for the reception. He said it would help with his expenses for the wedding. We looked at each other and saw no harm in this so we passed him our passports and he went into the duty-free store. He came out with a few boxes of liquor that he placed in the trunk, then returned our passports and drove us back to the hotel with an invitation to join in the celebration at 7 PM.

Thinking we'd maybe have a drink on our taxi driver at the wedding, we went to the lobby after dinner but there was no wedding reception scheduled that evening. Our taxi driver was able to load up on duty free liquor using our passports. Smart guy, but at least he did work for it adding to our adventure in Egypt and no harm was done.

The MV Excel was the first Red Sea Aggressor approved vessel to be in the water.

GARDENS OF MEMORIES~ON BANNERFISH COURTING

Soft coral walls, colored fish all around;
>   *This is where memories are sure to be found.*
Go underwater and seek solitude;
>   *Don't be surprised if you witness a feud.*
A bannerfish streaks with a look that could kill;
>   *He's found an intruder around his girl!*
Ring around Rosie, to retain her hand,
>   *"Get away from my gal," is his demand!*
He chases down till the new fellow leaves,
>   *Then back to her for a lecture on thieves.*
But not before checking, just to make sure,
>   *This guy is gone for good on his tour.*
A question to her is, "Who enticed whom?"
>   *"Why did you not shoo him out with your broom?"*
But she calms him down, and offers a stroll;
>   *Her female ways seem to take toll.*
This nature picture has no room for three;
>   *Gardens of memories, in open sea.*

The SS Thistlegorm

Another of the shipwrecks that we dove on while I was aboard the MV Excel in the Red Sea was the SS Thistlegorm. She was a British armed Merchant Navy supply ship during WWII. She was bound for Alexandria with her cargo including two locomotives and coal tenders secured to her main deck intended for the Egyptian National Railways. Below decks, she carried many dozens of Norton and BSA motorcycles, Bedford trucks each with three more motorcycles in the beds of the trucks to save space, Rolls Royce armored cars, Bren gun carriers, wooden cases of .303 rifles, and radio equipment among other things.

For safety reasons, the Thistlegorm was traveling in a convoy of ships. But due to a collision in the Suez Canal that was blocking the canal, the convoy had to stay put in safe anchorage near Ras Muhammed until the wrecked ships were removed. At the same time, German intelligence thought there was a large troop carrier in that area bringing more troops to Egypt. They sent two Henkel bombers to search and destroy that ship and the troops.

Having not found that particular ship, and while on their way back to their base, the pilots decided to drop two bombs on the largest ship in safe anchorage which ended up being the Thistlegorm. Both bombs hit the #4 hold which happened to have ammunition and bombs stored there. The explosion tore open the ship just past midship and peeled part of the top steel deck back like a banana peel and causing the Thistlegorm to sink with a loss of nine lives. The explosion not only blew the two locomotives off the main deck, it also blew the Henkels out of the air and into the sea killing both pilots.

In 1955, Jacques Cousteau found the Thistlegorm due to information from local fishermen. His crew removed a motorcycle, the captain's safe, and the ship's bell. A picture in the February, 1956 issue of National Geographic shows the ship's bell still in place as well as Cousteau's team in the "Lantern Room." After that, the Thistlegorm would remain a secret until the 1990's when Israeli fishermen told a local dive operator about its presence. That's when she became a well-known world-class dive site, but without her bell.

During both dives on the Thistlegorm, Karim had pointed out large, eight-foot long Jewfish, now politically correctly called Goliath Groupers. He told me the ship was large enough for a few of these to live inside in the various holds. On our dives, we also saw a turtle, a number of pipefish and nudibranchs, as well as many different species of surgeonfish. There was also a school of spadefish that meandered around the ship.

As we swam sternward from amidships on our first dive, we passed the wheelhouse then over the exploded hold that was non-existent now. We saw one of the Bren gun carriers lying amid boxes of ammunition and a second one way down in the sand. One end of the ship's driveshaft was sticking out over this area coming from the main section of the ship and we could see the other end about 60' away.

There were also some unexploded shells just past the demolished hold. Karim laid his arms across one of them and couldn't touch both ends at the same time, and he's over six feet tall. At the stern were a machine gun pointing into blue water and an anti-aircraft gun pointing towards the seafloor. The huge propeller sat in the sand at about 95'. We swam along the starboard side as we returned to the Excel. After Karim pointed out one of the locomotives in the sand, I filmed it as best I could then I caught Wayne giving me a big OK signal about this dive.

Before our second dive, Karim told me the currents can get strong at times on the Thistlegorm. When we went in for our second dive, the current was tremendously strong, so we swam into the current towards the bow at the beginning of the dive. Divers are taught that using one's energy in the beginning of the dive makes the return part easier and safer.

The anchor chains were still attached to their winches, then they threaded down through the hawse pipes. I filmed a shot down through the hawse pipes to the sand, then took a second shot of the chains running across the sand to the anchors still sitting where they had been when they were used during safe anchorage. Red Sea basslets danced in the current in the bright sunlight around the winches and chains on the bow that were covered with colorful soft corals. This was one of my favorite nature shots of the promo video I produced.

After fighting the current long enough, we rode it sternward a few feet, then dropped down into some rooms below the bow where there could be seen a dozen or more brand-new rolls of heavy-duty rope still tightly packed. Then we drifted further back to the main holds and dropped into the 20' square opening to get out of the current and explored more below decks. Straight down at the bottom, I could see the .303 rifles stacked together as if they were still in their wooden crates. But the wood had long since deteriorated and concretion was keeping the rifles together solidly.

As we explored the holds, I was amazed at the vehicles that hadn't seemed to shift at all from the explosion or even when it hit the bottom. All of the motorcycles were upright on their kickstands just as they were the day they were loaded, and the trucks still had minimal space between each of them. Schools of glassy sweepers flowed around the vehicles as we swam over them.

In another hold, there were airplane wings stacked against one another, probably meant for the small, one-man airplane body that sat upside down on the upper deck along with the coal tenders. In still another hold, there was a large pile of rubber Wellington boots, which were knee-high boots meant for the British troops.

Besides representing a war grave, the Thistlegorm displays intact original vehicles of the day as if it were a museum. Looking inside the trucks and jeeps, one can see the dashboards, springs of the seats and the tall gear shifts with the emergency brake handles still attached. This wreck dive was by far the most interesting wreck dive I'd ever done, and my subsequent research on her for my promo video production added even more captivation for me. On this trip, she became my favorite wreck dive in the world and still is to this day.

GARDENS OF MEMORIES~ON THE THISTLEGORM

Troop trucks and cycles; barbed wire tightly wound;
This is where memories are sure to be found.
Winches and davits and anchors and chains;
Bombs still attached to wee German planes.
She sailed with munitions packed in her stern.
One small torpedo left, no time to burn.
Her deck peeled back like a sardine can;
Below decks were exposed to all diving man.
Water rushed in and flooded her down,
Beginning the growth of her coral gown.
Now, eight-foot groupers swim through her hull,
And divers cast bubbles, leaving no lull.
Red Sea basslets dance on backgrounds of blue,
O'er rubber boots that belonged to the crew.
Machine guns' silhouette from sun above,
While yellowfin tuna get cleaned with love.
There's surgeonfish with scalpels, sharp as tacks;
Pipefish and nudibranchs, clownfish and jacks.
All of them settled in their home rent-free;
Gardens of memories, in open sea.

Discovery Channel Shoot

In September 1999, I received a phone call from a Discovery Channel producer from California. Bo told me he'd gotten my name from a chap named Greg Millinger who lived in Port Clinton, Ohio on Lake Erie. Bo was looking to have someone film a shipwreck in Lake Erie for his next program and Greg told him I was an accomplished underwater videographer and might be willing to tackle this undertaking for him.

Bo's program was about a fleet of schooners that had gotten caught in an early ice-over in Alaska in the late 1800's which crushed and sunk the ships. He had already taken an ROV (Remotely Operated Vehicle) with a camera to film the ships in Alaska, but unbeknownst to him, the seawater had taken its toll and there was nothing left of the wooden ships other than rolls in the sand where parts of the ships had been. These schooners were built in Manitowoc, Wisconsin in 1872.

In subsequent research, he found that there was in fact a shipwreck in Lake Erie named the Willis that had been built in the same shipyard at the same time as the fleet of schooners he was wanting to film. The 132' long Willis was intact having sunk in the cold, fresh water of Lake Erie on November 11th of the same year she was built. This would be the only footage he could get of a wooden ship that looked just like the ones he was documenting.

Bo asked me what camera I was shooting with, if I had a wide-angle port to obtain wide angle shots of the wreck and if I had HID lights because it would be important to have a high-quality camera and lights. Having recently purchased the 3-chip digital Sony VX-1000 in a Light & Motion housing with HID lights from Stan, I confidently told Bo what I had, including a wide-angle port and assured him my video lights were HID lights.

Pleased with my answers, he asked what I would charge him to meet him up there some weekend and spend a day filming the Willis for his documentary. I gave him a $1000/day cost including a half day prep for charging batteries as well as scuba gear and camera set-up, a half day clean-up of all my gear, plus driving time for me to get there and back from Cincinnati, plus all expenses. He was fine with my charges and sent me a contract to sign and return. We scheduled a weekend near the end of September for the shoot.

I'd dived in Lake Erie enough times to know the water is normally cold, which I don't particularly care for, and I knew that September would be even colder. I had a 6-mil shorty and john's wetsuit combination with hood and gloves, but decided maybe it was time for me to learn how to dive in a dry suit with warm thermal underwear inside. I had an instructor friend, Wolf Olsen, willing to teach me how to dive in a dry suit and another friend who let me borrow his dry suit for the training and video shoot.

I also called Greg to get a better idea of what this shipwreck looked like and how it was situated on the sand. He told me it was perfectly upright, sitting on its keel at a depth of 72'. I was keener to know how it pointed so that I could be totally aware of how the sun would hit the wreck and I could keep the sun coming over my shoulders for better ambient light shooting of the wreck when appropriate. He described its north/south position for me and told me what things are on the main deck so I could orient myself better.

I drove up on a Friday morning and about four hours later, checked into a cheap motel for the weekend. Greg and I went to a nearby quarry and did a dive so I could get some more bottom time using the dry suit. That evening, I met up with a number of old friends including Greg, Rod Althaus who owns New Wave Scuba Center in Port Clinton, and Steve Sheridan who owned the boat, "Scuba Recovery," that we'd use to get to and dive the Willis. We spent the evening planning the shoot over dinner and drinks. The team had obtained Aga masks for Greg and I, which are full face masks with communication abilities to each other as well as to the surface.

Bo took the red eye flight from California and was picked up at the airport early Saturday morning. He brought a monitor on the boat that I could hook my camera to via firewire so he could see my footage after each dive. Gear was already loaded on Steve's boat so when Bo arrived, we headed out of Port Clinton for the two- to three-hour ride to a few miles southwest of Pelee Point in Canada where the

Willis has rested on the bottom for 127 years.

Upon arrival over the Willis, Steve moored the boat while Greg and I geared up in our dry suits. I was still a little anxious about using the dry suit, but with more than 10 years of diving under my belt, I talked myself into believing everything would be fine. I had an assignment and I had to concentrate on getting that right since I was getting paid for this.

Before rolling off the boat, we checked our communications. Then I checked where the sun was located, rolled off, obtained my camera rig from Rod in the boat and followed Greg to the mooring line. Water temps were in the low 60° F range and visibility was probably 15-25' which to my knowledge, was normal for Lake Erie. With a trade of OK signs, Greg led the way down the mooring line.

At about 40', the water turned dark. Very dark. I pressed the button on my Aga mask so I could communicate and said, "Greg, you didn't tell me this would be a night dive!" He only shrugged and said sometimes the visibility is good and sometimes it isn't. I could only laugh about my serious questions about where the sunlight would be coming from, but yet no one mentioned that this could be the equivalent of a night dive. I was also realizing that there would be no great wide-angle shots of the shipwreck that Bo was wanting.

At about 60', we reached the port gunnel near amidships. Visibility was three to five feet at best with a lot of suspended particulate matter in the water. So, I turned on my lights and positioned them as far out as possible so as to not illuminate the backscatter. I turned on my camera and started shooting along the gunnel, as I swam towards the bow with Greg behind me. We passed many deadeyes and an occasional davit before reaching the prow.

Then we decided to head aft-ward and swim over top of the deck to see what other structures we could film besides the deadeyes. Since the zebra mussels had invaded and been taking over Lake Erie for many years, everything on the wreck was covered in layers and layers of zebra mussels. There were a lot of "piles" and vertical "stands" of zebra mussels but there was very little wood or iron to be seen anywhere. I also had many close calls with hidden davits and pieces of the mast reaching out from the dark trying to tag me as I swam past them.

After 40 minutes on the wreck, we decided to return to the mooring line and make our way back up to the boat. The air was chilly, so after drying off, we all huddled in the wheelhouse area and I hooked up the camera to the monitor and started playing my footage. Bo's face sunk as he watched the night footage of passing deadeyes and piles of zebra mussels. This wasn't what he had in mind at all.

Greg on the other hand was excited about the footage. "There's the capstan," he cried! "There's the anchor line! There's a pile of rigging!" All I saw was piles of zebra mussels and wondered what Bo would do next.

During our surface interval, Greg explained to Bo that sometimes the water at depth is as dark as night and sometimes the water turns over where it's darker at the surface and the visibility at depth is good enough to see beam to beam on the wreck, which was almost 28'. Bo asked if there was a time of year when visibility was better, but Greg explained that there's no predictability whatsoever. One never knew until arriving on the wreck what the visibility might be.

In an effort to salvage our trip, Bo asked me if I could get to the bow then back away from the bow on the port side and then down to the bottom so that I could rise up and swim towards the prow having it come into view. I assured him I could do that easily enough, so that was part of our plan for the second dive. I'd also get to the stern and film the single, tear-drop shaped porthole the Willis is known for.

Greg and I made our way down the mooring line a second time with a mission. I headed towards the bow with Greg right behind. Once at the prow I looked at Greg and signaled that I'd get away from the ship and drop to the bottom, then let him know when I'd start coming up and towards the prow. I'm usually pretty good at "feeling" where I am so I was confident this would be an easy shot.

As I got closer to the bottom, I put my hand down so that I could push myself up from the sand like I might always do in the oceans, then make my way up and towards the boat. As I touched the bottom, I kept descending as my arm sank into silt up to my shoulder! I quickly added some air to my drysuit trying desperately to keep my directional bearings in mind.

I pressed the communication button and told Greg I was on my way up and he acknowledged that he heard me. I thought I'd successfully not gotten lost in the cloud of silt I created and swam towards the wreck as I ascended with lights and camera rolling. Up a little, forward a little, up a little forward a little, up a little forward a little until I thought I should have been there by now. How could I have missed it?

I again pressed the communication button and asked Greg if he could see me and he said yes. I asked him where I was and he answered Lake Erie! At about that time I felt my ears popping quickly and all of a sudden, I was out of dark water. Crud! I needed to slow my ascent immediately with this stupid ballooning drysuit so that I could at least make a good safety stop before reaching the surface. I told Greg my plan and we'd meet on the boat.

I did my three-minute stop at 15-20' and surfaced about 20' away from the boat. Having only been down about 8-10 minutes, Rod asked if everything was OK. As Greg surfaced nearby, I just kept swimming towards the boat and climbed aboard. Rod asked me what happened, and I told him I'd missed the prow then began ascending too fast and had to abort the dive.

Bo asked me if I was ready to go back in to finish the shoot, but I knew I needed a break to gather my wits about me, but didn't want to say that to Bo. Fortunately, Greg was just then climbing up the ladder and heard Bo's question. Greg looked at me and I made my eyes as BIG and WIDE as I could while Bo was standing behind me. Knowing Greg was an instructor I'd hoped he might recognize my hint at being uncomfortable for the moment. I asked him what he thought about going right back in with my eyes still as wide as I could make them. Without missing a lick, Greg said he thought we should take some time on the surface before going back in again. Phew! Perfect! I gave Greg a knowing wink of thanks.

We did two more dives that day before heading back to Port Clinton. Visibility was the same and the zebra mussels never left. On our return trip to Port Clinton, Bo told me to itemize my invoice and mail it to him along with the video tapes when I got back to Cincinnati. Then he asked if everyone would be willing to try the shoot again some weekend in the near future, weather permitting. He wouldn't be back, but everyone else agreed to try again, hoping for better visibility on the Willis.

When I got home, I cleaned my gear, made copies of the tapes so I could keep a copy for myself, and sent my invoice and the original tapes to Bo. A couple of weeks later, I received Bo's check for my work.

But on our second shoot two months later, the visibility was still the same, water temperature had dropped to 48° F and the zebra mussels were still mostly there. However, there was an area around the tear-drop porthole where there were no mussels this time. I found this strange, but got great shots of the porthole and surrounding wood. I knew Bo would like this. The people who made a trip to the Willis earlier in the week to use Kevlar gloves to rub off the mussels, exposing the wood around the porthole, knew this as well.

The missing mussels remains a mystery to many people to this day, especially those in Canada who know it's against Canadian law to do anything like this to protected shipwrecks in Canadian waters. I know nothing. I only know that after mailing my second invoice and the tapes to Bo I didn't receive my paycheck in a timely manner like the last time.

After a few weeks of waiting, I emailed him but got no reply. I tried calling him but he wouldn't answer even after I left a message. I finally mailed him a letter requesting that he honor his word and pay me for my efforts on this second weekend. After all, it wasn't my fault the visibility was not good.

A month or two went by with still no check in hand, so I decided to try to contact someone from Discovery Channel. I'd talk to someone to tell them my problem and they'd tell me there are hundreds of producers and they had no idea who Bo was (I did give them his last name and the name of the program he was working on with a Discovery Channel grant). Then I'd be referred to someone else, then someone else, then someone else. I'd ask for supervisors, managers, editors, etc. each time getting no one who would help me.

I finally asked who is in management for Discovery Channel and was referred to a vice president. I told my story again only to hear the same answer I'd gotten from everyone else. There are hundreds of producers working on programs and she didn't know who Bo was and hadn't heard of the program. At that point I had an epiphany and told the lady OK, but if his program airs on Discovery Channel using my footage before I get paid, I'll definitely be a rich man. Then I told her goodbye and hung up. An overnight package showed up two days later from Bo in California with a check enclosed for the full amount he owed me.

GARDENS OF MEMORIES~ON THE WILLIS

Three-masted schooner on bottom aground,
  This is where memories are sure to be found.
During day, visibility can be like at night,
  Or maybe a turn can make it just right.
The Willis sits at seventy-two feet;
  Davits and deadeyes on gunnel so neat.
Her prow still reaches for lands yet to see,
  But she'll remain on the bottom of Lake Erie.
Her masts lie across her beam so wide,
  Ne'er to navigate another tide.
Captain's quarters filled to the top with silt,
  Gives little chance of finding a sword or its hilt.
Capstan and anchor chain covered with mussels
  Give little clue as to what were her tussles.
Exposed wood on her hull befuddled more than a few,
  But the deed turned out to be right on cue.
A teardrop porthole on her stern is quite nice
  While sister ships fade beneath the ice.
Discovery Channel shoot with credibility;
  Gardens of memories, in Lake Erie.

International Studies Program

Before spring break 2000, a Wilmington college professor contacted me and asked if I might be interested in being made an adjunct professor and help lead a group of 18 Wilmington College students on an expedition to an island in the Bahamas where there was a scientific research facility. The college called this their international studies program and the students would be given credit for the expedition. The trip was planned to coincide with their spring break and they also wanted me to film everything for future students to see what this program was all about.

Upon arrival on Lee Stocking Island, everyone was assigned dorm rooms at the Caribbean Marine Research Center. After unpacking, we all met in a meeting room for our orientation given by Dan Wood, a staff member at the research center. He explained about the layout of the research center and where we would get our meals, then about activities we would be doing, and rules the students would have to follow. Even though these were college students, there would be no fraternization between them and absolutely no alcohol, even though it was their spring break.

The next morning Dan met us at breakfast and told us he'd be taking us on a tour of the island and he'd teach us about the island, its history, and anything else that we saw or encountered. On the tour, we passed beaches that had piles of hundreds, if not thousands of sunbleached conch shells. These piles are called middens.

Conch is considered the national food of the Bahamas. Dan told us that the natives would surface dive for conch to feed their families then discard all of the shells in certain areas, which is why these middens were so large. Since conchs seem to represent the relaxed mood of the Bahamas, conch shells are used to create jewelry, Christmas ornaments and even line walkways or are built into cement walls for decoration. That evening we coincidentally had conch fritters at dinner, reminding me of my trip to San Salvadore.

As we were walking, Dan found a sea hare in a shallow lagoon and carefully picked it up to tell us what it was and share more facts about it. Sea hares feed on algae, so are usually found in grassy flats with scattered rocks just like where we were standing. As he put it back in the water, Dan gave it a small squeeze so we could see the thick, purple fluid it releases when disturbed, similar to an octopus inking.

During low tide, we passed an exposed part of the seafloor that is completely underwater during high tide. There were a number of different species of crabs crawling around and Dan identified each type and told us a little about them including what things they were searching for to eat. There were also some sea stars just waiting for the tide to return and Dan explained that if sea stars lose an arm, it will regenerate a new one.

The students were given time each afternoon before dinner to compile their notes from each day's activities into a journal. This journal, along with the extent of their class participation and a final paper would determine their grade. All of the students were very attentive as well as respectful of the environment and each other.

That evening at dinner, Dan and I discussed the day's activities then moved on to discuss where we were from. As it turned out, Dan grew up in a quaint little village east of Cincinnati only about four to five miles away from where I grew up and still lived. He took off a couple of years after college to study at the research center which is why he was working there.

The following day we took the group sea kayaking. Only a couple of the students had been kayaking or canoeing before, so Dan gave a crash course on the use of the paddles including how to steer, before assigning kayaks to everyone. Some were single kayaks and others doubles, where two students would work together to get to sea. The beginning of this trip was quite comical because some students continued to row in circles and others were bumping into other kayaks with little control. After a while, everyone got the hang of things and we traveled as a group out to sea for a few hours with only a couple of kayaks lagging a little behind.

Dan led us towards a small island an hour away from Lee Stocking Island. As we got closer to the island, he pointed to a small arched opening on the island just above water level. He explained that this wasn't visible at high tide but at low tide one could swim into the opening then dive down deeper in the water to follow a cavern of sorts until it opened up into a large open chamber underground.

He invited anyone willing to follow him into the arch then showed each of them how to swim through the cavern underwater to the chamber. It might not have been safe to surface in a chamber like this except there was an opening at the ceiling that allows fresh air to circulate in and out of the chamber. Without fresh air, this chamber would eventually fill with carbon dioxide and possibly other gases, which would not be breathable for anyone inside. Only half of the group were willing to take this leap of faith but those that did, enjoyed it immensely.

The next day we got into a couple of motor boats that took us to a number of different fairly shallow snorkeling areas. Dan taught everyone how to snorkel properly, then while we were snorkeling, Dan and I pointed out various marine creatures, identified them, and shared any knowledge we had of them. If anyone in the group saw something they found interesting, they'd call us over and ask about it and we'd tell them what we knew.

Of course, there were small schools of fish swimming by all the time and I'd direct any nearby student to get behind the school and swim towards me to separate the school as they swam through so I could film this for the video I'd produce. The students asked if there were any sharks around and we told them probably, but the sharks would be too afraid of us because we were bigger than anything they ate and they would therefore stay away. I think some of them didn't believe us but no sharks showed up that day.

What did show up was a three-foot barracuda. This isn't that large as far as barracudas go, but it did shake up some of the students. I'd seen it off in the distance and pointed it out to one of the students in hopes he would swim around behind it for a good shot that would make the barracuda look even bigger on video, which he was willing to do. As I was shooting this scene one of the other guys noticed the barracuda out of the corner of his eye and zipped through the middle of my shot faster than a speeding bullet, almost walking on water towards the boat!

Once he was safe on the boat, we all had a good laugh with him. I explained that the barracuda is a very curious creature but not aggressive unless something threatened it. He remarked that he saw the barracuda's mouth opening and closing while showing its teeth like it was going to attack, but I explained to everyone that the opening and closing motion is how they breathe. The fellow said he still wasn't getting back in this water to snorkel any more.

The weather turned rainy the next day so the students were sent to a library on campus and told to study about artificial reefs. Once they had a good understanding of artificial reefs and how they can create new habitats for many marine creatures, they would be asked to create their own small artificial reef in a small pond on the campus or under the dock where we first landed. As the weather improved and it stopped raining, we took the group to the dock and showed them the array of fish that were congregating around various discarded items under the dock.

Then the students spread out to look for things that might make good artificial reefs. One student found an old water heater near the pond and pushed it into the water. A couple of other students gathered as many discarded conch shells as they could carry and built an underwater mountain of conch shells in the pond as well as another one under the dock. Other students collected whatever they believed would provide protection and/or a habitat and placed these items in either the pond or under the dock. One student even thought of using some discarded tires she'd found on the center's campus.

During our last full day on the island, we visited the pond and dock to study and discuss whether the items the students chose were good choices or not. There were no fish around the water heater so the group decided this was probably not such a great choice and worked together to pull it back up on the shore of the pond. The conch shells in the pond also hadn't attracted any noticeable congregation of fish or creatures but the ones under the dock did have a number of fish staying close to the shells which enabled them to duck inside if danger approached.

The tires attracted a crab in the pond and more fish under the dock. When discussing why the shells in the pond didn't seem effective as an artificial reef but the ones under the dock did, the group decided that it might have something to do with the types of fish found in each ecosystem.

That afternoon each student returned to the meeting room to assemble their final paper describing their activities and what they gained from the expedition. The professor and I read the papers on the way back to the U.S. and discussed the trip. He was extremely pleased with what everyone seemed to have learned and everything else about the trip...except for the few guys who found a way to get some alcohol on the third evening there and got drunk enough to get caught. Go figure; they were college guys.

© Cricket Manuel

Here's Roger getting stock shots for the trip video the students will get.

ROGER ROTH

GARDENS OF MEMORIES~ON ARTIFICIAL REEFS

Sun-bleached conch shells piled in mounds,
    This is where memories are sure to be found.
A study of objects, then prove your belief
    Your object will make for a viable reef.
There are tires of rubber and blocks of concrete
    In hopes of completing a simple feat.
Some are formed and some chained together,
    While others are made to withstand the weather.
Old ships have been used after cleaning debris
    Then sinking them down so carefully.
Even cremains have been mixed into balls
    And placed in the sea to create fish malls.
A habitat new where there once was none,
    A place to call home for more than one.
Something for spawn to begin its growth;
    A benefit for man and marine life both.
Algae collects and becomes food for some fish
    While others await a much different dish.
Sustain ecosystems quite carefully,
    Gardens of memories, in open sea.

Southern Red Sea on the MV Excel

In early 2000, Wayne Hasson contacted me to compliment me on the promotional video I produced for the Excel the year before and asked me if I was interested in returning to the Red Sea Aggressor to tour the southern Red Sea. I told him of course and I gathered seven other friends from my dive shop to join me and fill half the boat. In May, we arrived at JFK around 2 PM to await our 6:30 PM flight to Cairo on Egypt Air.

Unfortunately, bad weather was setting in and the flight was cancelled. The next flight to Cairo would be the following evening at the same time. We were stuck in JFK airport along with thousands of other passengers. All of the hotels in New York were full but we were told that we could hunker down in Delta's Sky Lounge for the night. At least there would be some juices and snacks, and attendants brought us some blankets to use while sleeping in the chairs.

Since I was pretty much the trip leader for my friends, I spent most of the next day trying to track down our luggage to make sure it would be on our flight to Cairo that evening. This ended up being much more difficult than it sounds. It seems that no one at JFK or Delta or with Egypt Air knew where the luggage was but assured me that it would be on the plane when we took off.

However, when we landed in Cairo only three people found and claimed all of their luggage from the baggage carrousel. Four others only found one of their suitcases or dive bags and I didn't get my dive bag, or my suitcase or my pelican case with the housing and lights inside that I'd bought from Stan Waterman. The Excel's first mate Karim met us at the airport for the drive to Hurghada and assured us that most if not all of the missing luggage would catch up to us.

Instead of heading out to sea immediately, Capt. Ramy decided to do the first day's diving around Hurghada so that the missing luggage could be delivered to the dock and would be waiting for us when we returned from our first day's diving. But upon our return, only three of the seven missing bags were waiting at the dock and none of them were mine. What was I going to do now? I had my video camera in my backpack but that wasn't going to do me any good without my housing.

Wayne was very good about coming up with dive gear for me and another person who didn't get his dive bag. He also told me I was free to use one of the small video camera systems kept on board for just this purpose, even though the quality was nowhere near the quality of Stan's old rig. But my next dilemma was, what about my clothes, toothbrush, prescription mask, etc.?

All of the men on this trip were much larger than I was and I'd literally swim in their clothes if I tried to wear them. So, the women on the trip all donated clothes that I could borrow for the week and Wayne even gave me a pair of women's shorts and a man's T-shirt from the boat's boutique stock. Since this wasn't a beauty pageant, those were the clothes I wore for the week.

Since we couldn't stay at dock any longer to wait for more bags to show up, we headed south towards the Brothers Islands doing some diving along the way. We dove a wreck called the Salem Express twice then dove Panorama Reef where Wayne fed a large Napoleon wrasse a hard-boiled egg.

I used these three dives mostly to get acquainted with the boat's video camera and tweak some things in the housing between dives. We arrived at Big Brother Island in time for dinner. That's when we were told there would be no night diving around here because it was against Egyptian law to dive in these shark-infested waters at night. That's when the sharks would be hunting for food.

That statement hinted to me that we'd probably be seeing a number of sharks during our day dives which pleased me for sure. But that night after everyone turned in, I wasn't tired enough to fall asleep again, just like the last time I visited the Red Sea. I again spent most of the night catching up with Karim. I remember him telling me that if I ever came back again, he wanted me to bring him a nine-inch Panasonic TV/VCR combination for him and his girlfriend Irene.

Then, we talked about Irene who used his small boat, Argo, to deliver ice cream to the dive and snorkel boats in the Sharm el Sheikh area. I had met her the previous year when the ice cream boat came to the Excel. That day, Karim even invited me to go fishing with him and Irene for the afternoon. I still remember the round ring door handle that he rigged to flop down and make noise when a fish hit the line notifying them that they had a fish on the hook.

Irene was from Brussels and had met Karim while diving from one of the boats on which he worked. They hit it off well and she ended up finding a way to stay in Sharm el Sheikh. Karim told me Irene was doing fine and still working the ice cream boat. They were thinking of getting married soon but she would still work the ice cream boat even if she got pregnant. She became quite the accomplished boat captain through the years.

We also talked about some ass on the boat on this trip named Bruce (not my friend from the Cayman Aggressor III trip with Jean-Michel). Bruce had already aggravated almost every guy on the boat with his brash attitude and insulted every woman on the boat with his vulgarity. The first fellow that was to bunk with him asked to be moved to a different stateroom after only one night. Every time Bruce would loudly saunter up to the sun deck, his insults would clear the women immediately. He even bragged about his email address being "blowme@whatever.com."

As dawn approached, I was beginning to get sleepy but I knew I had to stay awake and keep diving with no naps in between so that maybe I'd sleep better that night. It didn't work on my last trip but I hoped it might finally work this time. Our first two dives at Big Brother Island were on a wrecked freighter by the name of Aida. It was covered with beautiful corals and inundated with tropical fish. Of course, there were also white tip and black tip sharks cruising around the wrecks as if keeping guard.

After lunch, we were going to dive on the northeast side of the 400-m long island where there would be fields of soft corals. I grabbed the boat's video camera I'd been using and loaded into the zodiac that would take us to the dive site. Unfortunately, we were on the shady side of the island, so not only was I using a video camera with less quality than mine, I also didn't have video lights nor sunlight to enhance the beautiful colors I'd see.

The soft corals seemed to take up acres of this side of the island.

As we were swimming over this garden of colorful flowing soft corals, I noticed Bruce using his brand-new video camera system as he swam through the soft corals…literally! Not above them like the rest of us. I shot video of him furiously kicking his fins through the soft corals while pieces of these corals sprayed up and about with every kick like a Montana snowplow throwing the snow to the side. It made me sick.

Even though I'd been tired all day from the lack of sleep, after dinner that night I was beginning to feel awake and not so tired again. I went to my cabin about 9:30 and tried to fall asleep. But by 11, I was still tossing and turning and hadn't fallen asleep yet. I went to the lounge knowing I'd find Karim there either sleeping on the couch or cleaning and straightening things. I told him about Bruce's ravaging swim through the soft corals and he promised to not only keep an eye on him and he'd say something if and when Bruce gets caught damaging anything on the reef.

Sometime around 3-4 AM I went back to my cabin, but only slept about an hour or a little more before waking up for the day. Our first two dives were on a larger freighter called the Numidia. Its cargo was train wheels and they were strewn about the reef. We were still seeing sharks guarding the wreck as well as the beautiful array of surgeonfish, scorpionfish and lionfish swimming through the corals growing on the wreck.

During lunch, Capt. Ramy moved the Excel to Little Brother Island. After lunch, Karim asked me if I wanted to do a blue water dive looking for hammerheads. I told him that I'd love to, but only if he promised to show me hammerheads. I'd never done a blue water dive like this before so I was a little anxious, but I had full confidence in my friend Karim thinking he'd probably done this many times before.

Karim and I left the boat and headed towards blue water away from the island. Once away from the boat, there was nothing to see but blue water above, below and all around. Occasionally I'd look at my depth gauge just to know where I was and it would usually read somewhere in the 70-90' depth range. Every once in a while, Karim would point into the blue at something. Half the time I couldn't see that far but swam towards it with my video camera rolling in hopes it would pick up whatever I wasn't seeing. Unfortunately, this video camera wouldn't pick these things up like mine normally would.

Then Karim got very excited and took off swimming hard while pointing straight ahead. There was no way I could keep up with him, but I followed as closely as possible until I began to see a large hammerhead emerge into view. Karim looked over his shoulder to make sure I was still keeping up with him and the two of us followed the hammerhead as best we could. Fortunately, it wasn't swimming fast nor was it necessarily trying to keep away from us.

All of a sudden it made a slow turn a little towards us and down. With Karim being next to me, I got close enough for my camera to get a good shot of the hammerhead. That's when I realized I could see the seafloor only five or so feet below the shark. That's also when a hand appeared in my viewfinder trying to pet the shark, which only resulted in it taking off like a rocket, ruining my shot.

As it turned out, the hand was Capt. Ramy's who just happened to show up. I only wished that he'd had waited another 10 or 15 seconds as my shot was just beginning to turn out great. When I began thinking about being this close to the bottom it made me realize I needed to look at my depth gauge. We were at 185'!

Well, that surely might put us into deco, so we made our way up the reef to shallower water ready to do any appropriate deco stops our computers displayed. Fortunately, as we got shallower, our deco time reduced and I had plenty of air left in my tank to finish my dive without asking Karim for his octopus. One of my friends that came with me on this trip almost always drained his tank down to 1-200 PSI then used his pony bottle to get back to the boat. It's a good thing he wasn't on this blue water hammerhead hunt with us.

By the end of the week, I'd still not gotten any more than one or two hours of sleep at any given time. I decided that I really needed to figure out how to deal with time zone changes, especially when traveling eastward. Now I try to stay awake on all flights as much as possible no matter how long the trip. This leaves me very tired and ready to sleep when I arrive at my destinations. This has worked for me ever since.

When we finished our diving for the week, we left Hurghada by bus and went back to Cairo to do a few days of sightseeing. Upon arrival at the same hotel I'd stayed in the year before, I walked down the hallway where the manager's office was who let me half-way off the hook for a very expensive long island iced tea. I knocked on his door and introduced myself after being invited in. I reminded him about that drink to show him that the Aggressor Fleet was still booking his hotel as I'd suggested. He smiled and gave me a knowing nod as he told me he remembered me and that drink very well.

We visited many of the same places I'd seen the year before when I was in Cairo, but the ancient history was still breathtaking. And we did visit some new tourist sites as well. On the third and last day Wayne suggested that we all meet for dinner together.

That night Bruce again obnoxiously stood out. When the waiter asked for his order, Bruce ordered steak and was particular about it being cooked very rare. The waiter apologized and told Bruce that the chef was not allowed to cook any meat rare. Bruce became very indignant and abusive to the waiter and told him to bring it the way he demanded. Reluctantly the waiter said he'd see what he could do.

Bruce got his rare steak while the rest of us tried to ignore him and enjoyed the evening together. The next morning, we boarded the bus that would take us to the Cairo airport. Everyone was on the bus except Bruce, so Wayne went back inside the hotel to find him. It turned out that Bruce was having some serious stomach and diarrhea problems, probably due to the uncooked Egyptian steak, but had no apologies for holding us up when he finally got on the bus.

As a matter of fact, every 10 minutes or so Bruce would ask the driver to pull over so he could use a restroom. We'd wait 10 minutes or more while Bruce took care of his business. But on Bruce's fourth request to stop, Wayne told him we couldn't stop again or we'd all miss our flight. Bruce begged and again got nasty about it, but Wayne stuck to his decision. Needless to say, when Bruce got off the bus, he definitely needed to change his pants as the dark stain was large and obvious, not to mention odorous.

When we arrived at the airport, I went directly to baggage services to see if they had recovered my luggage. They told me they had and took me to it. My housing pelican case had been opened, inspected and the housing was damaged due to someone not closing it properly.

This also left the Pelican case open (actually only zip tied shut) since the housing wouldn't fit inside the case without being closed properly. My suitcase had destination tags from Poland to Germany to France before it arrived in Cairo. My dive bag had tags from California to Australia to Japan to Spain before it arrived in Cairo, and I hadn't gone to any of those places on this trip.

All of the other missing bags were also there and claimed. Who would have thought that a 24-hour layover at JFK wouldn't be enough time to get all our luggage to Egypt Air and sorted properly so that it could be loaded onto our plane? Certainly not any of us.

© Cricket Manuel

Roger zeroing in on some beautiful flowing soft corals of the Red Sea.

Shipwrecks

Beneath the oceans, coral gardens abound,
    And this is where memories are sure to be found.
At these gardens a wary eye
    Is kept by the angels, curious but shy.

Where angels do swim in structures of man,
    There's still a touch of Nature's hand.
She blankets all with tender care;
    Reason and purpose are obvious there.

No matter how big or small one would be,
    These gardens display the guards of the sea.
These keepers will balance a need not so fickle,
    As memories are formed with (just) one little tickle.

Finding these keepers is not a hard task,
    And new memories form in the wink of a bass.
While searching the gardens, color catches the eye;
    Upon close inspection, they're bluer than sky.

Or some may be gold, still looking similar.
    How are they different and yet so familiar?
Nature's way is not always rough;
    In this case, it's a labor of love.

As new beds are placed on the floor all around,
  New creatures will come so they can be found.
By divers exploring this new chalet,
  Or others delighted with water ballet.

Artificial it was, but now it is real
  With myriad creatures from its mast to its keel.
There's not enough time to see all it holds,
  But memories see time taking its toll.

A floor that was barren now teems with life.
  Beauty so deep and no signs of strife.
There's more to be found in this garden of sea,
  And other ways to preserve memories.

From shore to shore as large as can be,
  Gardens of memories in open sea.

Walindi Plantation and the MV FeBrina

In October 2000, I visited Papua New Guinea planning on diving from the MV FeBrina with Captain Alan Raabe in order to create a promotional video for him. The captain is world-renowned for his fun antics, craziness, and superb knowledge of the Bismarck Sea. I'd also stay and dive with Walindi Plantation so I could include this land-based dive operation in the promo video, too.

I was able to convince my friends Cricket and Jerry to join me on this trip and I was looking forward to seeing them again. I'd visited them in Clearwater and dived from Jerry's boat more than a few times since I met them in Fiji. They like to take their boat out to the "middle grounds" where they do spearfishing. I met up with them in Sydney on the way to PNG, then we flew to Cairns before landing in Port Moresby, the capital of PNG.

Our last flight was to Hoskins airport on New Britain Island where we were picked up by a driver who took us to Walindi Plantation, about an hour away. The owner Max Benjamin and his wife Cecilie had been running this operation in Kimbe Bay since 1983 and they have warmly welcomed some of the world's finest underwater photographers and videographers ever since. Visitors stay in well-maintained cabanas nestled in the jungle and connected by curvy concrete sidewalks through the jungle that ultimately lead to the main office and dining hall.

Since Alan and Max had been the Best of Show prize sponsors for the Underwater Images Photo/Video Competition for five to six years, I was keen to produce a very nice promotional video for them. Their donated prize every year was a trip for two people to stay at Walindi for a day, then a seven-day cruise aboard the FeBrina, then three more days at Walindi after the cruise. This was reputed as one of the best prizes out of all of the international competitions combined and I used it as the Best of Show prize in the competition every year of its existence.

After the three of us settled into our cabana, we put our dive gear into large plastic bins and put them on our porch for the staff to pick up and carry to the dive boats for our dives the next morning. Walindi's dive boats are tinnies (aluminum-hulled) that can accommodate up to eight divers comfortably. After getting cleaned up, we went to dinner at the dining hall and had a couple of drinks at the bar.

The next day we did a couple of morning dives, then left our gear on the boat in the plastic bins for the staff to take to the FeBrina. We carried our cameras back to the cabana to recharge our batteries, repack our clothes, and get a shower. Then we left our luggage on the porch for the staff to carry to the FeBrina before we went to lunch at the dining hall.

After lunch, we boarded the FeBrina. Jerry went directly to Capt. Alan and reminded him that he had requested the larger stateroom located in the bow, below decks, and wanted to be sure that's the stateroom he and Cricket would get. Alan was somewhat taken aback that Jerry was so adamant on having that room. Alan was going to suggest to Jerry that the crossings were rough to take in that stateroom, but okayed the arrangement per Jerry's insistence.

I shared a room with Gerard. He was a doctor and lived on his large cattle ranch in the outback, not far from Sydney. Interestingly enough, I'd later find out that he didn't see sick patients. He'd only see patients that were well and healthy and teach them how to remain that way. He said he didn't want his patients to be exposed to sick people in his waiting room, which was pretty different than the doctors and their philosophies with which I'd been familiar all my life. Cricket said he looked like a gerbil, so we called him the Gerbil for the rest of the week. He didn't mind and seemed to like the attention.

Once everyone was aboard, including Gary Bell of National Geographic fame and his wife, Meri, Alan started the engines and we began cruising away from Kimbe Bay out into the Bismarck Sea. We would be visiting the Witu Islands and Fathers Reefs. We did a couple of day dives and a night dive before settling in for dinner and some good Australian wine graciously offered by Alan to all who were interested. After dinner, he took one of the empty wine bottles and told us that whomever can get the last drop of wine out of the bottle will win a whole bottle of wine for themselves.

To Alan's delight, we sat around the table for hours passing that bottle from one to another in turn until little by little, people just gave up and went to their rooms to turn in for the night. The first few drops dripped out quickly but as time went on, it took longer and longer for a drip to drop…but it always did drip. I don't remember who gave up last but I'm sure another drop could have fallen from the bottle with enough patience.

Throughout the 10-day cruise we visited world-famous dive sites like Dickie's Knob and Dickie's Place known for its fabulous muck diving. Muck diving consists of searching around in the sand and under debris for small creatures that many divers have never seen before. This was the first time I'd done muck diving and I found it quite enjoyable.

Our first dive at Dickie's Place was a shallow night dive along the shore. Since Cricket knew I was doing a promo video, she didn't hesitate to model for me, knowing what would work well for my video. She would give me time to shoot whatever I was shooting, then ease herself into my shot to look at the critter I was shooting. She did this when I was shooting a needlefish that night and the shot turned out fabulously since the needlefish remained next to her face when she approached it without darting away.

The next morning, we dove Dickie's Knob. We hit the water around 6:30 AM and found some beautiful anemones still balled up with anemonefish bouncing around and barely poking their heads out of the top. I think the anemones were still asleep since it was so early. Later in that same dive, we found a humphead parrotfish cleaning station. These magnificent fish can grow up to four and a half feet long and have a large, bulbous forehead.

After another reef dive, Alan took us back to Dickie's Place for more muck diving. I got a great shot of Gary readying for his shot of a pair of ghost pipefish trying to camouflage themselves in the turtle grass. Then I slowly zoomed in to the pair of fish and followed them with my camera as they drifted through the grass. I was careful to not disturb Gary's shot. When I zoomed back out to include Gary in the shot again, he had repositioned his body as he followed the fish, making this sequence as good as having two totally different shots that I could choose from for my video. The first half of this shot ended up being the opening of the promotional video.

During our surface interval, Gary thanked me for not disturbing his shot. Then he asked me if I had realized the male was pregnant. I told him I hadn't but I went right to my camera and replayed the tape and confirmed to myself what Gary had told me.

On the next dive at Dickie's Place, Cricket came up to me and gave me the out of air signal, then grabbed my octopus, as she showed me her air gauge reading almost zero. I was quite surprised as Cricket can do an entire hour-long dive and still have over half a tank of air left, but we'd only been in the water for about 15 minutes. We set our camera systems down in the sand knowing we'd be back for them and went back to the boat so she could switch tanks. But as she hung on the ladder, her air gauge was showing more air in her tank than what she'd shown me underwater.

I reached up and checked the knob on her tank that turns the air on and realized it wasn't open all the way, so I opened it and her gauge finally read that she had almost a full tank of air. Since the crew hadn't turned the tank on all the way, it made the air gauge not register properly underwater.

I'd never known this before but learned a valuable lesson at Cricket's expense. We returned to our cameras and got some great shots of anemonefish in an anemone quivering similar to the barred hamlets I'd filmed mating while diving in the Exumas. I was pretty sure that this was probably a courting dance for the anemonefish.

On our night dive that evening, we dove a site called Dickie's Reef. Cricket found a beautiful harlequin ghost pipefish which is probably the most colorful of all the pipefishes. Using the information Stan had taught me about my video lights, I ended up getting a stunning shot of it. After everyone else was finished shooting it, I went back to get more shots and caught it with a colorful banded coral shrimp sitting in the background.

After dinner and our night dive, Dickie Doyle came aboard to meet everyone as he always did when the FeBrina visited, and had a glass of wine with Alan. Dickie and his wife, Nancy, owned the cacao plantation on shore, hence the name of the dive site. If you don't know, the cacao bean is used to make chocolate.

The next morning, Alan took us out to a dive site called Lama Shoals where we did three dives. There were gigantic schools of big-eyed jacks and tuna swirling around each other. There could very well have been thousands of fish in this school. Since Jerry wasn't feeling too well, Cricket and I decided to do the dive together without him.

Cricket and I decided we'd swim in and through the school. Once inside the school, we separated and there was nothing else to see but the fish. Knowing about where Cricket was in my mind, I headed in that direction just filming the fish swirling about me. Then the fish would begin to part and Cricket would slowly appear out of nowhere. We went back and forth, and up and down, appearing and disappearing for over a half hour. Both of us thoroughly enjoyed this dive and the shots we took.

On the second dive that morning, I was underneath the school of fish as they were twirling round and round like a tornado funnel and I got a great shot of Gerard drifting up into the middle of this funnel by himself with the sun just off to the left of him! I'm sure he enjoyed that dive immensely!

For our third dive, we were told we'd need to find a place on the reef below to settle into and we could watch as hundreds of fish swam into a current above and in front of us. We were warned that there was a good-sized bed of corallimorphs on this reef where we'd want to settle down. These are a type of coral that are classified as cnidarians, which have stinging cells like jellyfish and anemones. We had to be very careful where we put our hands when we went to hold onto something.

When we got in the water for the third dive, the current had kicked up tremendously. Alan must have been rubbing off on me a little because I'd written in my logbook, "Bloody kickin' current, mate!" We settled down on a part of the reef where we could hold onto some rocks while we shot schools of jacks, tuna, and anemonefish swimming head-on into the current, getting nowhere. I never realized anemonefish left their anemones like this, but they reminded me of Nemo's father, Marlin, fighting the current trying to find Nemo.

That night, the weather got rough and Alan was up most of the night keeping the boat safe. Alan had anticipated this weather and had the crew tie ropes to large trees on the bank to augment the anchor.

But, during the night, the mooring ropes broke twice and the crew worked hard to get them retied and secure to no avail.

That's when Alan finally had them cut the ropes and weigh anchor to head towards the Father's Reefs. During the night, the seas remained rough. Since Jerry had been so insistent on getting the larger stateroom as soon as he boarded the boat, Alan decided that Jerry needed an attitude adjustment and told one of the crew to loosen an anchor that hung on the other side of the stateroom wall. It began swinging and banging on the hull to the rhythm of the waves. This kept Jerry up all night with a headache but after that prank, no one had any hard feelings and got along fine.

Joelle's Reef was named after Alan's daughter and was inundated with things to see. I filmed tiny thor shrimp dance around the tentacles of a tube anemone, a pretty freckled hawkfish, a very colorful mantis shrimp, a sailfin goby that continuously raised and lowered its dorsal fin for me, and a stand of bubble coral that looks like a congregation of large bubbles in a bubble bath. There were also unicornfish and surgeonfish everywhere.

I followed a lovely cuttlefish as it constantly changed colors, then let Cricket get her shots of it as I followed another one. Then we saw a hawksbill turtle munching on some coral in a nook. I filmed Cricket as she took her pictures of it and even caught her getting a shot of it yawning. Later that year, I talked Cricket into entering that shot into the Underwater Images Competition and she ended up winning a first place with a prize of a trip for one to the Bilikiki liveaboard in the Solomon Islands. Note that I didn't say anything during the judging about knowing her or anything about this shot.

Rest Orf was a dive site somewhat protected from the weather and not very deep, so we did our last afternoon and night dives there. My logbook pages are filled with critters I filmed on these dives including a banded snake eel, blue blanquillo, leopard flounder, seahorses, five different species of anemonefish, and two kinds of flatworms gracefully swimming over the reef, not to mention a half dozen nudibranchs. I also found an inimicus scorpionfish that mostly walks on the sand rather than swimming. I filmed it walking, then it stopped and slowly buried itself in the sand until only it was totally camouflaged with only its eyes barely visible. It was waiting to ambush its prey if and when any prey swam past.

The Flabellina Nudibranch is a colorful 2"-long sea slug popular in PNG.

The Gerbil and I decided to do a very early morning dive before the first scheduled dive and hit the water around 5:30 AM. The water was calm; flat as glass, and the visibility was marvelous. We weren't in the water more than five minutes and I noticed a stand of red whip corals that seemed to look familiar. It only took a few seconds for me to realize this was the exact same stand of whip corals that Patricia "PJ" Jordan had shot a couple of years before that won her the best of show prize in the Underwater Images Competition!

At the end of the dive, we swam back towards the boat. As I got closer, I could perfectly see the boat through the surface of the water and began filming as I approached. Just before getting to the ladder while still filming, I slowly lifted my camera out of the water and got a clear shot of the stern. This ended up being my final shot of the promo video for the FeBrina.

Our next dive would be the first morning dive for everyone else.

After telling Jerry and Cricket what we'd seen on our first dive, they went where we had been, and the Gerbil and I headed towards the bow of the boat and the mooring beyond. The first thing we spotted was a titan triggerfish over its nest. A titan triggerfish can be deadly when protecting its nest.

Its territory when nesting is actually cone shaped, from the nest up, so we knew to not swim in that imaginary area. Most people who might accidentally get inside that area might try to swim upwards to get away from the aggressive triggerfish, but the fish will follow to the surface attacking all the way. One must know to swim sideways and get out of that coned territory to be safe. My videographer friend Bruce, who I met on the Cayman Aggressor III, actually had a titan trigger bite a chunk out of one of his fins as he was protecting himself and getting away.

The Gerbil and I swam around the nest and found a part of the reef where there was a cloud of silversides rolling and tumbling above the reef. The Gerbil slowly swam into the school while I filmed him disappearing then reappearing without him even moving. As we made our way back to the boat, we passed a large school of batfish circling the reef. In our wide swim around the titan trigger, we came upon a charming clown triggerfish. Rest Orf may very well have been one of the prettiest dive sites of the trip.

Digger was one of the best spotters I'd ever dived with, and Josie was the lead divemaster and also a fantastic spotter. Their knowledge of the reefs and critters was only surpassed by Alan's. He'd assembled a great crew and many of them including Digger and Josie were still on board when I returned in 2005, as well as in 2015.

On one of the dives, Digger began finding small tube blennies on almost every coral head we passed. These one- to two-inch long fish live in holes in corals and usually a diver might only see their small head, possibly the size of a BB, barely popping out of the tube. But with patience and time, the tube blennies may come all the way out to feed on something small drifting by, and then quickly duck back into their tubes, tail first.

Our next dive was at a dive site named The Arches. During the dive briefing, we were told there was a large coral arch formation down around 90', and there were some freckled face blennies living on the top of the bommie. I decided to forego the deep part of this dive in order to spend more time at the top searching for the blennies. I looked up a picture of one in the ID book in the lounge so I knew what to look for.

The water was crystal clear and the sun was hitting the top of the bommie perfectly. As other divers began leaving the boat, I grabbed my land camera and got some shots of them as they swam away from the boat towards the bommie. The picture of these divers swimming across blue water, then above those beautiful corals was spectacular!

Many of the group went down to about 90' to see the arch, but once Cricket and I got in the water, we headed towards the crest of this flat-topped bommie at about 45'. The top was about the size of a basketball court. We circled the perimeter of the bommie first, then split up and spent most of the dive searching for the freckled face blennies and anything else we found interesting.

I finally found a freckled face, and he was the cutest blenny I'd ever seen. He's got a couple small "antlers" called cirri on top of its head, chubby cheeks and a pouty face with red freckles all over it. The one I found played hide and seek with me for the entire 15 minutes I was filming it, and I did get great shots of it every time it popped back out into view. I was extremely pleased with the footage I was getting and knew the promotional video I'd produce would impeccably portray the spectacular diving offered by Alan and the FeBrina crew.

On my last day in PNG, after my friends all left, I asked Max about doing some of the land tours they offer enabling me to include these in the promotional video for FeBrina and Walindi Plantation. He really liked this idea since no one else had ever suggested this. He arranged a driver with a small S-10 pick-up truck and a local gal, Shirley, to model for me. After breakfast, we headed out of the Walindi compound to tour around New Britain Island. Shirley insisted that I get in the cab with the driver and she jumped in the bed of the truck.

We drove for almost an hour as I watched the roads become less and less used and maintained until we stopped to talk to a native fellow in a field with his betel nut bag hung from his shoulder and his bright red teeth gleaming every time he smiled. (Chewing the betel nut creates a permanent red stain on one's teeth.) I was beginning to wonder if this decision to go out of the safety of the Walindi Plantation was a prudent one. What if I never returned? No one would have any idea where I was except possibly Max. I reassured myself by concluding I wasn't worth any ransom money anyway.

The native fellow was a friend of the driver and after they talked a minute or two and the fellow had given the driver some betel nut, we continued on our way through a field, then we turned into the jungle and drove down a little-used path. I did get a tad bit worried again knowing I had a family at home, but the adventure was getting too good to worry about the small things. The driver finally stopped the truck and we all got out. I was fairly glad as the driver had some pretty bad body odor that was beginning to irritate me.

We had arrived at the hot river where I sat in water heated by the volcano, leaning against worn boulders as if in a comfortable chair, while the hot water cascaded over my shoulders. Who would have thought Papua New Guinea would have a natural spa! I shot as much footage as I could until the steam fogged up the lens so much that it couldn't focus on anything any longer.

Shirley had been a great model diving into the large, deep pool and even using a rock to "wash up." She handed me one of the rocks and explained that this type of rock is what the natives use to bathe. She had me just rub it on my skin as if it were a bar of soap. I noticed that the driver had also been using one and hoped it would make a difference. When we got back into the truck, I was pleased to not detect any body odor from the driver.

Next, we visited a couple of plane wrecks that had set down in the jungle during WWII. The Talasea airport was nearby and was an instrumental airport in the war. These planes hadn't made it to the airport but were still almost totally intact. One was an NZ4522 and the other was a B25H Mitchellin. Shirley climbed in and around the planes while I filmed her and the planes.

In February 1942, the Japanese attacked Papua New Guinea and took over Talasea Airport. They used it until 1944 when allied forces carried out an amphibious landing to drive the Japanese out and re-take the airport. Having an airport in this area of the fighting gave the allied forces an advantage.

As we headed back to Walindi, we stopped at a local village and walked around while I interviewed and filmed the villagers about their family life in PNG, their schools and even what they did for entertainment. Walindi also offers other land tours but time didn't allow me to include any more than what we'd done that day, which had become another adventure, just as exciting as the diving had been. The only thing I didn't do on this trip to PNG that I considered doing was to chew some betel nut. I guessed that would have to wait for another visit.

Trumpetfish love to camouflage themselves in whip corals!

GARDENS OF MEMORIES~ON TUBE BLENNIES

One coral patch where tube blennies abound,
   This is where memories are sure to be found.
They reside in a hole as round as a pen,
   And keep to themselves in their own little den.
Macro they are, so you'll have to look close.
   If you're lucky at first, you may see their nose.
Be patient, my friend, to not cause a scare,
   Soon they'll reward your effort, so fair.
They'll pop their head out with eyes peeking all ways,
   Searching for food floating by during their days.
Farther out they may stretch for a better view,
   E'er keeping one eye coming back to you.
They may upside down, or they may right side up;
   But whichever it is, they're cute as a pup.
Quickly out and back in, a bite they will snatch.
   An awesome shot for photographer's catch!
Once you find one, you'll know where to look;
   Like learning to use a fish ID book.
In coral apartments, there's many to see;
   More gardens of memories in open sea.

Mahonia Na Dari –
Guardian of the Sea

After our 10 days of muck diving, shark diving, night diving and the like, we returned to Walindi Plantation where the FeBrina moors when not cruising. Some people including Cricket, Jerry and the Gerbil spent a day packing and doing various land tours before flying out the following day. I'd be staying a few more days, so I did some tinnie diving the first day back at Walindi. That evening at Walindi, we were entertained with a sing-sing where locals get together to sing and perform for Walindi guests. Most of the performers were the local school-aged kids.

The following morning Max introduced me to the director of the Mahonia Na Dari program. In 1997 Max and Cecilie partnered with The Nature Conservancy and the European Union Islands Regional Environmental Program to form a program called Mahonia Na Dari which, in the local language means Guardian of the Sea. This organization was formed to provide environmental education to the local community in order to understand and conserve PNG's natural resources and environments. It's a non-government organization (NGO) with its own Board of Directors and is based on property Max and Cecilie donated for this purpose.

The Mahonia Na Dari campus includes numerous dormitories for staff and/or international scientists who visit PNG to not only study the marine environment, but also to study things like the lumber industry in PNG, the Palm plantations, or even the Queen Alexandra Birdwing butterfly which is the largest butterfly in the world reaching up to almost 10" across. The campus also has a laboratory as well as a library for research purposes. Originally a Marine Environment Education Program (MEEP) was formed for local New Britain residents and students.

Being a former science teacher, I was very interested in this program and I asked to attend some of the classroom sessions with the instructor and students so I could document their program. At the time, there were about 12-15 students participating. Half of them were between the ages of 9-13 and the other half were aged 14-18. The theory sessions I attended and filmed using a tripod, were divided up into the two age groups and centered on the marine environment for both.

That afternoon I went out on a boat with the younger group who were going to be snorkeling with equipment provided by Max and Cecilie. They all had masks, fins, snorkels and dive slates. Their assignments for the day that were written on their dive slates included finding something that represented a symbiotic relationship, something that represented man's effect on the reef, and something that represented Nature's effect on the reef. As we left the dock, I noticed some of the kids looking at the disappearing shore with trepidation as if they'd never been that far from land.

On the way to the site where they would snorkel, I told the kids that I'd be diving nearby with them while they snorkeled. I also told them to come and get me when they found any of these things so that I could film them pointing out the fulfillment of their assignments to me and my video camera. The kids truly enjoyed ducking behind an anemone with an anemonefish while smiling at the camera to point at this symbiotic relationship they'd found and recognized. Others, surface dived down to fish nets entangled in the reef to show man's effect. Still more pointed out some bleached corals illustrating Nature's effect on the reef for the camera.

Later that afternoon, the MEEP director told me she had arranged a beach clean-up that I should consider attending. I ended up getting some great footage of not only the students but many of the locals cleaning debris from the beaches. Participants ranged from 4-94 years old and all of the debris that was collected was cataloged piece by piece and entered into an international database that would help discern where that debris originated, whether from local fishermen or things that would have come from cruise ships passing by and dumping their garbage into the sea.

It was obvious this program was working for the students and they were excited to learn about their greatest natural resources. I promised to put together a promotional video about the program so that it could be used to entice other students to become involved.

This video could also be used by teachers as a tool to teach about the marine environment. A third very important use was to show off the MND program so that donors could see what the program was all about and hopefully invest in it. When I finished this short program, I sent it to them on a few separate VHS tapes in hopes it would be beneficial for them.

I would find out years later just how well it was received and used.

The students would search for things like a symbiotic relationship between this 1"-long Sarasvati Anemone Shrimp and its host Anemone.

GARDENS OF MEMORIES~ON MAHONIA NA DARI

A teacher with students gathered around,
    This is where memories are sure to be found.
Cecilie and Max had offered the chance
    For kids to learn how to take a stance.
Conservation; a lesson on keeping it right,
    Will show them the way to carry the fight.
Guardians of seas they will become,
    All while having boatloads of fun.
Watching the shore as it fades away,
    With thoughts of snorkeling; in water, they'll play.
Find symbiosis and give me a smile,
    Fishnets on reefs, are all in a pile.
Water's too warm causing corals to bleach;
    Is saving them too far beyond our reach?
With good instruction, the students will learn
    How they can save them; an honor they'll earn.
Locals together, all ages alike,
    Up and down beaches they all did hike.
Cleaning and sorting all the debris;
    Gardens of memories in open sea.

Manatees: The Gentle Giants

Since we were already in Florida on a family vacation visiting my father, I decided it was a good time to travel inland a bit from the Naples area and visit Crystal River to snorkel with the manatees. My youngest kids had never seen them before and it only made sense to give them this opportunity since we were this close.

Every five years or so since I first started diving, I would plan a trip for myself to Florida to film the Manatees once the water started getting cold and the manatees started congregating near warmer water springs, like a famous one named Three Sisters at Crystal River. This time, along with my wife, I was taking my youngest daughter, Caitlyn, who was 14 and my youngest son Casey, who was 10, to see these Gentle Giants.

We left Naples very early in the morning so that we would get there just after sunrise. Once we arrived at Crystal River, I rented a john boat and life jackets for everyone. The kids already had masks, fins and snorkels since we have a swimming pool at home. I loaded my wetsuit, snorkel gear and camera into the boat and helped everyone on board.

My wife wouldn't be getting in the water at all and the kids probably could have swum in the Arctic Ocean without thermal protection. You know how kids are when it comes to swimming. Mine always got in the pool on the same day I'd open it after winter was over and spring was just around the corner.

As we motored out towards Three Sisters, I taught them how to look for the manatee noses barely breaking the surface of the water when they breathed. When we arrived at the mouth of the Three Sisters spring, the kids were seeing manatees under the water and getting excited about snorkeling with them since they looked so cute. After I put on my wetsuit, we all donned our snorkel gear and slipped into the water. I turned on my camera and looked around to see where I might want to begin shooting.

That's when I heard a blood-curdling yell for help. A manatee was getting closer to Casey and he was beginning to realize just how big these gentle giants were. They were surely MUCH bigger than he was and he wanted back on the boat ASAP!

I lifted him back up into the boat and tried to convince him that the manatees wouldn't hurt him. I explained that they only eat vegetation, not meat or people. Even Caitlyn, who was still in the water, was showing him how the manatees would just swim by and not bother her. But he wasn't going to have anything to do with any of this.

That's when a lady who was snorkeling and taking pictures nearby swam over. She had looked a little familiar to me from the first time I saw her, but I wasn't placing where I'd seen her before. Then she introduced herself as Lorraine Sadler and I remembered right away that I'd seen her a few months earlier at DEMA (the Diving Equipment Manufacturer's Association expo). She had just been inducted into the Women Divers Hall of Fame.

She started talking with Casey and telling him how cute the manatees are and assured him they wouldn't ever hurt him. Then she asked if she could take his picture in the water with the manatees. This so totally distracted him that he agreed and became her model for a while.

With Lorraine's help, he had become very at ease with the manatees. One of the manatees even came close to them and seemed to want to be petted, so Lorraine showed Casey how to tickle them under their flippers, which he enjoyed immensely. Of course, I was getting my own video of him and Caitlyn comfortably interacting with the manatees.

Once we finished shooting, Lorraine and I spoke a little further and I learned more about her and her accomplishments in the diving industry. That's when I decided that my good friend and mentor, Joyce Hayward, belonged in the Women Divers Hall of Fame as well. When I returned home, I immediately filled out and submitted a nomination form and Joyce was inducted by year's end, 2001.

The kids stayed in the water for another half hour before they started getting cold. I got them back into the boat and had mom get them dried off and dressed into some warmer clothes we'd brought for them. As we headed back to the dock, the kids continued noticing the manatee noses sticking up from the surface, trying to see who could find the most.

All in all, it was a great end to a great vacation.

GARDENS OF MEMORIES~ON MANATEES

Crystal River in winter; manatee around;
    This is where memories are sure to be found.
At crack of dawn, a work of art,
    Mother and calf will touch a heart.
With bodies so large, and flippers like hands,
    These gentle mammals are curious of man.
Met in the oceans by old salts of the sea,
    They foraged on grasses, these manatee.
With tails so flat and eyes forlorn,
    No questions arise how mermaids were born.
Manatee gardens date millions of years,
    But visits with them may conjure up fears.
With noses at surface like bowling balls,
    Population numbers continue to fall.
Propeller blades, careless bumps in the day,
    All take their toll; high prices to pay.
After today, their extinction does loom,
    Such a sad state, this arrow of doom.
All care must be taken; preserve manatee,
    And gardens of memories in open sea.

Joyce Hayward

I met Joyce Hayward in 1994 when my Gavia Scuba Club hosted our first annual ScubaFest for the Ohio Council of Skin and Scuba Diving Inc. (OCSSDI). She was one of the presenters, having been chosen by our Board from her "Application to Present" that she sent to our club for review.

Her bio in our 1994 program read like this: "Joyce Hayward is a Master Diver and Assistant Instructor. She is president of Bay Area Divers and on the Board of the OCSSDI where she serves as chairperson of the archaeological and Legislative committees. She is a Vice President of the Association for Great Lakes Maritime History and is Committee Chair of the Diver Coordination Committee. She is president of the Ohio chapter of Save Ontario Shipwrecks and serves on the Governor's Advisory committee for underwater cultural resources for the State of Ohio. She has given dive presentations all over Canada and the States. Her presentation will outline research opportunities, and organizations, training in class and pool, open water projects and how to become involved in a project or start your own."

That year I did a presentation on "Behavior and Ecology of Marine Life" but was much more interested in attending Joyce's presentation. I was keen to learn more about getting involved in the diving industry and felt her presentation would be a valuable lesson. Little did I know at the time that Joyce and I would become very close friends through the years.

Her mentorship with assembling slide shows to present winners of the international non-profit Underwater Images Photo/Video Competition turned out to be invaluable for me until I was able to do this digitally with my video editing programs years later. At the time, I knew nothing about slide projectors or adding music along with the projection, and this was her expertise, even giving multi-projector presentations.

Our friendship grew even tighter when we learned that we both taught school. Of course, I'd left teaching by that time, but Joyce was still teaching fourth grade in Bellevue, Ohio and was earning awards from mayors, governors and even a president for her activities. She would fast become my first hero in the diving industry.

I began to get much more involved in OCSSDI, by becoming a Board member, a Trustee and even Chairman of the Board a few years later. I figured if she had the time to devote to OCSSDI along with all the other things she did, I could make it my business to give back to Ohio, too. It took many years before she finally admitted that I'd become a hero of hers as well, having taken my video accomplishments to higher levels, mentoring other videographers and photographers, founding and directing the Underwater Images Photo/Video Competition, as well as things I'd been doing for OCSSDI.

Joyce obviously did most of her diving in the Great Lakes more than anyplace else. She became a shipwreck expert for the Great Lakes having researched, dived and photographed hundreds of wrecks. She dove with and consulted for authors like Gary Gentile, Chris Kohl, Bernie Chowdhury, and many more. This eventually led to her title of "Lady of the Lakes," and she was even highlighted in a PBS special, "The Great Lakes in Depth" for her work in shipwreck and marine biology education.

Any time I'd get invited to do a video presentation for the Bay Area Divers in Sandusky, Ohio, I'd stay at Joyce's house for the night then drive back to Cincinnati the next morning. Her guest room was filled with framed certificates from those mayors, governors and president I mentioned earlier. Seeing these would always motivate me to continue working on doing and giving back even more.

Joyce's presentations were always educational and well done. She could bring these shipwrecks alive even though they may have been on the bottom for decades or even centuries. Sometimes she would have the entire audience wiping tears from their eyes by the way she told the stories of those shipwrecks, their crews and families, and the losses suffered by all.

When Joyce was told that she had cancer, she decided to concentrate on her family and she gave up diving and everything that came with it. I offered to film her dozens of awesome presentations if she wanted to "present" them for me in front of my video camera so these fabulous stories could be archived in the way only she could do, but she very warmly declined my offer.

Her friends and I learned to respect her decision and while we were thrilled that she was still alive long after her diagnosis and prognosis, Joyce finally succumbed to her cancer August 26, 2009. In lieu of flowers Joyce asked for donations to be made to "Back to the Wild," which was a volunteer-based, non-profit wildlife rehabilitation and nature education center located in northwest Ohio. She was still giving back even in death.

Roger and Joyce discussing our presentations at ScubaFest.

GARDENS OF MEMORIES~ ON JOYCE HAYWARD

A woman who gives, Joyce Hayward is crowned,
    And this is where memories are sure to be found.
Decades of work shows her labor of love;
    Surely energy drawn from powers above.
Joyce's walls are filled with letters of thanks
    From presidents to mayors and all through the ranks.
She teaches and loves, and dives shipwrecks with friends
    To document lost stories, giving those true ends.
Her research and pictures have taught Great Lakes lore
    Of ships and lives we'd not heard of before.
Her slide shows draw tears from all who will listen;
    Every eye in the room guaranteed to glisten.
A mentor to many and hero to another,
    But most of all, she's a loving Mother.
A member, Women Divers Hall of Fame,
    Her accomplishments equal most others by name.
From classrooms to lectures to informal sittings,
    Weaving knowledge to all with her expert knitting's.
Touching thousands of hearts, memories ne'er to flee;
    Creating Gardens of Memories in open sea.

Grand Cayman

In January 2002, Jerry contacted me and told me he would be going to Grand Cayman with Cricket for some diving and asked if I wanted to meet up with them. They went there a couple of times a year and this time invited me to join them since they had reserved a condo that had an extra bedroom. I accepted his invitation and in March we met up in Grand Cayman.

The condo was on the ground floor and right on the beach overlooking the ocean. On certain days, we could even see the Cayman Aggressor moored at the northernmost point of the island that we could see from our beach. The dive sites in that area were popular ones and if the weather was bad, that was a good place for the Aggressor boat to stay moored until the weather changed.

Cricket and Roger on Jerry B.'s boat, going to dive in the Gulf of Mexico.

Jerry and Cricket always dove with the same dive operation every time they went down. That operation would bring the dive boat and pick us up from the beach in front of the condo for our two morning dives then drop us off at the same place when we finished our dives. That made it easy to carry our gear and saved us the drive into town each day.

Ever since I started diving, when speaking with other divers about our favorite places to dive, many always talked about the Cayman Islands being their favorite dive destination. But I never really felt that strongly about the diving in the Cayman's. I'd always had a good time there, but I never saw anything really spectacular (other than famous people) and the visibility was OK at best. Maybe I was getting too spoiled by the Pacific, Indo-Pacific and Red Sea diving that I'd been blessed with.

Our dives were all close to hour-long dives but they were again just typical Cayman dives to me. Nurse sharks were almost guaranteed at least once a day as were also green sea turtles, since the turtle farm was just around the corner. But there always seemed to be a lack of macro subjects which I'd learned to really enjoy filming after muck diving in Papua New Guinea.

On one of our surface intervals, Cricket happened to be looking in the water, then told me to quickly grab my camera. The surface of the water was inundated with sargassum and this one clump had some juvenile seahorses hanging underneath. We got in the water and started shooting. I'd never seen seahorses in the Caymans so it was fun to finally find some floating at the surface.

Sargassum is brown algae that originate in the Sargasso Sea in the Atlantic Ocean near Bermuda. Sargassum floats on the surface and is transported by the Gulf Stream. There are times that these algae can totally cover the surface like a large blanket, so has been deemed a headache to tourism boards. The sargassum can disappear as quickly as it appears.

Shooting the critters in the sargassum as it floated by was a great way to spend our surface interval. These floating rafts were havens for many different types of juvenile marine creatures. We shot pipefish, crabs, juvenile triggerfish and more. This was really a stay-in-one-place-and-let-everything-come-to-you experience!

After we were dropped off back at the condo, I contacted Jim and Lois who still lived on Grand Cayman. I had met them on the MV Excel/Red Sea Aggressor a few years before and thought it might be fun to see them again as they were a very nice couple. I'd emailed them before leaving the States to see if they'd be up for a visit and they agreed it would be nice.

Jerry and Cricket dropped me off at their home on the other side of Georgetown before they did some shopping. I spent a few hours talking about old times in the Red Sea and catching up on where we'd each been diving the last few years. They told me their children David and Janice were doing well and Lois was actively passionate about saving bats. She still is to this day but I've never figured out why. Maybe someday I'll learn a better appreciation for bats, but my experience with them is mostly when they inundate someone's attic and I have to figure out where they get in and fix those holes.

As I was getting ready to go back to the condo Jim asked me if I wanted to take a plane ride around the island. He had a small plane and could take me for a ride if I wanted. I told him I was interested but I thought my friends Jerry and Cricket might want to come along as well, if that was OK. He said that was fine and that we should plan to meet at the airport after our diving the next day.

Cricket wasn't interested, but Jerry and I met Jim at the airport as he was readying his plane. It was a single engine prop plane of some sort; I hadn't paid attention to the type, but it might have been a Cessna. Jim took off all of the doors and stored them in the hanger. Then he gave me and Jerry a pair of headphones to wear to protect our ears from the engine noise and told us to get in and buckle up. We taxied out to a runway and waited for the tower to give us clearance to take off.

The people in the tower recognized Jim's plane and they had an informal chat to catch up, then the tower finally gave him the go-ahead to take off. As Jim revved up the engine, he told us that he wouldn't need much runway to get off the ground. That was a total understatement as I think he might have only used 30' of the runway before we were airborne.

First, he flew over our condo where Cricket was standing on the beach waving to us. She took pictures of me hanging out the open door and I got video of her on the beach as well. Then Jim flew us around the entire island. We flew over Stingray City and could easily see the stingrays swimming about in the shallow blue water above the white sand. He pointed out all the famous peoples' properties and buildings as I hung my feet over the edge of the door frame and kept shooting video, sometimes with my feet in the picture just for fun to illustrate the lack of a door.

The flight around the island was a real treat that I'd not expected and it topped off another fun dive trip with Jerry and Cricket. Through the years, we were becoming quite close.

Here's a juvenile Cleaner Wrasse cleaning the tail of a Triggerfish.

GARDENS OF MEMORIES~ON SARGASSUM RAFTS

Small rafts of sargassum for miles around,
  This is where memories are sure to be found.
A single blade here and a few over there;
  They likely have youngsters in tow in their care.
Darting amid and among as they wheedle,
  Are pipefish the size of a long pine needle.
And swimming beneath in the shadows of grass,
  Are triggerfish testing their fins as they pass.
No larger than thumbnails, they tilt to the side;
  With hopes their low profiles help keep them alive.
Crabs have a grasp that last hundreds of miles,
  As might loggerheads, lobsters, and shrimp in piles.
Transparent comb jellies dance to and fro,
  With neon light ridges and colors aglow.
Coyly suspended from sargassum sails,
  Are one-inch long seahorses hanging by tails.
Some bright sunshine yellow, and some brown and tans;
  Living jewels at the surface of great expanse.
Like charms on a bracelet, all dangle quite free;
  Gardens of memories in open sea.

Business Class

In 2003, I earned my 9th international first place award for underwater video. This time it was again from the prestigious Los Angeles Underwater Photo Society's competition. My prize was a week aboard the Nai'a in Fiji. The winning short production was titled, "Papua New Guinea: Land of Diversity" and highlighted the Mahonia Na Dari program for the students of PNG teaching them about conservation of their greatest natural resource. It was a shortened version of the video I'd made for the MND program.

This prize was spectacular for me since back in those days, videographer winners may or may not get nice trips for prizes like the still shooters got (remember, one year I received a first-place prize in the video category of a close-up adapter for a Nikonis still camera). I had heard about a great dive site called E-6 in Fiji and since I hadn't visited it on my last trip, I was looking forward to diving it this time. E-6 is a bommie that rises 3,000' to within a foot of the surface that could be dived 10 times without seeing everything.

Since I'd met Jerry and Cricket in Fiji, I thought it would be great if they could make the trip with me again. I contacted Jerry and we decided to schedule this trip to be together again at the end of the year in November. I contacted the Nai'a staff to see if the dates I picked would be available to redeem my prize as well as bring two friends who would pay their own fare and they verified that my dates would work for them all the way around.

I would later find out that I coincidentally booked my trip for the same week Stan Waterman would on board. Indeed! This would be my second trip with Stan in Fiji, and he had become a great mentor to me and my video work. I would even be shooting with his old rig that he sold me after our first trip together.

After making those arrangements with the Nai'a staff, I felt the next thing I needed to do was to look into my airfare and begin booking that as well. I'd fly from Cincinnati to Los Angeles where I'd board

Air Pacific for the long flight to Nadi in Fiji. I realized that it was going to be a pretty good chunk of money, but I also appreciated the fact that my diving was free.

When I contacted Air Pacific, I asked to speak to a marketing person. Once Barb got on the line, I told her that I was going to Fiji to do promotional video work for a dive operation there and offered to share my footage with Air Pacific for its promotional purposes if they were interested. I also suggested that if they sent me air to air footage of their planes, I'd work that into my production for even more promotion of Air Pacific. She apologized and told me that they don't give tickets away for promotional purposes.

I told her that I'd be purchasing my ticket, but if she could bump me to Business Class, I'd do all the promotional things for Air Pacific I spoke about earlier. Since I'd done this once before with Qantas for my trip to Papua New Guinea and they accepted my offer then, I also shared that story with her during our discussion. She said she would be willing to do that, but it would only be on a space available basis. I told her that would be acceptable with me.

I hung up the phone on cloud nine, as you can imagine! Any Business Class seat on a long flight is as good as it gets. Especially if that seat doesn't cost any more than the standard economy ticket. It would be easy to work their air-to-air footage into my production and it might even make my production look that much more professional, to boot!

November finally rolled around and I was off to Los Angeles. Upon arrival, I grabbed my bags from the domestic carrousel and made my way to the international concourse, with quite the spring in my step I might add. I found the Air Pacific desk and waited my turn to get my boarding pass, hoping it would say "Business Class."

When the ticket agent called me forward, I handed her my itinerary and passport. Then I proceeded to ask her if she had information about my possibly being bumped to Business Class as arranged through their marketing department. She said she didn't see anything for now, but would issue my economy class ticket then look into the upgrade I mentioned, and call me back to the desk when she had more answers.

I told her that would be fine since I was there about four hours before my flight time. I wasn't in a hurry and wanted to show a sense of patience even though I was jumping out of my skin due to my anticipation. I put my checked bags on the scale and they were under the weight allowances, so she tagged then and put them on the conveyor belt, then handed me my economy seat boarding pass.

I stepped back to allow the next person in line to check in and decided to patiently wait until she could get the time to look into my request. About 15 minutes later, she called me back up and told me she found my request that had been accepted by the marketing department and they did in fact have a seat available in Business Class. Wahoo! I was going to again travel in Business Class!

That's when she looked over the desk at my legs and said, "Oh, I'm sorry sir, but you can't fly in Business Class wearing blue jeans. You have to be wearing slacks like khakis." HUH? Really? I remarked that my jeans were brand new and I was wearing an ironed white shirt embroidered with my logo on it, so it wasn't as if I was a slovenly bum wearing old jeans with holes in them.

She then offered to have my luggage brought back up so that I could exchange my blue jeans for slacks that would be appropriate for Business Class. Disappointedly, I reminded her that I was flying to a tropical diving destination with a weight allowance, and a second pair of long pants was not in my luggage, ever. This really presented a quandary I wasn't ready to accept.

She said there was nothing else she could do. If I had slacks, I could fly in Business Class. I told her I'd try to think of something and let her know if I came up with a solution. I figured that I was in Los Angeles international airport filled with stores selling hats, sweaters, shirts, belts, underwear, socks, shoes, purses and whatever other sundry items large airports have. And this concourse was huge.

So, I set out to find and buy a pair of slacks. I walked up and down those hallways three times on both sides. I went into stores and asked if they had slacks or knew of any store that might. Every answer was the same…No slacks.

I had pretty much given up hope. There was nothing in my luggage that I could use and nothing in the hundred or so shops around the concourse. How could such a small detail like this cause me to have to lose a comfortable seat in Business Class?

I was leaning up against a wall feeling like a rug had been pulled out from under me when a young, African American fellow came up to me. He seemed pretty inebriated and at this point, I wasn't interested in any discourse with him, but I couldn't seem to avoid his eyes as he approached me directly. "Excuse me sir," he began, "I was wanting another beer or two but the bartender upstairs wouldn't sell me another one, saying I was too drunk. If I gave you the cash, would you be willing to go upstairs and get me a couple more beers? My next flight is still about six hours away."

Eureka! Our plights might be finding an amicable solution after all! I looked this fellow over, and although he was walking on the cuffs of his khakis, the waistline was almost below his buttocks. Despite him walking on his cuffs, the pants looked clean and the pleats were well-ironed and it seemed we were about the same height.

I suggested to this fellow that I'd obtain and even pay for a couple of beers for him if he'd trade his slacks for my brand-new blue jeans. He looked me over and stated that he thought mine would be too small for him. I asked his waist size and he verified 32", the same as mine. Our height was the same. I told him I'd first get his beer, and then we'd trade pants in the men's room. If my jeans didn't fit him, he could keep the beer.

I got him a couple of beers from the bar and delivered on my end of the deal. We went into the men's room and exchanged slacks. His fit me perfectly, so I knew mine would fit him as well. He was good with the deal and I left a happy man again. I never did get his name, though, and hated to lose my new blue jeans, also. I'm definitely a jeans person rather than khakis.

Elatedly, I sauntered over to the Air Pacific desk and approached the lady who had helped me earlier. I showed her my slacks and she asked, "How did you do that? No one sells slacks in this airport." At first, I told her she really didn't want to know. But she had been such a help to the extent she could, I felt I owed her a funny story and to her delight, I relayed what had occurred. As she admitted that she'd never heard such a tale, she handed me my Business Class boarding pass and wished me a safe trip.

Once I boarded the plane and slid into my Business Class seat,

I looked around at the others sitting up there. I always like to watch people, and in this case, I try to figure out who is who and what they might do for a living. While looking around, to my surprise, there were at least six men and a few women wearing blue jeans, and some even wearing shorts! As it turned out, about five of those people were on the Nai'a with me that week.

I could only guess that if one paid for these seats, they could wear anything they wanted, but if it's a freebie of sorts as it was for me, one needs to be dressed for the occasion, a lesson I'll always remember. At that point, all I knew was that I was very appreciative of the staff of Air Pacific and I was on my way to Fiji, comfortably.

Roger (and Jerry B. in the background) filming over this pretty reef.

GARDENS OF MEMORIES~ON E-6 IN FIJI

E-6 is a dive site a half mile round,
    And this is where memories are sure to be found.
From three thousand feet to a foot of the surface,
    This seamount in Fiji flourishes purpose.
Soft corals caress with colors of care,
    Inviting cameras to images there.
Safaris can lead to an undercut wall
    Where sea fans and feather stars cover it all.
The nudibranchs crawl and the flatworms dance,
    Displaying their splendor as they prance.
Small blennies and crabs peek out from their holes,
    While parrots eat corals, and take their tolls.
Scorpionfish watch as filefish stalk.
    Then shrimp become dinner; mostly their fault.
Whitetips cruise by with thoughts of their prey,
    Suggesting we'd meet another day.
When I thought the thrill of the dive was spent,
    With no sight of land, to the boat I went.
Then schools of 'cuda spiraled around me,
    Gardens of memories in open sea.

The Nai'a

I met up with Jerry and Cricket at the airport in Nadi, Fiji and we made the long bus trip to the dock where the Nai'a was tied. Rob Barrel is the owner and welcomed us aboard then showed us to our staterooms. Rob would be joining us on this trip along with Stan Waterman and his travel/dive buddy Nancy McGee, so it promised to be a great trip all the way around again. I've found when the owner is aboard, things usually happen perfectly.

Little by little, others began showing up to the boat. As it turned out, about six of the people who were seated in Business Class on my Air Pacific flight to Nadi from Los Angeles showed up in their jeans and shorts to join the trip. I'd later share my story with them about hunting for decent slacks in LAX and they got a good laugh from it as well.

Before I left Cincinnati, I'd asked others on a pro and semi-pro underwater photographer's forum about their recommendations on any given dive sites in Fiji that the Nai'a might visit. One fellow told me about a file clam at the dive site named Mellow Yellow that looked a lot like cookie monster and he had just found this a few months earlier. This really piqued my interest so I asked him if it would be possible for him to describe where I might find this clam.

He emailed back and told me it would be very easy for me to find the file clam and I wouldn't miss it once I saw it. He described Mellow Yellow as being a pair of underwater mountains, or bommies, that had a saddle in between them at around 40-50' deep. He said if I found the saddle, I should look towards the smaller bommie and Cookie Monster would be right there. This sounded pretty simple.

On our third day, our cruise director Josh told us that our plan was to dive Mellow Yellow before and after lunch for our second and third dives of the day. I told Jerry and Cricket about the file clam and said I'd be trying to go straight to that saddle. They were game for this as well and agreed it was a good plan for us.

As soon as we hit the water, we could see the two peaks rising from the depths. We swam towards the saddle between them, and noticed that there was a very nice sandy area in the middle of the saddle. We positioned ourselves looking towards the smaller bommie and I immediately saw the file clam. It was uncanny how much the growth on and around this file clam did in fact make it look just like Cookie Monster with a soft coral hat!

We all shared time shooting Cookie Monster to our hearts' content. Sometimes if someone got too close to the clam it would close its shell and we'd have to wait a minute or two until it opened back up to get the Cookie Monster effect. Once we finished our shots, we continued on to experience more of what Mellow Yellow had to offer. As we shot many different species of butterflyfish and even a large titan triggerfish, I began thinking more about Cookie Monster and was getting what I thought would be a good idea for a novel video shot.

At lunch, I asked Josh if there might be an extra lens cap anywhere around the boat, adding the thicker it was, the better. I didn't want to take one from any of the photographers in case it got lost. Josh found an old, thick one for me and my plan was beginning to take shape.

I told Cricket and Jerry that I was going back to Cookie Monster at the beginning of the dive then I'd catch up with them after getting some shots I wanted. When I got to the saddle, I positioned my video camera so that it would capture Cookie Monster perfectly from the side. I turned the camera on and hit "record." Then I took the lens cap and offered this black "cookie" to Cookie Monster from its front. As the lens cap got closer, Cookie Monster would close its mouth, as if to say, "No more cookies!"

I did a number of takes so that I could have a choice of shots to use. Of course, it took a while since I had to wait for the clam to open again after each take, but it was all well worth the time and effort. That evening, after Stan showed one of his trip videos from Guadeloupe Island, I shared my footage of Cookie Monster with the group. Everyone was giggling and Stan was definitely impressed with my idea that wouldn't have given the same effect for a still photographer.

The next day our diving was planned for sites around Wakaya Island. It was an early dive and many of the anemones were still closed into their tight balls with their bright, almost fluorescent green skins glowing in the morning sun. Jerry, Cricket and I had fun trading anemones to shoot while the anemonefish peeked out from openings in the tops of the balls.

We also saw green morays, blue ribbon eels and even hammerheads on a couple of dives around the island. At one point I was filming a Dampier Stonefish that was sitting perfectly in a nook of the reef looking straight towards me. As I was about to finish my shot it swam away, so I let it swim out of the picture. But before I turned off the camera, a second stonefish swam into the picture from the background and settled itself into the exact same nook posing exactly as the first one had sat. It was almost like beauty pageant competitors taking turns modeling. Another right time, right place shot for me as if I'd directed the stonefish in a movie!

After spending the day at Wakaya Island, we moved on to Nigali Passage where we did a drift dive with plenty of black tip, silver tip, and gray reef sharks swimming and even sleeping on the sand where larger currents were flowing. Our last dive there was a shark feed that I always enjoy. Fortunately, the bait was placed in an area that was a little protected from the known ripping currents of Nigali Passage.

For our third dive of the day Rob and Josh asked the group if we might want to do an exploratory dive at the mouth of a river to see if it might be worthy of becoming a new dive site. Everyone was agreeable to the idea so we jumped in. There was a lot of turtle grass and pretty low visibility being as close to the river mouth as it was, so we all separated and went our own ways to see what we could discover.

It was more of a muck dive because of all the silt, and unfortunately there wasn't even much marine life in the muck. I did get a few shots of flagfin and gold speckled shrimpgobies. Then my battery showed no more power left and the camera turned off. (I must have forgotten to change the battery after the last dive again.) I was on my way back to the Nai'a when I noticed a very small juvenile octopus sticking out of a small hole on top of a four-foot diameter coral head in about 15-20' of water.

Since I didn't have any battery power left, I sat my housing down in the sand and began slowly interacting with the little guy. It allowed a close approach as I got almost nose to nose with it. Then I slowly brought my finger towards it, and when it didn't disappear, I started to caress it between its eyes. It seemed to really like this as it came up out of its hole even farther. Rats! What a great shot I could have gotten with my camera placed on top of the coral head if I'd only had any power left.

That's when I noticed the Nai'a was almost directly above me so I grabbed my housing and ascended to the dive deck trying to keep my eye on that one coral head. Josh was on the dive deck and took my camera from me. I asked him if his video camera was close and if it was ready to shoot. He said it was so I told him my battery was dead and asked him to come back down with his camera and film something.

As we descended, I realized that the boat had drifted somewhat and I could no longer see the coral head. I held up a finger telling him I'd figure this out and kept looking. I was hell-bent on finding that coral head. Finally, I saw an irregularly shaped Elkhorn coral I'd seen before and knew I was close. A few seconds later I located the coral head and saw the octopus still on top seemingly waiting for me to return and pet it some more.

I pointed to it and signaled for him to watch and start rolling tape. As I petted it, I could hear him kind of squeal as he realized what I was doing. He positioned himself perfectly and got a great shot that he showed everyone during lunch. I asked him if he would copy the footage for me if I gave him a tape to use, which he did. It wasn't until I returned home that I realized his video camera was filming in PAL and I needed NTSC footage. It would be years later before I finally had an editing system that could convert the footage from PAL to NTSC and make it usable.

That afternoon we visited nearby Lovu Village for a tour of the village and their school, then a Kava ceremony in their community hall. I shot almost an entire hour tape on that visit. I got great footage of one of our crew presenting gifts we'd brought from home for their school kids, then the chief welcoming us to his village, telling us we were now family. This was followed by dancers and musicians of the village putting on a show for us wearing their native regalia and make-up, as a few other villagers began mixing up a large wooden serving bowl of kava to share.

Some people say that kava tastes like dirty dishwater but I wouldn't know as I've never tried drinking dirty dishwater. But I will admit it looks like dirty dishwater. The kava ceremony begins with a villager filling a small wooden bowl from the larger one and bringing it to a guest who claps twice to receive the bowl. The server claps three times as the guest drinks the kava and returns the bowl. The guest will then hand the bowl back to the server and clap three times to thank him.

Kava is made from the yaqona root by powdering it, then placing it into a mesh bag and constantly squeezing it in the bowl of water as if it were a large tea bag. Kava seems to be a Fijian inebriant and may leave one's tongue a little numb for a short time. Each night after most guests went to sleep, the crew would invite me to join them on the bow of the Nai'a with their instruments for singing and more kava, which was great fun.

Being an early riser, I was the first guest to enter the lounge the next morning. Rob was already there and told me that he had been contacted by the World Wildlife Fund (WWF) telling him that there might be a Minke whale stranded inside an atoll on an island that was close to us. Rob had the boat moved in the night so that a few of us could go to the island and speak with its chief about the whale. If there really was in fact a whale stranded, we'd have to get his permission to swim in his bay. Rob, another guest, and I got in a zodiac and headed towards the island around 5:30 AM.

We were directed to the chief's home by one of the village fishermen on the beach and were subsequently invited in for tea. We sat on a large rug together on the floor and the chief verified that there had been a Minke whale stranded inside the atoll for a couple months. He then gave us permission to bring all our guests to snorkel in the bay if we wanted.

We returned to the Nai'a and told the rest of the guests what was going on but Rob explained that if we snorkeled with the whale, we'd lose a couple of planned morning dives. Everyone was quite interested in this adventure and we decided unanimously to forgo those dives. We loaded up into two zodiacs and proceeded to the bay. The chief arranged a fairly large truck to meet us after our swim in the lagoon, as the tide would be lower when we finished snorkeling and the zodiacs would need to be empty to get over the top of the atoll.

As we entered the bay, we saw four or five of their boats in the bay overflowing with villagers waiting our arrival. Each boat looked like it could have been a boat full of immigrants leaving Honduras. The villagers seemed to be as excited to have us there as we were about being there. Once we were all in the water, a boatload of people all of a sudden started pointing in one direction telling us the whale was over there!

We'd swim in that direction, but sometimes saw nothing until another boatload of people started pointing in a different direction. Then we'd change our direction and go that way. Finally, as a group we were able to spread out enough to keep track of the whale as it swam in the bay. Everyone got some good shots of the whale and we had a great time spending the morning swimming with a Minke whale.

That evening we decided that since the coral of the atoll was so close to the surface even at high tide, the whale must have been washed inside the atoll during a big storm with waves large enough to carry it over the coral. Rob verified the whale's presence to the WWF but also told them there was probably nothing that could be done to release the whale without damaging the coral. According to Rob the next time I saw him, the whale must have stayed alive in that bay for another five or six months before finally starving to death.

Minke whales are baleen whales which normally would filter feed plankton from the water. Since there wouldn't be that much plankton in the bay, this whale must have found a way to adapt its feeding habits and probably began feeding on small fish and/or crustaceans to have lived as long as it did while trapped in the bay.

After our snorkeling excursion with the whale, we did another exploratory dive nearby. The visibility was immensely better than our first exploratory dive and I was even able to film a couple of lined bristle-tooth surgeonfish courting each other. After about five minutes of them quivering and twirling around each other, they swam off, presumably to have a little privacy and possibly make babies; or so I'd like to think.

The next morning, we moored around Namena Island. There was a cleaner shrimp on the wall of the island that Rob's wife Cat was able to get to jump into her mouth and begin cleaning inside as if she were another fish. I was hoping to try this and Josh told me he'd take me to it.

When we got there, Josh pointed to the shrimp. I turned on my video camera and handed it to him so he could film this with my camera. I took a deep breath then took my regulator out of my mouth, leaned in close to the shrimp and waited. The shrimp quickly jumped into my mouth tickling the inside of my cheeks with its antennae and I could feel it picking at my teeth and gums. When I needed to finally breathe, I barely gave my jaw a closing twitch and the shrimp jumped back to where it came from on the wall, and I put my regulator back in my mouth. Once back on the boat, I joked about possibly skipping my next dentist appointment.

I was ecstatic about this interaction. I've been on many dives where I've been able to get cleaner fish and shrimp to jump to my hand, but I'd never had one jump in my mouth. I was finishing another dive trip with more firsts! Cookie Monsters, whales, and shrimp, oh my!

Roger & Stan at breakfast on the Nai'a. (Note the pics on the cabinets of the guests and crew, making it easier to learn everyone's name!)

GARDENS OF MEMORIES~ON ANEMONE BEDS

Fiji anemones sporting their clowns,
    This is where memories are sure to be found.
In mornings, these beds are curled up in balls
    Awaiting their usual sunrise calls.
As they unfurl, the clownfish appear,
    Swimming through tentacles brushing quite near.
These arms have a sting keeping most at bay,
    Protecting the clownfish throughout the day.
Those fish that scurry upon your approach,
    Reach these safe arms, then dare your encroach.
There's others that hover in cover of arms;
    Harder to photograph, harder to harm.
Maybe a crab and a shrimp live there, too!
    Tiny they are, but they surely see you.
Offer these tentacles bits of fresh fish,
    And watch them devour their favorite dish!
As sunlight decreases, the beds will close,
    Sometimes with clowns still showing their nose.
Cozy in there, I suspect it would be;
    Gardens of memories, in open sea.

Georgienne Bradley
and Jay Ireland

Georgienne Bradley and Jay Ireland founded the non-profit Imaging Foundation (later to become SeaSave.org) and in 2004 they advertised a photographic expedition to Puerto Rico in May where they would help people with their photography. They would be teaching how to get better shots as well as how to enhance these shots using photoshop for digital manipulation, which was fairly new at the time.

I'd known Georgienne and Jay for at least six to eight years through my friends Gayle and Rich with the EPIC competition. I had also invited Georgienne and Jay to be keynote speakers for my Gavia Scuba Club's ScubaFest 2000. That year they also helped judge the international, non-profit Underwater Images Photo/Video Competition.

It seemed to be a no-brainer that this might be a good trip for me to take. They probably wouldn't be able to help much with my video but it would be good to travel with them and get to know them better. Furthermore, Jay did do some filming at times so maybe this could be a chance to show them my work; who knows, some day they may ask me to join them on an exciting shoot somewhere exotic.

I roomed with a fellow whose nickname was Shack and he was from the Tampa, St. Petersburg, Florida area. He retired from the US Navy after about 21 years, and then had just recently retired from the US Postal Service after 20 years with them. He had been doing a lot of photography above and below water as well as being a fairly adept actor.

Ana Martin and Bonnie Smith were both from Seattle, Washington. Bonnie was just beginning to take pictures underwater. Ana was a good photographer and was currently also volunteering for the Imaging Foundation with Jay and Georgienne.

When Ana found out that I was from Cincinnati, she told me about her favorite restaurant in Cincy that she would always make a point of visiting when in town a couple of times a year, then asked me if I'd ever heard of Montgomery Inn, a place that serves some of the best barbecue ribs in the world! I gave her a knowing smile and told her I'd grown up in Montgomery which is a suburb of Cincinnati since 1960, and I know the owners very well. I lived only about three miles from the restaurant and the owners' children grew up with me, albeit a couple years younger. It's also where I took Jim Church for lunch the day we met at the Cincinnati airport for the ScubaFest event in '98.

The afternoon we arrived in Puerto Rico, Georgienne and Jay introduced themselves to those who didn't know them yet and gave everyone a better idea of what to expect throughout the week. We'd do two day dives each morning and a couple of night dives during the week. There would also be a nature hike or two in the afternoons looking for an endemic frog on the island that was supposed to be pretty cool-looking. We'd meet for lunch after the morning dives, then we would have a workshop where anyone could share their photos. Jay and Georgienne would show how photoshop could totally enhance their shots, no matter how bad they were originally.

Since I'd directed the Underwater Images Photo/Video Competition for nine years so far, and always had to be on the lookout for "photoshopped" pictures, I personally wasn't a great fan of photoshop. At the time, I was pretty much old-school. If your pictures weren't that good, you needed to learn whatever it takes to take a better picture, not make a better one on a computer by covering up one's mistakes.

After breakfast the next morning, everyone took their dive gear and cameras to the dock and split up into two dive boats. Shack, Ana and Bonnie were in the same boat as I was along with Jay and another couple. On the way to the dive site Bonnie began feeling seasick and lost her breakfast into the ocean.

As soon as we arrived at the dive site, Jay suggested she get in the water as quickly as possible and he'd hand down her dive gear, which they did. Once in the water, she was fine and completed the dive. But once back on the boat for our surface interval she began getting sick again. The next dive site wasn't far away and as soon as she got in the water she started feeling better again.

On this second dive, while still fairly close to the boat, I'd seen a squid that I wanted to film. I waved off Jay and gave him an OK signal telling him I'd stay here for a while. He gave me the OK in return and led the group on the rest of the dive.

I started filming the squid and was pleased that it didn't seem that interested in squirting away like most squid might do. Actually, even when I got close, it pretty much stayed around this one three-foot tall gorgonian. Occasionally it would drift 5-10' away and I'd follow while filming it. But after a short while, the squid returned to that same gorgonian and then would duck down, tentacles first, below a small coral head at the base of the gorgonian. It would stay there for about five seconds then back out and hover next to the gorgonian again.

At the time, I had no idea what it was doing, but I thought if I filmed this behavior, Georgienne or Jay might know. I ended up staying with my new friend for the entire dive until the group returned and I pointed out the squid to Ana and Bonnie. Then I left them alone to their photography. Since I was close to the boat I still hung around finding and filming crabs inside vase sponges and corkscrew anemones with small cleaner shrimp dancing around the tentacles.

Once back on the dive boat I asked Jay about the squid behavior. He said he didn't notice it, but he was pretty sure it sounded like the squid was probably laying its eggs each time it went tentacles first beneath that coral head. That might also explain why it remained in that one area for so long. Squid usually lay all of their eggs in one place. On one hand I was delighted to think that I might have possibly filmed it laying its eggs, but on the other hand I was disappointed that I hadn't gotten the shot of the eggs actually being deposited.

The next day Bonnie was too weak to dive and missed the dives that day. The third day she'd do the dives and get sick while on the boat as she did the first day. Then she'd predictably again miss the following day's dives.

One evening after dinner, Georgienne and Jay planned on taking us on a boat ride to Bioluminescent Bay. There were about five of us interested. After it got dark, we loaded into a boat and headed for the bay. It wasn't long before we could tell we were there because the wake of the boat was lit up like an over-decorated Christmas tree as we cut through the water. At one point the boat stopped and we got into the water and floated on the surface waving our arms and legs to make bioluminescent angels in the water. Unfortunately, my attempts at filming this didn't work. Unfortunately, my video camera wouldn't pick up the bioluminescence.

Bioluminescence is light produced by a chemical reaction that occurs in organisms. The yellowish light that fireflies emit is a good example of bioluminescence on land. Dinoflagellates are a type of plankton in the ocean that gives off a blue-green bioluminescent light. You may have experienced a small flash of light or two on night dives when waving your arms in the water. At Bioluminescent Bay, you wouldn't see only a flash or two, but an entire solid wave of light as if you had an entire wing under your arm.

On our last dive day, we returned to the dive site where I'd seen the squid and I spent half the dive swimming around trying to locate that tall gorgonian. Even if the squid wasn't there, I could at least get a good shot of her eggs. I had a perfect picture of that gorgonian in my mind but I never did find it. After a while, I decided to just get back to doing a regular dive and began searching for a new subject to film.

Out of the corner of my eye I noticed a movement but when I looked in that direction, I couldn't see anything. Then I noticed a pile of shells next to a small coral head and immediately thought maybe I'd seen an octopus. As I got closer, I could see the octopus in a hole under the coral head holding a larger shell that it was pulling in front of itself to hide.

I backed off and waited a while until it began to emerge from the hole then swim across the reef. I followed and filmed it as it jumped from one coral to another. Then I saw it spread its tentacles over a conch and I suspect it was going to eat the conch. Unfortunately, my camera battery had run down and I didn't have enough power to film it eating. After a while, it left the conch with a couple of hermit crabs hanging out nearby, probably wanting to upgrade their shell homes. The octopus swam back to the hole under the coral head where I'd found it.

Not long afterwards, a second octopus showed up and the two began interacting with each other. But Jay was waving everyone to the boat and I couldn't stay any longer to see if they might be engaging in a little foreplay; at least that's what I wanted to imagine anyway.

When I got back to Cincinnati, I went online and ordered two slabs of ribs and a bottle of their secret barbecue sauce from Montgomery Inn and had them shipped to Ana in Seattle just in time for her birthday.

ROGER ROTH

GARDENS OF MEMORIES~ON THE OCTOPUS

Freshly eaten, shells in a mound;
    This is where memories are sure to be found.
A nearby den with a shell at the door;
    All the rest were dropped to the floor.
It may not be seen, but in plain sight,
    The octopus watches, and then takes flight.
With pulses of water, it shoots through the sea,
    Ever changing its colors, randomly.
As trailing arms catch up to land,
    It's colors mottle to match new sand.
As it stalks, and moves quite wary,
    It suddenly jumps without tarry.
It wrestles in currents during light of day,
    A blanket of arms engulfs its prey.
A dinner of conch was meant to be,
    And waiting hermits upgrade for free.
The octopus slinks to its two-inch hole
    To squeeze itself in under that knoll.
Its eye will soon be peering at me;
    Gardens of memories in open sea.

Sea Level Education
at Anthony's Key

Before I went to Puerto Rico I was contacted by Dan Wood, the fellow I'd met in the Bahamas when I was an adjunct professor for Wilmington College. He had moved back to the neighborhood where he grew up not far from me and was currently teaching science at a prominent private school close to him. He told me that some of his junior high students were finishing up their open water certification classes and would be going to Anthony's Key Resort in Roatan, Honduras for their open water dives. Dan wanted to know if I'd be interested in going as a co-leader and also to film the group's trip.

I was glad to be visiting Anthony's Key since they had been founding sponsors in the Underwater Images Photo/Video Competition and remained on board for all 15 years I ran the competition. Haydee Galindo was my contact for this prize each year and I'd see her at DEMA every year. Her parents started the resort many years before. I'd never been to Anthony's Key, so I was looking forward to meeting the rest of the family, including her father Don Julio, who started the business and her two brothers who were always on site.

A month after returning from Puerto Rico, I was in the Greater Cincinnati Airport meeting the students and some of their parents and even a grandparent who had all taken the certification class. After the introductions, I began filming the group at the beginning of their adventure.

This would be a marine biology class like no other for the students. They would do two dives in the mornings with instructors doing the required open water exercises, then spend the afternoons in a classroom with Dan and others learning identifications of fish, corals and sponges. They also learned about various marine behaviors, turtles and their nesting habits, and even quite a bit about dolphins.

A couple of the students and parents had completed their basic open water certifications the year before with Dan and were now working on their advanced certifications. I stayed in one of the bunkhouses on the hill with a group of the boys and Dan stayed with the other group of boys. A couple of the moms stayed with the girls' groups and the rest of the adults stayed in nicer accommodations on the cay.

After the students did the necessary drills for their certification, the instructors would take them around the reefs and show them whatever they could find as I filmed everything. On one dive, I found a grouper in a cleaning station and motioned for a couple of the kids nearby to come over and see. After the grouper left, I held my hand next to the coral head and finally the cleaner goby jumped onto my hand and began cleaning it.

Once back on the boat I explained what cleaning stations were. I also added that sometimes the cleaners would jump on a hand and other times they wouldn't, so one just had to be patient. On the next dive, I noticed one of the boys with his hand out like I'd shown them, so I turned on my camera and approached him hoping to get the shot of the cleaner on his hand.

That's when I noticed that his hand was next to a corkscrew anemone and I quickly grabbed his arm and pulled his hand away from the anemone. He looked at me with a questioning glare so I pointed at the corkscrew anemone and wagged my finger back and forth telling "no," then I pointed to my temple in an effort to get him to remember this and I'd explain later. He didn't realize that besides the Pederson's cleaner shrimp around a corkscrew anemone there's likely also a snapping shrimp that had it come out, it would have surprised him enough to swallow his regulator. It could have hurt him as well had the shrimp touched him when it snapped.

These are also known as pistol shrimp. Their claws have evolved in such a way that one side of the claw can be cocked like hammer of a gun. When released, it snaps to the other half of their claw creating a large powerful wave of bubbles that can stun their prey and even break a glass dome port of an underwater camera.

Each day the students would log the names of the fish, corals, sponges and critters they'd seen that day. They might be told what the fish was or they might have to look it up in an ID book. By the end of the week, they were to have no less than 100 new species listed that they could recognize. Most of the kids had way more than that and could easily recognize most of them. I was quite impressed.

Each morning at least one of Don Julio's sons would be sitting on the deck in front of the dining hall. Julito and/or Samir would greet all the guests staying at AKR to make sure everyone was happy and had no problems. Paco was a parrot that they always had with them. I was warned that Paco sometimes isn't nice to men, especially men with beards so I should just be aware of this. Yet every morning, Paco would walk around the railing behind the benches that surround a large deck, then jump up on my shoulder for as long as I sat there. The brothers agreed that there must be something special about my demeanor that Paco picked up, since it didn't once try to bite my ear.

On one dive, I'd found a spotted drum swimming in its territory and called over a couple of the kids to show them. It swam back and forth and back and forth, but never left the safety of the nook in which it was swimming. Back on the boat one student asked me why the spotted drum didn't swim away when we were watching it and I explained about the safety it felt in its territory and that all spotted drums predictably acted this way.

One afternoon half-way through the week, I followed the kids into the Research Institute for Marine Science (RIMS) building that the Galindo's had built. We were going to listen to a lecture on dolphins and I was going to film the lecture. The kids learned about countershading for the dolphins' protection and camouflage. They also learned about echolocation, a sort of bio sonar. Then they were told about the dolphins that were kept at Anthony's Key in open pens with which the kids would eventually interact.

After the next day's dives and lunch, the group went to the dolphin area and the trainers taught the students a little about the hand signals the dolphins would react to. The students learned how to make the dolphins jump or dance on their tails or even dance while a student held the dolphin's pectoral fins. After each trick the students would feed the dolphins a fish as a reward.

After this, everyone snorkeled in the dolphin pen and even took pictures of themselves with a dolphin lying across their arms at the surface while I filmed all of this. Even the Grandfather Ed, who was also getting certified, got in on the act. Later, Dan and I and the advanced students went out on the dive boat for a third dive of the day; this time with two of the dolphins playing and doing tricks in open water.

That evening Dan took me and the advanced divers on a night dive. There was a new moon so the night was dark. On the way to the dive site, Dan explained that there are crustaceans called ostracods that do their courting at this time of the month. The ostracods are about the size of a sesame seed. The males rise into the water column then give off a substance and enzymes that combine to form little droplets that shine with a bioluminescence that's supposed to impress the females. As they produce more and more of these droplets, they combine to look like falling pearls in the water.

Once we arrived at the site, we got into the water then descended to about 30' to wait. There's no special time that the ostracods start or stop so it's just a matter of luck to see them. The water was black so we had to pay special attention to our buoyancy and depths for safety reasons. Then the droplets started falling and sure enough it looked like bright blue-white strings of pearls floating down from seemingly nowhere.

At the end of the week, all of the students received certificates for completing their certification as well as their assignments to learn more than 100 marine creatures. The kids even learned a lot about the behaviors of many of these creatures.

For many years, Dan's school always studied the oceans just before Christmas break. They would have the students pick a salt-water fish and make a report on it. Dan would invite me in to show a video to all of the seventh-grade classes of various types of fish I'd filmed in the Red Sea. Then I'd talk about the video and answer any question they might have. Every once in a while, a student would recognize one of the fish in my video because it was a fish they reported on.

I suggested to the teachers that I could give the teachers a list of the fish in the video and they could in turn make that a list the students could choose from. This way all of the students were sure to see their fish in the video making it more meaningful to them. I really enjoyed being back in the classroom like that.

GARDENS OF MEMORIES~ON CERTIFICATION

Parrots and dolphins in the same town;
This is where memories are sure to be found.
Flight to an island called Roatan;
Families together was always the plan.
Learning to dive were kids and their dad,
Grandpa and moms weren't all that bad.
Dive in the morning to practice a skill;
ID's of the creatures all brains would fill.
Afternoon classes to learn about turtles,
Each of the students work on their hurdles.
Dolphins will jump with the wave of a hand,
Give a new signal, on tails they will stand.
Reward them for tricks by giving a fish,
Has to fulfill every student's wish.
Swimming with dolphins playing in pens,
Learning marine life 10 by tens.
School on vacation was never so fun,
While riding on boats in tropical sun.
Certified divers they all would be;
Gardens of memories, in open sea.

Revisiting Papua New Guinea

In 2005, I was invited back to Papua New Guinea to update promotional videos for Walindi Plantation and Mahonia Na Dari as well as create a promotional video for Loloata Island Resort, Tufi Dive Resort and Star Dancer that was based out of Walindi at the time. As I planned my trip, I put out an email to all my diving friends to offer a good price for diving with any of these operations while I was there. Interestingly enough, Bonnie from Seattle got back to me and said she was interested in diving from the liveaboard Star Dancer.

I was kind of surprised that she was thinking about living on a boat for eight days when she could hardly spend 10 minutes on a dive boat in Puerto Rico without getting sick. She said she'd be bringing the seasick patch medicine and was hoping a bigger boat might not be as unstable in the water. As it turned out she made the whole trip without getting seasick.

I flew to Port Moresby which is the capital of PNG then took a puddle jumper flight from there to Tufi where we landed in a grass field lined with villagers and wild hogs. Tufi Province is on the mainland of PNG and is surrounded by fjords.

The resort sits atop a large hill overlooking one of these fjords, with the dive operation and house reef down at the bottom of the hill. Divers are guaranteed to see mating mandarinfish on night dives at the house reef. Fortunately, the staff did drive divers up and down that hill so we didn't have to walk.

The back porches of the rooms and the outside dining hall all overlooked the fjord. I enjoyed looking down and watching some of the men standing in their narrow dugout canoes (not outriggers) and poling themselves around a lagoon with their spears. When they saw a fish, they'd spear it. I'm sure I couldn't have stood up in the slim canoe, let alone spear a fish while standing.

Besides the typical reef diving, our dives also included a Japanese plane wreck, but the visibility was somewhat poor. The best part of the diving at Tufi was their house reef. They said they had guaranteed mandarinfish and possibly mandarinfish mating every night. Not only did we get that, but the night dives were more like muck diving where we hunted for small critters in and under the sand, in and around logs in the water, and in or around even pop cans that had been littered by uncaring natives.

The diving and staff at Tufi were great, but the land tours were even more impressive. Tufi offered bird watching for Birds of Paradise and other interesting species, fjord cruises either on motor boats or outrigger canoes, and village visits to a couple of different native villages. William was a pretty knowledgeable local and volunteered to guide many of these tours.

We took an afternoon to explore the fjord in an outrigger canoe with one of the locals paddling that was pretty neat. Once we got to the end of the large part of the fjord, we kept paddling up a stream through the jungle. The silence on the water mixed with the sound of the birds and creatures in the jungle is something I'll never forget.

William was from Kofure Village, so on another afternoon we chose to visit there before visiting Jebo Village the same day. This time we took one of the motor boats. Upon arriving at Kofure, the elder of the village, Chief Davidson Yariyari, came to greet us then led us to a small open building with tables and chairs, and one of the villagers brought some fresh fruit for us to snack on.

I explained to Davidson that I was doing promotional video work and wanted to share what village life was like with other divers in hopes that they would want to come and visit. While we were snacking, a half dozen of the villagers showed up in their native regalia including loin cloths, spears and headdresses. They were enjoying dancing and singing for us while I filmed their show.

Then we grabbed some water from the boat cooler and William and Davidson showed us around the village. Most of the men of the village were out fishing and the women were smoking a few dozen fish atop a large grate over a small smoky fire. William explained that smoking the fish allowed them to keep the fish for longer periods of time without it getting spoiled.

Each family had their own hut built on stilts and small gardens with a variety of vegetables surrounded by flowers. The village also had a primitive guest house with handmade cots for sea kayakers and tourists to stay as long as they pleased. I think they charged $1/day and that included eating meals with the villagers. Davidson even showed us their cemetery and explained the various trinkets that were placed around the graves of their ancestors that meant something.

Then we got back in the boat and headed towards Jebo village. Since Chief Davidson was good friends with the elder of Jebo village, Chief Lancelot Ginari, Davidson came along for a visit. I drank another bottle of water on the way in an effort to stay hydrated. I had done a couple of dives that morning and it was a hot afternoon, so drinking water was a must.

Upon our arrival at Jebo's white sandy beach, I noticed a young fellow coming down the beach with about four or five lobsters hanging from his hands, so started filming right away. Then Chief Lancelot came to the beach to greet us and was glad to see Davidson. Lancelot showed me around his village including their own guest house which they were quite proud of since it had a shower next to it. The shower was actually nothing more than a large wooden barrel filled with water.

Later, we walked to the community hall which was a platform made of trees with a roof over it. The platform was large enough to probably hold a few dozen people sitting closely together. As I started to lift my leg up to the platform, I started getting pretty dizzy and told William I wasn't feeling quite right.

They helped me up to the platform and told me to lean against one of the posts. Another chap brought me some huge chunks of pineapple and a coconut filled with fresh coconut milk. They encouraged me to finish all of this and promised I'd feel better since they believed I was getting dehydrated. Surprisingly enough, within only about 10 minutes I felt much better.

Both chiefs had been educated by missionaries when they were young, which explained their knowledge that was fairly extensive. Since they were so excited about my filming them and the thought of my productions bringing more guests, I asked them about the guest houses and what these guests might be bringing to their villages that could upset a balance of their own ethics and morals that had lasted for generations.

They admitted that the more outsiders showed up, the more difficult it became to keep the younger generation in line. Some outsiders did in fact bring drugs at times and at other times seemed to instill a jealousy in some of the "rascals" causing them to begin stealing. This was something the villages never had to deal with before. But the outsiders bought souvenir trinkets made by the villagers, adding income to the village. Outsiders also brought more attention to an annual Arts and Crafts Fair for Tufi Province that was growing in attention.

From Tufi, we flew back to Port Moresby where we were met by Chet Moore and a driver who took us to a boat that would take us to Loloata Island Resort for a few days. Chet Moore is from California and does a lot of marketing all over the U.S. for all of the PNG dive operations.

Loloata has a flatter area at one end of the island where the rooms are located and the rest of the island is a large hill. A walk around the perimeter of the island can take a couple of hours. Wallaby's and peacocks freely roam the island. I needed to be careful walking at night because any time I stepped near a wallaby that I didn't see was there, it would quickly jump away startling the heck out of me. The staff also had a baby cuscus which is an Australasian possum.

The jetty is about 100 yards long, so you can imagine how shallow the water is at this end of the island. A five-minute boat ride gets you to some very interesting muck diving. Further away, the dive sites included some wrecks as well as walls and reefs. Rare pygmy seahorses could be found at a couple of different dive sites, and there were plenty of other macro critters like shrimp, crabs, and pipefishes, including the beautifully colored harlequin ghost pipefish. On one dive, I filmed a large titan triggerfish eating a triton's trumpet snail. That was a little sad since the triton's trumpet snail is known to eat the Crown of Thorns sea stars that ravage the reefs by eating the corals.

One of the wrecks was inundated with a school of silversides below deck. They sparkled and glistened as the school flowed in waves. They'd part for a passing diver then meld together again once the diver was gone. Every once in a while, a barracuda can be seen drifting into the school. Schools of fish like this are always fun to watch, but sometimes difficult to film.

After visiting Loloata, we flew from Port Moresby to New Britain

Island where we'd stay at Walindi for a day. Then Bonnie, Chet and I would board Star Dancer the next day. Chet also shot video so we roomed together and Chet did a lot of dives with us while we shared subjects for the next eight days on Star Dancer.

Most of our diving would be around Rabaul on the east side of New Britain Island. This would be different than the dive sites FeBrina usually visited even though Alan Raabe was now a co-owner of Star Dancer along with Max Benjamin from Walindi. They had purchased the boat from Peter Hughes. Rabaul saw more than its share of action during WW II and was later buried under a foot of ash due to the eruption of the volcano, Mt. Turvurvur in 1994.

One dive we made was on an Aichi E 13 A "Jake" plane which was a long-range Japanese reconnaissance seaplane. The plane was upside down on the reef and I got a great shot of Chet reaching out and opening the bomb bay doors exposing two bombs that were still inside. Schools of razorfish and threadfin butterflyfish swam around the plane.

Another dive site we dove was named Two Tanks because of the two Mitsubishi Chi-Ha tanks that weighed 15 tons each and were equipped with a 57-mm short barrel cannon as well as a 7.7 mm machine gun. Then we dove on a "smart" barge that the Japanese used to transport equipment (smart because it has its own motor).

As we ascended to do our safety stop after diving the smart barge, I looked up to see a dozen or more dugout canoes on the surface from three different villages. Some of the canoes had kids hanging over the sides looking underwater to watch us divers as we came up. We could tell the kids were having as much fun as we were!

After getting back on board, I quickly grabbed my land video camera and began interviewing the divers as they came up and stepped onto the dive deck. Chet's first statement to me was that he thought we were the village entertainment since there were so many canoes around. When I asked Jeff Yonover what he liked about the dive, he looked around at all the canoes and said, "Coming up!"

After this dive, we moored near shore but were awakened in the early morning hours by a lot of large waves buffeting us about. It seems that being in the ring of fire can leave you prone to earthquakes and that's what caused the large waves even though we were so close to shore around Rabaul. It turned out that the epicenter of the quake may have been less than 50 miles away from where we'd moored.

Due to one of the dryers catching fire on Star Dancer the night before, we would tour the area and stay the night at a hotel in Rabaul while the dryer was fixed and made safe so it wouldn't catch fire again. We toured the old city of Rabaul that had been buried in Turvurvur's eruption. Most of the buildings had collapsed due to the amount of ash on the roofs. The 10'x10' concrete safe of the bank was still intact but the bank building itself was gone. The theatre was also missing but there were still spools of film strewn about its concrete porch and steps.

Then we were taken higher up the mountain into the jungle where we toured many of the underground caves used by the Japanese for their protection during WWII. These caves were extremely extensive in their construction. Caves used for the troops included nooks for cooking with very small holes in the ceiling that led to the jungle floor where smoke could escape into the middle of the jungle and not give away their entrances.

Other caves were used as hospitals or military headquarters. Still more caves were built on the edge of a bay with their openings camouflaged by trees and well-placed undergrowth. Floating inside were numerous Japanese vessels built like tanks and included cannons.

That night while settling in at the hotel, we felt a big rumbling and the manager of the hotel came to get us explaining that a nearby volcano was erupting. He asked if we wanted to pile into the back of his pick-up truck with some chairs and get closer to watch the night show happening across the bay. Bonnie and I and two others piled in with our cameras and he drove across huge fields of volcanic rock and ash seemingly in the middle of nowhere until we could see the volcano. It was spewing bright red embers and ash. The manager told us that the embers we were seeing were probably the size of a Volkswagen!

After a day's cruise from Rabaul we returned to Walindi where we'd do a few dives the first day back. The next day, we and many of Walindi's guests were given a tour of the Mahonia Na Dari campus and then we all attended a presentation by a new director I'd never met. The presentation was meant to generate donations to help sustain the program.

In this presentation, the new director Anasei Bein explained the MEEP program and was proud to tell us that this curriculum was now being used all over Papua New Guinea, not just New Britain Island. It was now reaching close to 150,000 students and teachers. This was a far cry from the dozen or so students from New Britain Island I'd filmed five years before. The director also had some charts showing the finances of MND and explained how the Board of Directors ran this NGO.

Throughout the entire presentation, the director would occasionally look at me directly into my eyes then look away as she spoke. Every time she looked my way, it almost seemed as though she knew me or something, but I'd never seen her before that I could remember. At the end of the presentation the group of 30 or so began filing out the door of the classroom thanking the director as they left.

Bonnie and I were the last to leave the classroom. When I got to the door to shake her hand goodbye she again looked directly in my eyes and asked if I was Roger Roth. I surely didn't see that coming, but answered that I was and asked if we'd met before. She said we hadn't, but she recognized me from my picture on the back of the VHS tape case that houses the production they still use that I'd produced after my first visit there. She walked to the bookcase and pulled out the tape to show me.

Now I was really surprised. Not only did she recognize me but they are still using my production years later! Then she asked if it might be possible to get some new VHS tapes as the ones they are still using is pretty worn out in places. (We all know how poorly those VHS tapes play once they get old.) I asked her if they had DVD players and she told me they did. I promised to get her a dozen DVD's as soon as I could and I'd bring more every time I returned. She was delighted; I was moved and humbled.

GARDENS OF MEMORIES~ON SILVERSIDES

Exploring a wreck with silversides around;
    This is where memories are sure to be found.
One room is empty, but drop down a floor,
    And fireworks' bursts will greet at the door.
Like glistening clouds of glitter, they gleam;
    These little fish flitter to and fro as a team.
Flowing in through a porthole, they circle the room;
    But with camera in hand, there's no way to zoom.
They're moving too fast as the whole school moves slow,
And a river of them starts heading below.
A diver emerges, thus thinning the school,
    But they're keeping their distance; their golden rule.
As soon as she passes, they fall back in ranks;
    With silversides aswirl here to ballast tanks.
Then a seam in the school parts it side to side,
    And a 'cuda appears with time it will bide.
It's there to protect a ready-made meal;
    Protection the silversides readily feel…
Unless they're a snack that just had to be;
    Gardens of memories, in open sea.

Flying First Class

While planning for this last trip to Papua New Guinea, I decided to see if Qantas Airlines would bump me to first class if I promoted them in the same way I promoted Air Pacific on my flight to Fiji to dive from the Nai'a. I contacted their marketing department and made the same offer. Qantas accepted my offer, but again, only on the space available terms. Thinking of that long of a journey, it was fabulous to know I might be spending at least some of my flights in first class!

I flew Delta to Los Angeles where I'd catch my first flight to Sydney on Qantas. I had to obtain my economy boarding pass, then wait to see if there would be space in the first-class cabin for me, just as before. I was glad when the stewardess invited me back to the counter for my first-class boarding pass.

Needless to say, the 11-hour flight to Sydney was very comfortable in first class. I only had to remember to stay hydrated by drinking lots of water in between any alcoholic drinks. My next flight would be from Sydney to Cairns. I wasn't going to be too disappointed if I didn't get into first class on this second Qantas flight since it was shorter, but I still kept my fingers crossed. Fortunately, there was again room in first class and I flew to Cairns where I'd fly a puddle jumper with Air Niugini to Port Moresby.

On my way home after my diving in PNG, the flight to Cairns was almost empty, so I again had no problem having my boarding pass bumped to first class. When we landed in Cairns, we had to disembark so the plane could be cleaned. Then we'd re-board the same plane in an hour. After that flight and waiting in the airport in Sydney, it was close to time for boarding the flight from Sydney to Los Angeles, so I approached the desk and asked about my possible bump to first class.

The stewardess told me the flight was pretty full, so I'd have to wait until she was sure there was a seat available before she could print a new boarding pass for me. I politely smiled and told her that was no problem. I stood back against a nearby wall where she could see me and kept that smile on my face. A few minutes later, some fellow was approaching the desk wearing his suit and loosened tied while loudly talking on his cell phone and waving his arms.

As he stood in front of the stewardess, he continued to talk on his phone, almost yelling at whomever he was talking to, sounding like some big shot CEO or something. When he finally hung up, he asked about getting a seat in first class and the stewardess told him the same thing she told me. His reaction was to tell her he had to have a seat in first class, so she should make sure that happened, as he walked away to answer another phone call.

About 10 minutes later, he returned and again almost demanded he get his boarding pass for first class. The stewardess politely told him it would only be a few more minutes and she would let him know. A couple minutes later, she called me over and handed me my boarding pass for first class. I thanked her very much and happily strolled to the gate to board the plane.

About five minutes later, the other passengers began boarding the plane walking past me while I drank my Jim Beam on the rocks. When I saw that loud-mouth guy start to walk past me, I hoped he wouldn't be sitting close to me as I didn't care much for his demeanor and I also figured he'd probably be on his phone bothering everyone. As he walked past me, he gave me a pretty nasty look, then continued all the way through first class to the economy class section. I guess it pays to be patient and nice.

After arriving in Los Angeles, I flew Delta to Chicago. I only had one more flight from Chicago to Cincinnati and was anxious to get home. When I went to the desk in Chicago for my last boarding pass, I was told the plane was having mechanical problems and the flight might be delayed. Go figure. My last flight to get home after flying 30 hours so far, and it was going to be delayed

After Delta announced three separate hour-long delays, we were finally told the next flight would definitely leave in three more hours when the replacement plane arrived. I was getting very tired and was thinking I could have rented a car and been home before the next plane arrives had I known this when I first arrived in Chicago. I went to a restaurant for a sandwich and beverage to pass the time.

After eating, I looked at the departure schedule and saw that my departure gate was changed to a gate in one of the hallways, so I went there to wait. There was a white-haired pilot with a small, white mustache and very friendly smile standing next to me for a while, leaning against the wall in the hallway. Since he only had a briefcase with him, I guessed he was going to be on the flight but not part of the flight crew.

A stewardess finally showed up and began announcing the boarding zones. I was in zone four, so would be one of the last to board. When I handed her my boarding pass, she told me my carry-on pelican case with my housing inside was OK, but my backpack was too large to fit under the seat and would have to be given to the crew to be put with the other checked baggage.

I explained to her that I knew it would fit under the seat since I'd flown on this exact type of plane a few weeks earlier and the backpack fit just fine. She got upset with me and told me she knew her job and it wouldn't fit so I had to leave it with her. I politely told her that I had $10,000 worth of cameras in my backpack and the cameras wouldn't be protected with other suitcases stacked on top of it.

I tried to appeal to her caring side, if she had one, by telling her that I'd been flying over 30 hours and also waited six hours there in Chicago for this final flight home. I told her that I wasn't trying to be trouble for her, but I knew the backpack fit under the seat. Out of the corner of my eye, I could see that pilot was watching all of this, but was staying out of it.

She wasn't accepting any of my explanations or appeals and told me it wouldn't fit under the seat as it was. She told me if I didn't leave the backpack with her or divide it up, she was calling security, and began picking up her phone. I asked if she might have a plastic bag that I could use to divide up what was in my backpack, but she said she didn't without looking for anything. I asked her if I could possibly take the clean garbage bag out of the small, empty garbage can next to her, and she angrily told me absolutely not!

Then I got an idea and took off my long-sleeve shirt, took my cameras out of the backpack and wrapped them tightly in my shirt, then tied the sleeves together. When I asked her if this was OK, she angrily scanned my boarding pass and told me to go, then began speaking to the other pilot. I felt pretty silly walking down the aisle of the plane wearing a T-shirt in January in Chicago, but I was also pretty aggravated.

When I got to my seat, I began unwrapping my cameras and returning them into my backpack. The pilot who had been standing next to me walked past and settled into a seat across the aisle and one row back. After I finished packing my cameras into the backpack, I very easily slid it under the seat in front of me, then turned to look at the pilot to see if he noticed, while I put my shirt back on. He gave me a large, knowing smile and nodded, almost telling me he understood, or maybe even complimenting me on my patience.

At least that made my heart feel better. I settled in for the two-hour flight home looking forward to a hot shower and my own bed. Four years later, almost to the day, I saw that pilot on TV and learned his name. His name was Chesley Sullenberger and he had just landed his plane safely in the Hudson River, saving all 155 people aboard. I would never have forgotten a friendly face like his and when I saw him on the news, I knew immediately I'd seen him before.

The beautiful Porcelain Crab is no larger than 1.25" in diameter.

Meeting Bob Adamov

During the summer of 2005, I was vacationing in northern Ohio around Port Clinton on the Lake Erie shore and I made a point of contacting my old friend Rod Althaus who owns the New Wave Scuba Center there. He and his wife, Jenny, met me and my girlfriend Patti for dinner at a restaurant a few blocks from his home and dive shop. Hanging out with Rod is always a good time and usually means a respectable amount of alcohol may be involved. I did say respectable.

At the end of dinner, Rod suggested we have another round of drinks. Patti said she wanted to go back to the house where we were staying with her sister and family, but she had no problem with my staying as long as I could get home safely. Rod suggested that I go home with him since he lived nearby. I could sleep on the couch and Patti could pick me up in the morning. The ladies went home and Rod and I ordered another drink.

While we sipped on our drinks, Rod told me that a mystery thriller novel author had contacted him and wanted to meet with him to consult on an upcoming book over breakfast the next morning and thought it would be a good idea for me to join them. I said it sounded like fun as long as the author wouldn't think I was intruding. Rod said he didn't think it would be a problem.

The next morning, we met Bob Adamov at the specified restaurant and ordered breakfast. Bob told us that the hero in his books is an investigative reporter living in Washington but he spends a lot of time with his Aunt in Put-In-Bay, a popular party island in Lake Erie not far from where we sat. He explained that he likes using real places and even uses real people that he's met; sometimes using their real names and sometimes changing the name a little bit.

To illustrate this, he told us a story he'd used in his last book about a waitress with large breasts that he'd actually met at a real restaurant in northern Ohio which he named and Rod recognized. Her name tag said CC. Whenever she served Bob anything, she'd always lean way over. When Bob asked the waitress what CC stood for, she told him "Community Cleavage" and Bob immediately asked her if he could use that in a book! CC said she had no problem with that.

Then Bob went on to ask us about boats and motors that are used around Lake Erie, wanting actual popular boat manufacturers, motor types, sizes, etc. Then he described a scenario about a boat sinking somewhere in the lake with drugs in a duffel bag on it and his hero would dive down and recover the drugs.

His questions to us included things like where could that boat actually have been and what could have caused it to sink (like an underwater rock). He also wanted to know what could have been on the boat that the hero could use to replace the drugs so he could leave the duffel bag on the boat. Another question was what type of scuba gear would his hero be using (manufacturers, colors, etc.). Rod and I agreed that Bob surely was thorough with his research, and always seemed to ask the right questions to keep the conversation moving.

Somewhere along the line I mentioned one of my videos about the Tibbett's wreck off Cayman Brac that I'd produced after following Jean-Michel Cousteau around the wreck for a couple of dives. Bob said he'd love to get a copy. I promised to send him one when I got home. A few days later he called me and told me the video had given him some great ideas for another book. He asked when I might go to Grand Cayman again and if he could tag along the next time. I told him I didn't have any plans to go, but I could surely just schedule a trip there and we could go together whenever he wanted.

He suggested Pirate's Week in December since that would be a party week as well. I agreed that was a good idea and we made the plan. I suggested we stay at Cobalt Coast Resort so I could go diving with DiveTech while he was in Georgetown doing his research.

At the annual Shipwrecks and Scuba Conference in Sandusky about a week before we left, Bob asked where Cobalt Coast Resort was located on the island. I showed him a map and pointed at the main road around the island, then asked if he saw the little town of Hell. So far, he was with me, so I told him Cobalt Coast was on the other side of Hell.

Bob almost fell off of his chair when he excitedly told me that's going to be the name of his next book! I asked him what was and he said it would be, "The Other Side of Hell." He had been playing with the name Cayman Connection, but didn't like it. It's funny how serendipitous our discussion was.

The following week, we flew to Grand Cayman and Bob rented a car. I was glad he was driving because driving on the other side of the road always confused me. We drove to Cobalt Coast to check in, then went to our room to unpack.

Bob had a list of places he wanted to go for his research like the Royal Caymanian Police, the National Archives, the Ministry of Finance and Banking, the Wreck Bar at Rum Point, Calypso Grill on Morgan's Harbour and more. He also had a list of people he wanted to interview including Nancy and Jay Easterbrook with DiveTech, Rod McDowell with Red Sail Sports, Adrien Briggs at Sunset House, a treasure hunter by the name of Mongo Marich and more. All of these people were Caymanians who had lived on the island most of their lives so they would be a treasure chest full of information for his research.

Bob had already heard my stories about Nancy at DiveTech and how she helped with my rebreather problems, so after we unpacked, we went to find Nancy and Jay so I could introduce them. Bob told them what he was doing and asked if they had a little time to sit down and help him out. They had the time, so we sat and talked about the island, people, places, funny occurrences…anything that Bob might use to enhance his readers' experience. The conversation flowed easily with a lot of information and with good humor, too. Just as he did when I first met him, Bob took notes continuously on his yellow legal pad.

Another place on Bob's list that he wanted to visit was Durty Reid's Bar. Reid Dennis was a Viet Nam vet who had lost his leg in the war and returned home to Grand Cayman to open a bar. This sounded like a good place for us to start after we left Nancy and Jay, so we drove back into town to see if Durty Reid might be at the bar.

We went in and Bob asked the bartender if Durty Reid might be there. The bartender replied who's asking, at which time Bob introduced himself and told the bartender that he was doing research for a book. The bartender then pointed over to a table near the front window and said Reid's over there. There were three fellows sitting at that table and one was in a wheelchair.

We walked over to the table and Bob asked which one might be Durty Reid. The fellow in the wheelchair said he was. While we were still standing, Bob introduced himself to Reid and the group. Bob explained that he was doing research for an upcoming book and wanted to talk with Reid about things that may have happened on the island through the years he lived there that might fit into his book well. Reid just sat there.

One of the other fellows finally invited us to sit down, so we did. That gentleman introduced himself as Steve Foster (Foster's Market is the largest grocery in the Cayman Islands) and told us the other fellow was Mark Rice of Rice Communications. As Bob put his legal pad on the table and pulled out his pen to hopefully start taking notes, Reid asked if we wanted something to drink. Bob got a coke and I ordered a long island iced tea. It was a vacation, wasn't it? Anyway, Bob was the one who had to get the stories straight.

As the bartender got our drinks together, Bob tried to get Reid more interested and helpful by describing the type of books he wrote and fun things he included in his books. Then Bob asked Reid how long he had lived on the island. Reid's answer was all his life. Next Bob asked Reid if he had any funny stories about any of the old-timers on the island and Reid said of course.

I have to admit I'd never seen Bob at a loss for words but he seemed to be running out of things to ask that might engage Reid and I could also see beads of sweat actually beginning to form on Bob's forehead. I think Steve might have noticed this as well so he spoke up and said he could tell us a funny story about Reid.

He told us about the night they were playing darts with many tourists in the bar watching the match. Half way through the game Steve threw a dart but instead of hitting the target, the dart buried itself into Reid's leg and almost everyone in the bar gasped. Reid reached down and calmly pulled the dart out of his leg and handed it back to Steve. That's when Reid chimed in and told us most people didn't know he had a wooden leg.

Everyone at the table laughed. I think between Reid giving the punchline of the story and Bob's wonderful belly laugh, Reid finally loosened up. He began to tell us more stories like the time he placed his wooden leg on the bar of another establishment since it was bothering him one evening. By the end of the night, Reid got so drunk that Steve and Mark had to carry him out and take him home. The next morning the janitor went to the bar early to clean up and when he turned on the lights, he saw a leg sitting on the bar with no body attached and went crazy. He immediately called for the police and an ambulance. Once they arrived, one of the policemen looked closer at the leg and realized it must have been Reid's

After a couple of hours and a couple more drinks we thanked the guys and asked if we could come back another time to listen to more stories. All of them agreed that would be fine as they had plenty more stories to tell. As we got into the car to return to Cobalt Coast, Bob spoke about how slow everything started but how much information he'd gotten and how much fun he'd had by the time we left. I totally agreed.

Each day I'd do a couple of morning dives with DiveTech while Bob went into town for his research visiting the places on his list. Then he'd come pick me up and we'd drop in Durty Reid's for more stories. Reid insisted on always buying our drinks and even our lunches while he and Steve and Mark entertained us with some of the funniest stories we'd heard. It was like our own private comedy club.

Reid told us about the time some guy was making moves on a pretty gal in the bar one night. After a while that guy took her into the small men's room (only one toilet) and began to have his way with her. Someone must have tried to walk in and caught them, then quickly stepped back out. But the guy didn't stop doing what he was doing until he was finished. Reid said he got a standing ovation when he came out.

That afternoon on the way back to Cobalt Coast, Bob decided we needed to do a dinner cruise on the local pirate ship, so he stopped and got two tickets for that evening. We had brought pirate paraphernalia with us, so we dressed up and went to the boat for dinner. The dinner was good, the rum punch flowed freely and the pirates and wenches on board all had a good old time.

After going to Reid's for the last three days, and him buying our drinks and lunches, we decided to have lunch somewhere else. We didn't want Reid and the boys to think we were trying to take advantage of their hospitality. We picked a restaurant in a strip mall and walked in. A waitress told us we could choose any table we wanted and she'd be right there, so we chose one back in a corner.

Even before the waitress came to our table, Steve noticed us from their table in the bar area and called us over to join them. Who would have thought that we'd pick a restaurant at random and end up running into the three of them again? Needless to say, we enjoyed more of their stories that day and we got to pay for our own lunches as well as theirs.

While we were waiting for our sandwiches, Reid told us about a movie he'd produced entitled The Cayman Triangle. I don't remember much of the story as it really didn't make much sense, but Steve dressed up like Tarzan in a leopard leotard and Mark posed as a statue in the middle of a square in Georgetown. Somewhere in the movie there was a sword fight. What I do remember well is how proud Reid was of that movie.

Bob asked if he had a copy that we might borrow to watch and Reid said he thought he did but it was the last VHS copy he had so we'd have to be very careful with it. We followed them back to Reid's bar and picked up that copy assuring him we'd take good care of it. We took it back to Cobalt Coast and watched it with Nancy and Jay and a couple of other staff members. It was stupid and funny, and we could only imagine how much fun they must have had producing it.

Roger & Bob Adamov bartending for Cobalt Coast Resort employees' party.

That night Cobalt Coast was having their staff Christmas party, so Bob and I offered to bartend. This way, the bartender could enjoy the party as well. At first, they said that wasn't necessary but it didn't take long to convince them to let us help. We donned Santa Claus hats that lit up and we worked the bar half the night. It was a good thing I knew how to make drinks because Bob had no idea, so he ended up mostly being the server.

The next morning, DiveTech was hosting a treasure hunt dive at the Cobalt Coast house reef. Any divers on the island were invited and there were tokens around the reef with numbers on them that corresponded with prizes on tables that were lined up on the patio. I'd found quite a few tokens and one of the prizes I'd received was an 8-Reales silver coin from a shipwreck named the Rooswjyk. That was pretty cool.

That afternoon, Bob and I visited the Wreck Bar at Rum Point and a couple of other places on his list. While walking the beach, I noticed a piece of driftwood that would make a good sign. There were a lot of these types of driftwood signs on the island that pointed in any given direction. One sign might read something like New York 1511 miles as it pointed north.

Bob asked me why I wanted that and I told him that I'd noticed the fire code occupancy sign in Durty Reid's and thought it might be a good idea to give Reid a sign to hang above the men's room that said, "Occupancy One." We went back to Cobalt Coast and got some paint to make the sign. I also asked Nancy if she might have an old VHS tape that she didn't need, even if it didn't work anymore. She found one for me and I told her she'll love the story when I tell her about it later.

The next day we went back to Durty Reid's to return the Cayman Triangle tape. When we got there, Reid and the boys were in the back room with at least six other good ol' boys sitting around a large table. Reid invited us in, told the bartender to bring us our drinks and asked us what we wanted to eat. We tried to decline but when that didn't work, we relented and ordered lunch.

Then I handed Reid the Occupancy One sign and suggested he hang it above the men's room door to keep guys in the bar from taking women in there. Everyone in the room burst out laughing. I guess the story was well-known among their friends, too. Mark took the sign right away and hung it above the men's room door for Reid.

While sitting in my chair I unwound a foot or two of the tape from the old VHS tape Nancy gave me, and wadded it up in my palm, keeping just a little bit between my finger and thumb. Then I stood up and announced to Reid that I'd also remembered to bring his last VHS copy of the Cayman Triangle back to him. I handed him the VHS tape case, but as he grabbed it, I held onto the tape and started backing away.

With tape still coming out of the case as I backed up, there was a huge gasp by everyone in the room! Then there was total silence with everyone looking at me. Reid's face was as red as a beet with anger. I'm guessing everyone in the room must have also known about the movie as well. I waited a second or two, then pulled out the real Cayman Triangle tape from my belt behind my back and told him here's the real tape and it's still working just fine.

I'd bet Nancy and Jay back at DiveTech could have probably heard the laughter that ensued. There was no doubt that Bob and I had been accepted as one of the good ol' boys at Durty Reid's. Fortunately, our time with Durty Reid turned out much better than the first few minutes we'd spent with him.

Steve Foster, Reid Dennis, Mark Rice, Bob Adamov and Roger at Durty Reid's.

As we headed back to Cobalt Coast, I asked Bob to stop at Artifacts, the shop that had donated the silver coin I received in the treasure hunt. When I got inside, I told the owner and his wife that I was the lucky recipient of their gracious donation for the treasure hunt. I also told them about my experience with the Underwater Images Photo/Video Competition and how I always told my winners to be sure to thank the sponsors of the wonderful prizes they were awarded. Finally, I told them I wanted to buy another coin from the same shipwreck to show my appreciation to them. I still buy a coin from them each time I go to Grand Cayman.

Earlier in the day, Bob had gotten us two tickets on the Jolly Roger Pirate ship for drinks and dinner and a sunset cruise. We donned our pirate outfits and tally-ho'd for the evening. Bob is definitely one to have a good time no matter where he is even though he didn't drink alcohol.

The following night was the last night of Pirate's Week and Nancy and Jay invited us to join them on their boat for the fireworks in Georgetown harbor. We donned our pirate outfits again and we fit right in with everyone else. There were hors d'oeuvres and rum punch on the boat and the fireworks were beautiful. It was a great way to celebrate the end of a fun and productive week from the other side of Hell.

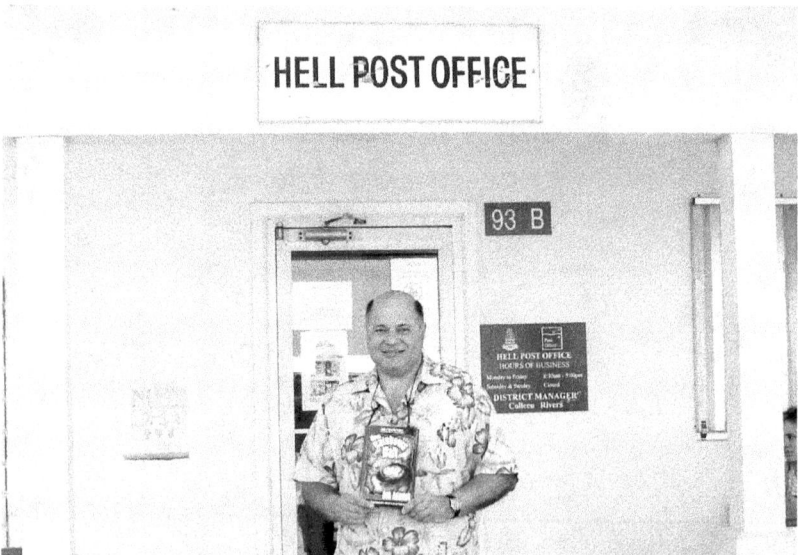

Bob & Roger on their way to the Other Side of Hell.

GARDENS OF MEMORIES~ON BOB ADAMOV

Meeting an author in Port Clinton town,
    This is where memories are sure to be found.
Breakfast at table with pad and pen,
    Adding a story every now and then.
The tape of a wreck caused his ideas to flow,
    A trip to Grand Cayman would help him to know.
Look on a map and see the burg Hell,
    More thoughts start ringing that lovely bell.
Research and people fill up his day,
    All this has become his own form of play.
Some not so easy with beads of sweat,
    Ending in laughter from broken cassette.
Wooden leg that has stories, start with a dart;
    Being left on the bar was not quite so smart.
Small glass of rum punch forever to sip,
    With pirates and wenches aboard pirate ship.
Bartending a party just to help out,
    Serving their drinks or drawing a stout.
Driftwood sign allowing just one,
    Enhances the trip filled with so much fun.
Visits and interviews, his potpourri;
    Gardens of memories, in open sea.

Wonders of the Oceans

When Bob Adamov wrote, "The Other Side of Hell," he asked me to write an ecological statement about our oceans that he could use in his book. The following is the ecological statement I wrote for him.

For eons, our oceans have been the most stable ecosystems on earth. Water temperatures, salinities, and amounts of sunlight have changed little through this time lending to the development and stability of the marine life we have come to love as scuba divers. But divers aren't the only ones who need to be aware of and protect this stability.

In the past few decades, numerous practices have had adverse effects on our oceans. These include, but are not limited to shark-finning, bottom-trawling, long-lining, by-catch waste, over-fishing that does not support sustainability of many species, and more. Shark-finning results in removing the apex predators from marine ecosystems which will soon cause a total imbalance in the food web. Bottom trawling devastates marine habitats on the seafloor, and the tonnage of by-catch that is thrown overboard is mind-boggling.

Because of irresponsible dumping, our oceans now have eddies of garbage floating in them that stretch for hundreds of miles that most people don't even know about. An example of this is the "Eastern Garbage Patch" located 800 miles north of the Hawaiian Islands. Much of this patch is made up of non-biodegradable plastic.

Costal development of resorts and hotels is causing silt runoffs worldwide that are smothering, choking, and ultimately killing corals and sponges. With the disappearance of these coral and sponge habitats, other marine creature populations are diminishing. Better development planning is necessary to alleviate this catastrophe from getting worse.

For our own protection, we need to preserve our ocean environments which are instrumental in keeping carbon dioxide levels within the limits we need to live. For our own protection, we need to help sustain marine population levels in order to have fish in our diets, keeping us healthy. For our own protection, we need to learn more about the oceans and fall in love with them.

Why should we learn more about the oceans and fall in love with them? Jacques Cousteau once stated, "People protect what they love."

This is the type of Barrel Sponge that Jean-Michel Cousteau went into headfirst.

OCEAN BEAUTY

The oceans are full of wonders and grace,
　　With life galore in Neptune's face.
And each of these creatures will live and die,
　　What's in between will catch the eye.
There's color and shapes, some large and some small,
　　Pillars of coral, short and tall.
Whales, rays, and turtles all share this domain,
　　Beauteous fit as planned; sustain.
Barrels and vases, these sponges are soft,
　　Cleaning shrimp wait, in and aloft.
Stonefish faces only mothers would love,
　　Beauty seen as a soaring dove.
Cuttlefish glisten fluorescent at night,
　　Hunters retreat at dawn's first light.
A scorpionfish so ugly and gray,
　　With beautiful fins on display.
Living around, in vast water expanse,
　　Many display their courting dance.
Carefully balanced, beautifully tended;
　　A realm so real never ended.
What value is there, is seen by us all,
　　Listening for that beckon call.
And when it is heard, with our hearts drawn nigh,
　　There's nothing more we can beautify.

About the Author:
Roger Roth

ROGER ROTH is a former science teacher who has been diving and filming underwater since 1988. He's earned nine international first-place awards for underwater video production and has authored dozens of educational videos for schools and educational outreach programs around the world. He has also created dozens of promotional videos for international scuba diving destinations. A partial client list for Roger includes the Discovery Channel, the U.S. Navy, the Nature Conservancy, Aggressor Fleet, LTD., Jean-Michel Cousteau, and the Ocean Futures Foundation.

Roger was also the Founder and Director of the international, non-profit Underwater Images Photo/Video Competition. Since its inception in 1998, he has raised and donated over $90,000 for marine conservation and scholarships.

THE POEMS IN THIS BOOK were mostly written after video was taken of those exact scenes described. I had originally hoped to produce poetic videos of beautiful underwater scenes, but with no less than four different video cameras and that many formats in just 12 years of diving, it was difficult to arrange those lower quality video formats in a meaningful manner.

Recognizing that you have read about a few of my adventures in only the first 12 years of my 32-year diving career thus far, keep your eyes open for *Adventures of a Landlocked Diver II* where my escapades continue and even grow in excitement!

To order more books for friends and relatives or to order Roger's underwater films on DVD, go to **www.RogerRothProductions.com**!

www.ingramcontent.com/pod-product-compliance
Lightning Source LLC
Chambersburg PA
CBHW062105270326
41931CB00013B/3224